GLAZES FOR THE POTTER

The front cover illustrations show the following range of glazes:

Top   Bowls by Emmanuel Cooper, with blue and green glazes (from left to right): (1) stoneware bowl with turquoise matt glaze; (2) crater glaze recipe (barium carbonate 25, nepheline syenite 50, china clay 10, quartz 10, cryolite 5 + copper carbonate 1, rutile 2); (3) stoneware bowl and (4) porcelain bowl with blue/green glaze (china clay 30, whiting 25, feldspar 40, flint 5 + cobalt 1, rutile 1, copper 0.5).

Centre   Test tiles of glaze recipes (see Appendix 2).

Bottom   Bowls with white glazes by Emmanuel Cooper (from left to right): (1) matt white/brown glaze (feldspar 15, whiting 5, zinc 2, barium carbonate 8, ball clay 5) on stoneware bowl; (2) white glaze (feldspar 50, dolomite 25, china clay 20, whiting 5) on porcelain bowl, with copper carbonate sprayed lightly on top of unfired glaze to give a green flush; (3) same white glaze on porcelain bowl, with manganese carbonate painted thinly onto unfired glaze to give a pink flush; (4) zinc speckle glaze (nepheline syenite 70, clay 10, flint 10, zinc 5, dolomite 5, whiting 5) on stoneware bowl.

GLAZES

for the potter

Emmanuel Cooper
&
Derek Royle

CHARLES SCRIBNER'S SONS · NEW YORK

Thanks are due to Ted Sebley for so patiently taking the photographs used in the book, and to Simon Adamczewski for allowing the photograph on the back cover to be reproduced. Harrison Mayer Ltd have kindly supplied illustrations of equipment and have offered much helpful advice throughout, for which we are very grateful. Our debt to all potters, teachers and students who have helped either directly or indirectly in the production of this book is duly acknowledged: it is to them this book is dedicated.

© Emmanuel Cooper and Derek Royle 1978

Library of Congress Cataloging in Publication Data

Cooper, Emmanuel.
    Glazes for the potter.

    British ed. published under title: Glazes for the studio potter.
    Bibliography: p.
    Includes index.
    1. Pottery craft. 2. Glazes. I. Royle, Derek, joint author. II. Title.
TT922.C66 1978   738.1′44   78-16586

ISBN 0–684–16021–8

Contents

Introduction

Pottery glazes form a special section of the group of substances called glass, and this book explains how they can be made, understood and used. Glazes are fired onto the surface of pots or ceramic objects and they cannot be considered without reference to their purpose, the clay on which they are to be used, or the temperatures at which they are to be fired. This book explains the methods used by the studio potter; these are often different from those used in the pottery industry and major differences will be pointed out where they occur.

Glazes fulfil a wide variety of functions. At the most practical level they provide a smooth, waterproof covering which can be easily cleaned and which renders a hygienic surface for domestic pottery. This, however important, is the least the studio potter wants from the glazes he uses.

Some potters want the quality of the glaze to be paramount in their work. Others are concerned primarily with shape and only add glaze to enhance this. A potter making repetition domestic ware needs glazes which are not only attractive but mature reliably over a fairly wide temperature range and are consistently reproducible. From this point of view, raw materials which are in very limited supply have only restricted use. Some potters want glazes on which they can paint designs or apply transfer decoration, others want cool blues, pale greens, rich reds or bright yellows. Every potter wants to use a glaze which is as much a personal statement as the making of the pot itself, and even when using industrially prepared glazes, it is finally the use of glaze rather than its recipe which will be the most important consideration.

It would be useless to claim that this book will contain all the secrets of glaze making; such a book would ignore the basic fact that potters, like the best cooks, develop their own touch and this skill comes out of a thorough knowledge of the materials which are available and how they react when mixed together. By following the sequences explained here from start to finish, students coming fresh to the subject as well as experienced potters, will acquire a good knowledge of basic materials and how they behave in glazes, together with guidelines on how to develop their own glazes and effects.

Users of electric kilns far outnumber users of other types of kiln although their special needs are often neglected in favour of the more exotic flame burning kilns. Much of what is written here is directed to the makers of oxidized stoneware, though the methods and tests are equally applicable to any sort of kiln firing.

There are basically two approaches to the study of clays and glazes; one is by trial and error, known as the empirical method, and the other is by the scientific method in which results are predicted by calculation. The Chinese could be said to be perfect exponents of the empirical method. Over many hundreds of years, Chinese potters developed their skills and techniques using the available raw materials. They knew nothing of glaze calculation, yet in terms of technical success their work has no equal. However, with the scientific knowledge now at our disposal, it would be inconceivable not to use it as best we can. The present understanding of the structure and behaviour of atoms and molecules and the mathematical calculations which can reveal such changes are fascinating and open up many possibilities for the glaze chemist which trial and error, with its time consuming methods, denied. Few potters, however, are such mathematical wizards as to be able quickly to understand and use such knowledge. Being for the most part practical people, potters need to combine actual experiments with scientific calculations so as to get the best of both worlds.

Part One
MAKING THE GLAZE

I

Pottery Processes

First let us consider the potter's basic material, clay, and the processes used to achieve different effects. Clay has two main characteristics. The first is its plastic malleable quality which enables it to be worked by a wide variety of methods and, in so doing, to take on almost any shape. The degree of plasticity varies from clay to clay as well as being dependent upon the amount of water present in the clay. When the water is removed by drying, the clay becomes hard and retains its form. It can, however, be returned to its plastic state by the addition of water. The second characteristic of clay is its ability to become hard and resistant to the effects of water when heated to a temperature which is usually in excess of 800°C (1472°F).

Most studio pottery is fired first, in the biscuit (or bisque) firing, to a temperature around 950–1000°C (1742–1832°F). In this firing the clay changes into a porous, absorbent but hard substance, which can be handled easily, and, for most pots, can be covered in a liquid glaze. Some pots, such as plant-pots, are completed at this stage. However, most pots have a second firing called a glaze or glost firing, in which the pot is covered with a fairly smooth and often waterproof surface. The temperature of this second firing determines the type of pottery which is made. In the pottery industry, the biscuit firing is taken to the higher temperature, and the glaze firing to the lower temperature.

Traditional processes, often used by the studio potter, involve building or forming pots without the use of mechanical equipment. This includes such techniques as slab building, coiling, squeezing and pinching. Moulds, too, are used for pressing or casting clay, and the wheel for making thrown pots.

Decoration on clay can be done at almost any stage of production. Before the clay has been fired, it can be burnished (polished) or incised. Clay can be applied or, in a liquid form, known as slip (or engobe), can be trailed on the surface of the pot. Biscuit ware can be painted with colouring oxides, as can the surface of fired and unfired glazes. Glazes can be applied either singly or one over the other. Enamels, sometimes known as on-glaze decoration, are specially prepared low-temperature glazes which are painted on the surface of the fired glaze which is then fired a third time. Enamels have the advantage of offering a wide range of bright colours, but they are less durable.

Before considering how glazes are made, the different sorts of pottery that exist need to be considered and classified into different types. The effect of heat on clay must also be explained as this plays a vital part in determining the type of pottery made.

Many eminent ceramists, writing about the processes involved in making pottery, have worked out elaborate ways in which the different sorts of pottery can be classified. It should be pointed out, however, that industrial pottery is often classified on a system based only on the temperatures to which the ware has been fired. For the studio potter, such a classification lacks the required flexibility and a broader method has to be used. Some sort of classification is important for several reasons: materials must be used which will operate at the required temperature, kilns must be suitable, and certain effects can only be obtained at certain temperatures and under certain conditions. In other words, different types of pottery, broadly speaking, display certain characteristics which, if recognized, enable the effect to be produced more easily.

For the purpose of this book, the most convenient classifications are those which are based on the temperature to which the pot has been fired and the degree of vitrification which has occurred in the body. Vitrification is the word used to describe the bonding together of particles of clay to form a solid glass-like state. During the firing process, the clay changes from being relatively soft and easily breakable into a tough, hard material which will not disintegrate in water. Most people are familiar with the effect of heat on clay. Building bricks are perhaps the most common and useful example. The fired bricks vary in colour from bright terracotta to dark reddish-brown or grey-black. Unglazed, the bricks have a roughish surface which can just be scratched with a nail. Though physically strong, the bricks are brittle and can be broken easily with a sharp blow from a hammer.

Similar building bricks fired to a higher temperature lose their bright colour and become darker; their surface, which acquires a slight shine, is harder and cannot be scratched with a nail. In such bricks, a greater degree of vitrification has been achieved together with increased physical strength.

Different clays are affected differently by the same amount of heat. At 900°C (1652°F), for example, some clays give bodies which are physically soft and porous, while other clays at this temperature are well vitrified and have great physical strength. Pottery made in primitive societies is often made from clay which becomes hard and vitrified at a relatively low temperature of about 800–900°C (1472–1652°F), for few primitive societies are able to fire their pots to a temperature much in excess of this. In contrast, most clays used by the studio potter are still soft and porous at this temperature.

THE EFFECT OF HEAT ON CLAY

Although the physical changes which occur in clay when it is fired can easily be recognized, the theoretical processes which affect the clay minerals are not so fully understood. The transformation of soft plastic clay into a hard, tough, durable and often beautiful material is a highly complex process. Different terms are used to describe the firing process such as baking and burning – the former implying transformation, the latter destruction, though firing involves decomposition of materials which recombine in new ways.

Stage 1

In its plastic state, clay contains approximately 25% water; when dried out to room temperature, up to about 5% remains. During the first stage of firing, this physically combined water is driven off as steam and water vapour. This is known as the drying or water smoking period. Because the volume of steam is many times that of water, the rise in temperature during this part of the firing must be very slow. A rise of no more than 1°C (3°F) per minute is considered workable. Ample ventilation is needed in the kiln to let the steam escape. In primitive firings, this 'preheating' period is often accomplished by burning hay or straw inside the pots or by standing them in the ashes of a bonfire. Clay which is made up of fine particles and contains no non-plastic materials, such as grog or sand, is more liable to explode if the initial temperature rise is too rapid.

Stage 2

Starting around 200°C (392°F) and lasting until approximately 800°C (1472°F), the clay crystals are partially decomposed and the water which is chemically contained in the structure of the clay is given off as steam. Different clays react at various temperatures. With the clay mineral kaolinite, rapid loss of water occurs between 450°C (842°F) and 600°C (1112°F). A cubic foot of pots can give off as much as a pint of water. Gases which are formed from other materials are also liberated; for example, carbonates give off carbon dioxide with a corresponding weight loss in the clay. It is important that the atmosphere of the kiln should have sufficient ventilation to allow these changes to be completed before the temperature rises above 600°C (1112°F). Even a slightly reducing atmosphere will prevent these changes being completed and this can result in defects such as bloating or blistering occurring later in the firing. Iron is, perhaps, the material most affected by the lack of oxygen. In a reduced atmosphere it becomes ferrous oxide which has a strong fluxing effect on the clay as well as becoming darker in colour. For certain effects, reduction is deliberately induced, as, for example, in the production of vitrified blue bricks which, though more expensive to fire, have greater physical strength as well as their distinctive colour. All the processes which involve the loss of water or gas must be properly completed before vitrification of the clay takes place. Vitrification seals the clay and, if it takes place too soon, will prevent the completion of the reactions resulting in bloating or blistering at higher temperatures.

As well as chemical changes resulting in the decomposition of the clay, changes also occur in the crystalline structure of the clay. Around 573°C (1063°F) the quartz present in the clay changes in size with an increased volume of up to 3%. During this change the temperature rise should be slow enough to allow this to take place without damage such as cracking. Other components of the clay will start to react together though such reactions are slow to reach completion. The rate and degree of the changes will depend on the intimacy of the mix and the presence of other components, some acting as accelerators, while others retard or even prevent reactions.

Between 600°C (1112°F) and 700°C (1290°F) some sintering of the clay takes place. In this process microscopic welding together of the clay particles occurs without the aid of a liquid phase. It is the first source of strength of fired clays. Clay used by the studio potter has little physical strength at this temperature, even though it has undergone irreversible changes. Further changes are necessary to achieve strength and hardness.

Stage 3

Vitrification, which is the conversion of some of the minerals present into glass, involves further complex chemical and physical changes, not all of which are fully understood. Liquid formation in clays can occur at a temperature as low as 770°C (1418°F), but in most commonly used clays, little glass is formed below 1000°C (1832°F). In clays containing feldspar vitrification begins around 1150°C (2102°F) and is unlikely to be completed until 1300°C (2372°F).

In the full-fire stage which begins around 800°C (1472°F), the temperatures can be increased more rapidly without danger to the clay. Chemical and physical changes begun earlier now proceed at a more rapid pace and new changes are begun. If the temperature is sufficiently high, or prolonged, any molten liquid which is formed rapidly enters the pores in the more refractory materials. The higher the temperature, the more complete the reactions become. Silica, present in the clay, enters into solution. During the production of vitrified material the chemical changes cause simultaneous physical changes. The total volume will decrease and as the pores are filled with molten liquid porosity will decrease. The colour of the clay may darken, and according to the amount of liquid formed, there will be an increase in hardness and strength. Most clay used in the workshop vitrifies between 1100°C (2012°F) for red burning clays and 1300°C (2372°F) for hard stoneware clays.

The temperature range in which clays will vitrify, starting with fusion and extending to the loss of shape, can be as narrow as 30°C (86°F) or as wide as 300°C (572°F), depending on the fluxes present. Magnesia, for example, extends the range. A good working clay has a fairly wide range of, say, 100°C (212°F). The ideal point is reached when all the required reactions and other changes are completed or have been carried out to such a degree as to give the articles or materials the requisite properties.

Maintaining the top temperature for a time, known as soaking, allows the heat to penetrate completely, which increases the amount of fused matter, reduces the number of pores between other particles, and renders the material more impermeable. Too much soaking or too high a temperature may well result in the formation of too great an amount of liquid, which causes bloating or boiling of the clay, often with a resulting loss of shape and eventual sagging or squatting.

Stage 4

Cooling is an equally important part of the firing process and, if fully understood, can be constructively used. Too rapid cooling can cause cracking, known as dunting, while too slow cooling can cause materials in fusion to crystallize out. At top temperature most clay is slightly soft and the glaze liquid. Reactions between the body and glaze form an integral part of the strength of the finished work. Cooling from a temperature of around 1250°C (2282°F) can be rapid to 1100°C (2012°F). This will prevent crystallization of cristobalite, and lessen the tendency of the glaze to come off the edges of the pot (known as shelling). Rapid cooling also encourages the development of clear glazes; slow cooling encourages crystal formations with opaque or matt effects. By 1000°C (1832°F) the clay body behaves as a solid. At 573°C (1063°F) and between 300°C (572°F) and 200°C (392°F) further physical changes occur in the silica, and both points need to be passed slowly. At 573°C (1063°F) the quartz in the body changes back to its smaller state with a corresponding contraction. Between 300°C (572°F) and 200°C (392°F) a further contraction takes place of approximately 3% in volume. Too rapid cooling between these temperatures may cause pots to crack or 'dunt'.

Less refractory clays are those which will only withstand a temperature of, say, 1100°C (2012°F) to 1150°C (2102°F). A typical example of this type of clay is red terracotta clay and clays used for building bricks and roofing tiles. Such clays are usually rich in materials such as iron or alkalies, and often have a high silica content – sometimes in the form of sand. In these clays liquids form at relatively low temperature. Highly refractory clays are capable of withstanding much higher temperatures. Such clays may contain high proportions of alumina or silica with a low proportion of fluxing materials present. Fired to a high temperature, the amount of liquid formed in the highly refractory clay may be equal to that formed in the low refractory clays fired to a lower temperature. A typical example of a highly refractory clay is fireclay which has a large silica content; it is often used in the production of furniture for use in kilns and sometimes added to clay bodies to raise their firing temperature.

TYPES OF POTTERY

The amount of vitrification which takes place in a clay is determined by the temperature to which that clay has been fired and the composition of the clay. For the studio potter, it is convenient to divide ware into three major groups, though there are other types which fall outside such a method of classification. Earthenware, stoneware and porcelain form the three groups, and are generally defined within certain limits of temperature and degree of vitrification. Essentially, it is the body, rather than the glaze, which is the basis of this classification with its porous or non-porous qualities. The porosity of a given body can be measured by first soaking a pot of known weight in water for a number of hours, then weighing it again. The increase in weight expressed as a percentage of the dry weight of the pot is a measure of its porosity.

Earthenware

A general term used to describe pots fired between about 1000°C (1832°F) and 1150°C (2102°F) and with a measurable level of porosity. In some primitive types of pottery the ability of earthenware bodies to absorb water which subsequently evaporates is utilized in water containers. In these vessels, the evaporating water keeps the water cool and fresh in hot weather. Earthenware was undoubtedly the first sort of pottery made; it was unglazed, porous and fired to a maximum temperature of around 900°C (1652°F) to 1000°C (1832°F). Such wares range in colour from dark brown or black to orange, red and yellow to pink and cream. With the development of kilns, probably in Mesopotamia around 3000–2000 B.C., greater control over the kiln atmosphere was achieved and with the use of glass, around 2000–1500 B.C., it was possible to render the pots waterproof and, at the same time, introduce an almost limitless range of decorative effects. Glaze technology slowly spread throughout the Near East and China and was eventually passed into Europe.

Today earthenware has, typically, four main characteristics:

1   It is fired no higher than 1150°C (2102°F) and usually no lower than 1000°C (1832°F).
2   The body is porous with a range of porosity between 5% and 15%. Characteristics of the body itself are its porosity and its mechanical weakness. Because of this, much earthenware is made thicker than wares which are more vitrified and therefore stronger. Exceptions to this are the naturally-occuring red clays which are rarely capable of withstanding a temperature greater than 1150°C (2102°F), at which point they are well vitrified and have considerable mechanical strength. Such bodies are usually fired to 1100°C (2012°F). More refractory types of clays which are fired to the lower earthenware temperature lack strength and are highly porous. Earthenware bodies can be mixed by the potter or bought ready-prepared from the pottery suppliers. Such bodies can have a wide vitrification range and vary in colour from cream to brown or black. Wedgwood's Basalt ware, for example, had a particular mix which rendered it completely vitrified at low temperature.
3   Earthenware glazes tend to lie on the surface of the pot. When broken the cross-section reveals little interaction between the body and glaze. Though a certain amount of interaction has taken place to keep the glaze in position, the intermediate layer is extremely fine. Earthenware pots are usually biscuit fired before being glazed.

4   The low temperature range of earthenware allows a wide variety of brightly coloured glaze pigments to be used, both mixed in the glaze and applied either under or on the glaze. For this reason, the technique of glazing earthenware is compared with that of the painter, while the technique using more vitrified clays and a limited and often a more subdued range of colours is compared with that of the sculptor. It is perhaps significant that when painters have decorated pottery, they have chosen to work with earthenware. Perhaps Picasso is the most famous of these painters, though Jean Miro, Gauguin and, recently, John Piper have all experimented with some success on pottery.

Stoneware

Stonewares are fired to temperatures over 1150°C (2102°F) usually to a maximum of around 1400°C (2552°F). Average stoneware temperature is between 1250°C (2282°F) and 1300°C (2372°F). At these temperatures, most clays become hard, vitreous and non-porous. It is easy to see why such bodies are called stonewares. The Chinese originally developed stonewares some 2000 years ago. At first the pots were glazed only by the action of the ash from the wood used to fire the kiln. At temperatures above 1200°C (2192°F) wood ash reacts with the surface of the clay to give a type of glaze. Glazes using feldspar were later developed by the Chinese. In Europe, stonewares were made first in Germany in the Rhineland. High-fired wares washed with a slip of fusible clay were made as early as A.D. 1000. Around A.D. 1300–1400 it was discovered that salt, introduced into the kiln at high temperature (1200°C (2192°F)) volatilized into sodium and chlorine. The chlorine escaped up the chimney as a gas, and the sodium combined with the surface of the clay to give a thin coating of strong glaze. Simply made, the saltglaze enabled pots to be made more thinly and was produced in large quantities up until 1800. Stoneware, like earthenware, has four main characteristics:

1   Stoneware is fired to a temperature over 1150°C (2102°F) and below 1400°C (2552°F).
2   Common stoneware clays used by the studio potter vitrify to a high degree at the usual working temperature which is around 1260°C (2300°F). A body can be said to be non-porous if it absorbs no more than 3% water. At 1150°C (2102°F) only partial vitrification takes place but over about 1200°C (2192°F) most stoneware clays become sufficiently vitreous to be called stonewares. With increasing temperature the body softens slightly and a good working body gives a wide operating range before deformation and eventual squatting takes place. Some highly refractory clays will retain, even at normal stoneware temperature, a marked degree of porosity, and though technically stonewares, do not fulfil all the basic conditions of that material. Some ancient Chinese wares, too, have a degree of porosity which exceeds that normally found in stoneware. For example, the Tzu Chou, Chun and Kuan ware of the Sung Dynasty.

3   Unlike earthenware glazes, most stoneware glazes do not lie as a separate layer on the surface of the pot, but interact with the clay to form an intermediate layer between glaze and body. This layer can usually be seen in a cross-section of the pot. This bonding of glaze and body gives stonewares added strength and can, when well fitted, increase the mechanical strength of the ware considerably. At stoneware temperatures, certain materials present in the clay give colour and textural effects which need consideration when bodies are being planned. Such materials also have a noticeable effect on the glaze.

4   At stoneware temperature, certain metal oxides used as glaze colourants burn off. The result is a more limited palette for the stoneware potter though the number of subtle variations are almost endless. Colours in stoneware glazes tend, therefore, to be those obtained with iron oxide and range from blacks and browns to greens, blues and yellows. Many of the bright colours of earthenware tend to be excluded. The quality of stoneware glazes, too, can vary widely for, unlike earthenware, the glaze need not necessarily be waterproof and, as a result, more textured surfaces can be used. Stoneware glazes, too, are more affected by the atmosphere in which the pots are fired. If the amount of oxygen present in the kiln is restricted either by burning a flame or limiting the flue outlet, then what is known as reducing conditions occur, and certain characteristic effects can be obtained. For example, in reduction, any iron oxide present in the body or the glaze will give blues, greens and blacks. In a kiln supplied with plenty of oxygen, yellows and browns will be produced. Copper oxide in reduction can give red, in oxidation, green. A reducing atmosphere also has the effect of lowering the melting point of various materials. Again, iron oxide, which is present in most clays, will, in its reduced ferrous state, act as a powerful melting agent in the body.

1 Amanda King. Press-moulded bottle using clays with coloured oxides added. Transparent glaze poured down centre, fired in saltglaze kiln. A rich textured surface coloured dark blue and brown with saltglaze flashings.

Saltglazed stoneware has many of the main characteristics of ordinary stoneware, though it is produced by a slightly different method. Made from clay with a high silica content, saltglaze stoneware is fired once only. Around 1200°C (2192°F) common salt is introduced into the kiln, where it vaporizes into its two major constituents – sodium and chlorine. The sodium reacts on the surface of the pot to form a thin but extremely hard layer of glaze, while the chlorine passes up the chimney. Iron oxide in the pot will encourage the formation of a brown glaze. Characteristic effects of a saltglaze surface are mottled, textured surfaces, ranging in colour from cream orange and brown or pale green. Surface textures similar to that of orange skin are often produced.

Porcelain

Like stoneware, porcelain was developed originally in China and is considered to be the finest achievement in the art of the potter. The secret of the manufacture of porcelain was not understood in Europe until the eighteenth century when it was produced first in Germany and then in other countries of Europe. True porcelain is, like stoneware, fired to a high temperature, usually over 1200°C (2192°F). However, porcelain is made from a specially mixed body which does not occur naturally and includes china clay (kaolin) and cornish stone (petuntse). The resulting body, when fired, is white, translucent and gives out a clear ringing note when struck. Because of the amount of vitrification which takes place in the body, it has great mechanical strength and is capable of being made extremely thinly. This not only gives porcelain its characteristic delicate appearance but also enables the development of the full translucent effects of the porcelain.

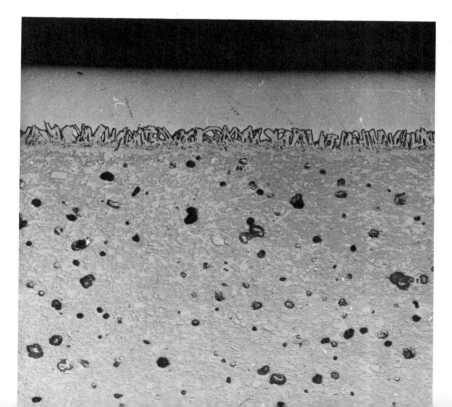

2 *American Commercial porcelain. Polished section (reflected light) × 200. Top white layer is glaze, the jagged layer is the reaction between the glaze and body below.*

True, or hard-paste porcelain, is fired to a temperature over 1200°C (2192°F) and rarely exceeding 1400°C (2552°F). A thin layer of clear or semi-opaque glaze is normally applied so as not to obscure the translucence, though sometimes opaque and coloured glazes are used. Some porcelain glazes fired in a reducing atmosphere will develop delicate pale blues and greens. In an oxidizing atmosphere, pale yellows, creams and browns are produced.

Low temperature or soft-paste porcelains have been made in Europe since the eighteenth century and are made industrially. Soft-paste porcelains are non-plastic and very difficult to work by hand. Though similar in appearance to hard-paste porcelain, having a highly vitrified body and considerable translucency, they lack the subtlety and depth of colour which can only be obtained at high temperatures. There are two main types of low-temperature porcelain: china and bone-china. Bone-china is a particularly English product and is made by adding calcined animal bone to a mixture of china clay and cornish stone. It is biscuit fired to about 1200°C (2192°F) and subsequently glaze fired to a lower temperature. China is made by adding a specially prepared flux in the form of a frit to a mixture of china clay and cornish stone. Biscuit firing is to around 1150°C (2102°F) followed by a lower temperature glaze firing.

High fired porcelain wares are difficult to produce for several reasons. Firstly, the necessity of using a large percentage of materials which are non-plastic, like cornish stone, or have a low level of plasticity like china clay, gives a body which is difficult to handle by the traditional methods of the studio potter. Such bodies can be made more workable by the addition of ball clays, but only at the risk of losing those qualities of whiteness and translucency inherent in the nature of the material. Secondly, the highly vitrified body, usually with a level of porosity of about 1%, quickly collapses if only slightly overfired and, in any case, is prone to distortion and warping, especially if thinly made.

Raku

Originally developed in Japan, raku describes a method of manufacture rather than the finished result. The technique dates back at least to the eighteenth century when it was closely associated with the religious ceremonies of Zen Buddhism. Basically, raku involves putting glazed pots into a hot kiln, allowing the glaze to melt and then removing the pot, while still hot, from the kiln. Cooling can be done either rapidly, such as by placing the pot in water, or slowly by letting it cool in the air.

Depending on the glaze effect required, the red-hot pots can be reduced by burying them in such things as sawdust, leaves or newspaper; a subsequent plunge in water rapidly cools the pots and prevents reoxidization. The glaze firing process takes little longer than thirty minutes when the finished results can be admired. Apart from the speed at which the effects can be obtained, the other main attraction of raku is the wide range of effects and colours which can be achieved at the low temperature and by the reducing effects. Ware made by the raku process is unlikely to be waterproof and it is a technique reserved for the production of decorative rather than functional pots.

2
Glaze Materials

At first sight all the materials, minerals and chemicals available in the potter's laboratory seem to make the difficult work of constructing a glaze almost impossible. Two easy courses can be followed. One is using manufacturers' ready prepared glazes. This is a straightforward process which, if the glazes are mixed, applied and fired according to the manufacturers' instructions, usually give very reliable results. The second easy alternative is to mix up glazes according to known recipes. Most potters have favourite recipes which they have found suit their particular needs, and many will pass on their recipes. Other potters guard their recipes and will not divulge them. However, the beginner will have no difficulty in finding many recipes which seem to offer interesting possibilities. Some will provide reliable, though often dull, glazes while the majority will not work at all, or will give results far from the recipe description. Materials from different sources and firing conditions in different kilns present such a wide series of variables that no results can ever be guaranteed.

If all a potter needs is a range of workable glazes, then glaze recipes will probably provide some answers. However, they will not fulfil the basic desire of most potters to know what the materials are, or what their particular function is in the glaze, or how the glaze can be adjusted. Chemistry text books will provide particular information such as chemical formula, origin and so on, but to the inexperienced potter such knowledge will only be of academic interest without a measure of practical experience to substantiate it. The sort of information which will be of greater use to the potter, is how these materials react when heated to high temperatures in the kiln, and more importantly how they behave when mixed one with the other. Such information is relatively easy to obtain, and provides a solid basis of knowledge on which to devise glazes suited to particular requirements and taste.

Some materials can be melted at very low temperatures without the aid of a kiln. This can be demonstrated by a simple experiment. On a looped piece of platinum wire, fastened in the end of a wooden stick, place a small amount of borax powder and hold it in the top part of a gas flame. Gradually the powder will melt and a clear glass bead will form. Other

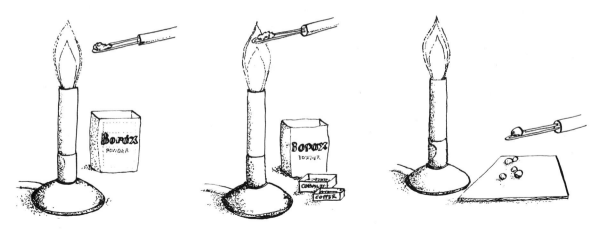

Diagram 1　Making glass beads.
  (a) Melt household borax powder in a gas flame, holding it in the platinum wire loop at the end of a glass rod.
  (b) The glass bead can be coloured with metal oxides.
  (c) Place the beads on an asbestos sheet to cool.

materials can be tested in a similar way, but it is unlikely that they will melt at the low temperature which can be obtained with this method. Glazes cannot be made by quite such simple means, for a glaze must not only become very much like glass, but must stay on the surface of the pot. In other words the glaze mixture must have a sufficiently high viscosity. It must have the ability to resist running off the pot, yet retain the ability to cover the pot's surface, and spread itself evenly by absorbing dribbles of glaze. Few glaze materials used singly possess all these qualities.

3 Tile 12 in. × 12 in. showing the effects of glaze materials fired alone at stoneware temperature. The fourth material from the left, top row, is colemanite.

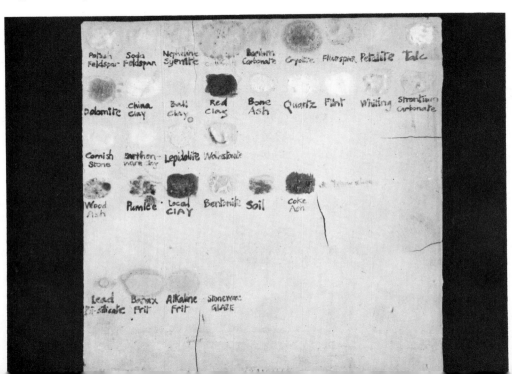

The first practical step, however, is to test on their own all commonly available materials at the temperature to which you intend to fire your pots – say, 1100°C (2012°F) earthenware and 1260°C (2300°F) stoneware, in either an oxidized or a reduced firing. Materials used by the stoneware potter are listed in this chapter and most are commonly and reliably available. Other, more specialized materials which are available only in limited quantities, are listed separately. Full lists of materials available from the potters' suppliers are listed on page 171. Most suppliers provide free catalogues which are well documented and contain much useful information concerning their materials.

For the tests a set of test tiles and pieces need to be made and biscuit fired. Use the clay intended for the workshop and prepare flat tiles about 25 cm (10 in) square, marked into squares with each square having a slight depression, strips about $20 \times 5 \times 1 \cdot 5$ cm ($8 \times 2 \times \frac{1}{2}$ in) thick and triangles about 20 cm (8 in). Vertical test pieces are essential. These can be made from folded slabs with score marks to show how the glaze will mark. Before firing, all tests should be labelled in a position which will not be messed up by any glaze failure. This can be done with either a mixture of manganese dioxide and water or black underglaze crayon. Adequate labelling avoids confusion and enables tests to be usefully consulted well after the original firing.

TEST ONE: TESTING MATERIALS SEPARATELY

Mix each material to be tested with water and paint this mixture in the squares on the tiles in two thicknesses. Label each material using a mixture of manganese dioxide as a marking ink, or black underglaze crayon (paper records usually get lost) to make a permanent record.

The various materials are most easily considered in four different sections. In the first section are the more common minerals; in the second section are the natural materials which occur in limited quantities; in the third section are the manufactured materials; and in the fourth section are the soluble materials.

Section one

This will contain such materials as potash feldspar, soda feldspar, nepheline syenite, flint, dolomite, wollastonite, fluorspar, lepidolite, talc, whiting, china clay, ball clay, red clay, barium carbonate, bone ash, colemanite, cornish stone, petalite, cryolite. The fired results, although not indicative of how the materials will act together, can, by observation, be broadly classified in three major groups.

In *group one* are the materials which have shown most reaction. Many will have become very glassy and spread over a wide area. Often some volatilization will have taken place and the surrounding area will be coloured by orange or brown 'flashing' due to the volatilized material reacting with the surrounding clay. Some materials will have spread over a considerable area.

Group two will contain the materials which have undergone a more limited reaction and have become vitrified and glassy whilst remaining fairly opaque. They are, in fact, highly viscous. Included in this group will be materials which have been affected by the heat to the extent of reacting with the clay body. Some materials will have become hard and vitrified without becoming shiny or glossy. In some cases bonding between the clay and the mineral will have taken place.

In *group three* are the materials which have not been affected by the heat. Their appearance is almost unchanged. Little or no bonding with the body has ocurred and the material can easily be lifted or scratched as powder from the tile surface. Such materials are said to be refractory.

On the tile illustrated on page 13, the materials listed above fired to 1260°C (2300°F) give the following results:

Group one: colemanite, cryolite.
Group two: nepheline syenite, cornish stone, dolomite, lepidolite, potash feldspar, soda feldspar, whiting, barium carbonate.
Group three: talc, china clay, ball clay, red clay, bone ash, flint.

Section two
Materials listed in the second and third sections can be tested in a similar way. Of the materials listed in section two, many are available from the pottery suppliers but because their chemical make-up varies from batch to batch and is so complex as to defy simple chemical definition, each batch has to be tested separately. Into this section come the natural materials such as wood and coal ash, local clays, red and yellow ochres, granite dust, and pumice (volcanic ash).

Section three
The third section is made up of materials which are commercially prepared, and have known and reliable composition. This section includes the commercially prepared glazes and the frits. Frits are mixtures of two or more materials which are heated until they melt into a glass, quenched in water and ground to fine powder. Fritting is carried out for several reasons. Some materials are poisonous and dangerous to handle, for example, lead compounds, which, whilst insoluble in water, are soluble in dilute acid both before firing and, in some cases, after firing. In the human body lead is a cumulative poison, so it must be handled carefully and be well balanced in a glaze. Lead solubility must be kept to minimum levels specified by law and fritting can eliminate this problem. (A full explanation of this can be found in chapter 8.) Glazes with a high clay content sometimes crack after drying when applied to biscuit ware; part of the plastic material can be calcined to reduce this. Some of the plastic materials should be left raw to help glaze suspension and increase the handling strength of the dry glaze. Some compounds, such as whiting, which give off gas on heating (in this case carbon dioxide), can cause pinholing and bubbling in the glaze. Fritting can reduce this tendency.

The pottery industry uses some glazes which contain a high proportion of frit and such glazes have certain advantages. For example, they mature evenly, present few crawling problems, such as may be caused by excess of plastic material in the mix, are extremely reliable in use, and rarely cause pinholing. For the craft potter such glazes are of limited interest; their chief value lies in the excellent base they provide for making other glazes. In this section the lead and leadless frits, and the clear and opaque glazes are tested.

Section four

For the experimental potter a fourth section can be made from the so-called 'impossible' materials. These are the soluble materials which if added to a glaze batch would partly or wholly dissolve in the water. This is undesirable in a standard glaze for several reasons. During glazing some of the soluble salts are drawn into the body of the pot and in the firing can cause bloating (boiling and swelling of the body). During the drying of the glaze some of the soluble salts migrate to the surface of the pot, especially to the edges and rims, and during firing affect the glaze at these points. Apart from the difficulties of obtaining an even glaze coat, more salts are dissolved in the glaze liquid as it stands in the barrel; as glaze is used from the batch its composition over a period of time is changed and unreliable glazes result. Such materials can reliably be added to a glaze in fritted form as explained earlier. However these soluble materials offer possibilities for certain effects, which can be useful to the interested glaze maker. Soda ash (sodium carbonate) potasium carbonate and borax are perhaps the three which offer a wide range of possibilities, though they can only be used in small amounts in the test as they all have a tendency to spread widely or volatilize alarmingly. Test these materials by sprinkling on the tile. It is difficult to get an even coating of the powder; grinding the materials in a pestle and mortar will give a more workable dust. All these materials will melt and volatilize and can quite clearly be classified as type one, and their use is described in chapter 8. Some of these soluble materials also form the basis of Egyptian paste. This is a non-plastic mixture of fluxes, quartz and feldspar with a little clay. From this mixture small models or pots are worked. During drying the soluble salts migrate to the surface and in the firing form a thin skin of glaze on the surface.

Results of all the tests (1260°C 2300°F):

Section one materials

Group one: colemanite, cryolite
Group two: potash feldspar, soda feldspar, cornish stone, neph-
                      eline syenite, dolomite, lepidolite, whiting, barium
                      carbonate, petalite.
Group three: talc, china clay, ball clay, red clay, bone ash, flint.

Section two materials

Group one: wood ash, red ochre
Group two: granite, volcanic ash
Group three: —

Section three materials

Group one: lead frit, alkaline frit, borax frit, stoneware glaze
Group two: —
Group three: —

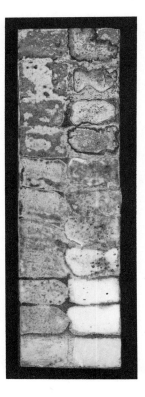

In general, group one materials are too fluid to constitute a glaze alone, group three are completely unsuitable and consequently, group two are the most promising materials on which to base a glaze. It is worth trying some of the group two materials individually as single glazes: merely mix the material with sufficient water to form a thin cream, pass through an 80 mesh sieve and dip onto a small pot. The results will be quite close to many of the early Chinese glazes which were developed over 2000 years ago. Because the materials are not plastic an even coating will be difficult to achieve; where the glaze is thick it will be milky and opaque, where it is thin it will have a tendency to craze. More useful results will be obtained by mixing materials from groups one and two or groups one and three in line blends.

4 Milky opaque crazed stoneware glaze, 100% cornish stone.

5 Milky crazed and bubbled stoneware glaze – 100% feldspar.

6 Line blend of feldspar (left) and whiting (right). Workable opaque and transparent glazes fall between the limits of feldspar 90–60% and whiting 10–30%.

TEST TWO: BIAXIAL BLENDS

	A	B	C	D	E	F	G	H	I	J	K
Raw material A	100	10	20	30	40	50	60	70	80	90	—
Raw material B	—	90	80	70	60	50	40	30	20	10	100

By mixing two materials together in the proportions suggested in this diagram to cover the wide range of possible variations, a good idea of how they will work as glazes will be obtained. Whilst the results of tests made by these methods are excellent indications as to possible glaze compositions, they cannot be regarded as giving useful glazes until particular mixtures have been tested on pots using standard glazing methods. Blends of materials can be done quickly and reasonably accurately by one of three methods.

1   The first method is the most accurate though the slowest; in each test the dry ingredients are weighed, mixed together in water, and passed through a sieve.
2   The second method uses proportions of the dry ingredients measured by volume before mixing and sieving. Successful results are calculated as weights.
3   The quickest method is to blend the materials wet from prepared mixtures of equal quantities of water and the dry ingredients. Each test is blended together in the stated proportions by taking spoonfuls.

When mixed, the test glazes are painted or poured on the tile in two thicknesses to gain a maximum number of results. As a general guide the applied glaze thickness should be about $\frac{1}{16}$ inch. Some glaze materials, such as barium carbonate, thicken the glaze while others tend to need far less water to make them manageable. It is useful to begin with measured liquid and solid ingredient amounts (especially for the wet blends) and adjust the mixtures to give the correct densities. An average thickness of liquid glaze is like that of single cream and will cover the hand without smothering it.

Some mixtures will provide workable results and the following are worth testing at stoneware temperatures:

    feldspar and whiting
    dolomite and red clay
    feldspar and colemanite
    red clay and feldspar

On the whole, however, mixtures of more than two materials are more workable; they provide glazes which are easier to apply, are more reliable, mature over a wider range of temperatures, and give greater consistency of results. Mixtures of several materials tend to melt at a lower temperature than any one of the materials used alone, and, generally speaking, the greater the number of materials used, the lower the melting temperature becomes. Materials chosen from those in group one will have a marked effect on the behaviour of materials chosen from groups two and three. However, it will be found by experiment that mixtures do not always react as predicted. In the example of feldspar and whiting it is only in the proportions of 80–20 respectively that a glaze is formed. As the proportion of whiting increases the result is not a greater melt but the reverse – the mixture becomes more refractory. The point at which the greatest degree of melt occurs is known as the eutectic point. This is a term derived from two Greek words meaning to melt readily, that is, to melt at a low temperature. A familiar example of a eutectic is that produced by adding salt to ice to cause it to melt. The eutectic mixture occurs at a 20% salt addition and further additions of salt have no more effect. A particular feature of eutectic behaviour is that usually the more components which are involved, the lower the eutectic temperature achieved. (This effect is amusingly demonstrated by Wood's metal which is an alloy of tin, lead, bismuth and cadmium in the ratio 1:2:4:1, which melts at 60–65°C (140–150°F). When fashioned into a seemingly ordinary teaspoon and put into a cup of hot tea the melting spoon is very alarming.)

Mixtures, therefore, of more than two materials will offer the glazer the possibilities of many more eutectics and the opportunity to adjust the proportions of the chosen ingredients to get a wide variety of effects. With this in mind blends of three and four materials enable many of the permutations to be tested together and the results, though often on a small scale, are useful pointers to good workable glazes.

TEST THREE: THREE LINE BLENDS

Ideally a full test should be made. This involves 66 tests and consists of three tests of single materials, 27 tests of two materials and 36 tests of three materials, as follows:

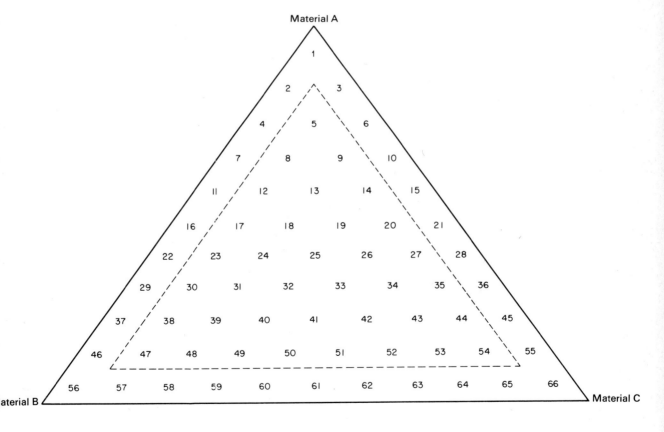

Diagram 2   Triaxial blends: the total number of tests is 66 – omit the biaxial tests to give 36 tests. Table 1, page 21, gives the proportions of each material.

Making the glaze

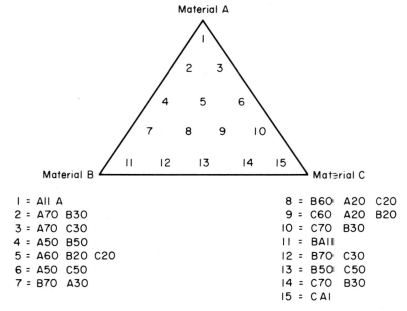

1 = All A			8 = B60 A20 C20
2 = A70 B30			9 = C60 A20 B20
3 = A70 C30			10 = C70 B30
4 = A50 B50			11 = BAll
5 = A60 B20 C20			12 = B70 C30
6 = A50 C50			13 = B50 C50
7 = B70 A30			14 = C70 B30
			15 = C Al

Diagram 3   A simplified test.

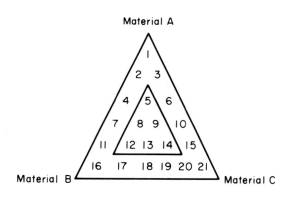

1	All	A = 100		11	A = 20	B = 80	
2	A = 80	B = 80		12	A = 20	B = 60	C = 20
3	A = 80	C = 20		13	B = 40	A = 20	C = 40
4	A = 60	B = 40		14	B = 20	A = 20	C = 60
5	A = 60	B = 20	C = 20	15	A = 20	C = 80	
6	A = 60	C = 40		16	All	B = 100	
7	A = 40	B = 60		17	B = 80	C = 20	
8	A = 40	B = 40	C = 20	18	B = 60	C = 40	
9	A = 40	B = 20	C = 40	19	B = 40	C = 60	
10	A = 40		C = 60	20	B = 20	C = 80	
				21	All	C = 100	

N.B. All tests total 100

Diagram 4   A medium test.

Test no.	% blend	Test no.	% blend	Test no.	% blend	Test no.	% blend
1	100 A	18	50 A / 30 B / 20 C	33	30 A / 30 B / 40 C	48	10 A / 70 B / 20 C
2	90 A / 10 B	19	50 A / 20 B / 30 C	34	30 A / 20 B / 50 C	49	10 A / 60 B / 30 C
3	90 A / 10 C	20	50 A / 10 B / 40 C	35	30 A / 10 B / 60 C	50	10 A / 50 B / 40 C
4	80 A / 20 B	21	50 A / 50 C	36	30 A / 70 C	51	10 A / 40 B / 50 C
5	80 A / 10 B / 10 C	22	40 A / 60 B	37	20 A / 80 B	52	10 A / 30 B / 60 C
6	80 A / 20 C	23	40 A / 50 B / 10 C	38	20 A / 70 B / 10 C	53	10 A / 20 B / 70 C
7	70 A / 30 B	24	40 A / 40 B / 20 C	39	20 A / 60 B / 20 C	54	10 A / 10 B / 80 C
8	70 A / 20 B / 10 C	25	40 A / 30 B / 30 C	40	20 A / 50 B / 30 C	55	10 A / 90 C
9	70 A / 10 B / 20 C	26	40 A / 20 B / 40 C	41	20 A / 40 B / 40 C	56	100 B
10	70 A / 30 C	27	40 A / 10 B / 50 C	42	20 A / 30 B / 50 C	57	90 B / 10 C
11	60 A / 40 B	28	40 A / 60 C	43	20 A / 20 B / 60 C	58	80 B / 20 C
12	60 A / 30 B / 10 C	29	30 A / 70 B	44	20 A / 10 B / 70 C	59	70 B / 30 C
13	60 A / 20 B / 20 C	30	30 A / 60 B / 10 C	45	20 A / 80 C	60	60 B / 40 C
14	60 A / 10 B / 30 C	31	30 A / 50 B / 20 C	46	10 A / 90 B	61	50 B / 50 C
15	60 A / 40 C	32	30 A / 40 B / 30 C	47	10 A / 80 B / 10 C	62	40 B / 60 C
16	50 A / 50 B					63	30 B / 70 C
17	50 A / 40 B / 10 C					64	20 B / 80 C
						65	10 B / 90 C
						66	100 C

Table 1   Triaxial blends.

Selecting materials

Mixtures of three materials chosen from group three will give poor results. Mixtures of materials from group one only will usually give over melted results. Two classic mixtures which incorporate one material from each group are:

Feldspar, whiting and flint.
Feldspar, whiting and china clay.

Other suggestions are:

Feldspar, dolomite and china clay.
Whiting, china clay and ball clay.
Cornish stone, whiting and china clay.

7 Test No. 42, dry white yellow opaque glaze, nepheline syenite 20, whiting 30, china clay 50, which responds well to small additions of colouring oxides, though the high amount of china clay may cause crawling problems. These could be overcome by substituting 25 parts of calcined china clay for the plastic china clay.

8 Test No. 9 – white opaque glaze with white spots and craze lines, nepheline syenite 70, whiting 10, china clay 20.

Interpreting results

From the results of triaxial blends, the effects of increasing or decreasing amounts of various materials can be plotted on a chart:

1   From the results of the test blend, on a triangular chart, can be marked the areas in which the glaze has crazed, the areas in which the glaze is matt or shiny and the areas where no glaze has been formed.
2   Try to work out what excess of materials causes these various glaze states.
3   Mark on the chart any eutectic points, that is, the points at which the greatest degree of melting has occurred.
4   Try to identify any of the physical effects of glaze such as crawling, shelling or peeling.

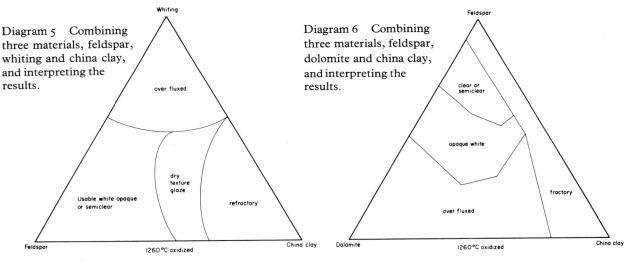

Diagram 5   Combining three materials, feldspar, whiting and china clay, and interpreting the results.

Diagram 6   Combining three materials, feldspar, dolomite and china clay, and interpreting the results.

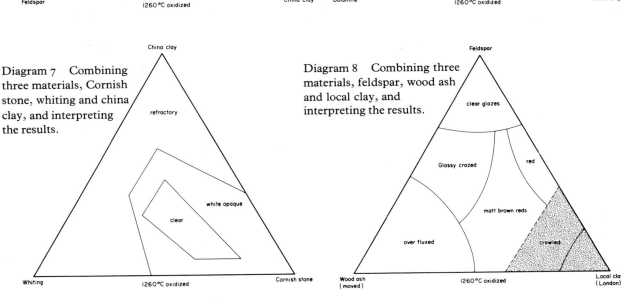

Diagram 7   Combining three materials, Cornish stone, whiting and china clay, and interpreting the results.

Diagram 8   Combining three materials, feldspar, wood ash and local clay, and interpreting the results.

TEST FOUR: MIXTURES OF FOUR MATERIALS

Mixtures of four materials present an almost infinite range of possibilities to the potter. Such an extensive list of glaze formulations enables many of the basic requirements of handling and firing needs of the glaze to be satisfied. Blends of four materials are not so easy to plot as the blends of three materials on a result diagram, but nevertheless with careful selection of the four ingredients to represent the groupings of materials limited results can be plotted.

Two sets of tests are given here, one involving 36 tests, the other 12; often it is the subtle proportions between the ingredients which provide individual glaze preferences though the plan with the smaller number of tests will indicate the sort of results that are possible.

Classical combinations of materials would be:

Feldspar (any), whiting, china clay and flint.

There are many combinations of materials which will provide a wide variety of glazes and other suggested combinations are:

Nepheline syenite, feldspar, china clay and whiting.
Nepheline syenite, barium carbonate, china clay and whiting.
Feldspar, whiting, dolomite and china clay.
Feldspar, talc, dolomite and china clay.
Nepheline syenite, barium carbonate, china clay and dolomite.

Percentages listed here on the four materials blends show the maximum amount of any particular ingredient is 50%. This does not entirely reflect all the possibilities which exist as a glaze may have 70% of a single ingredient.

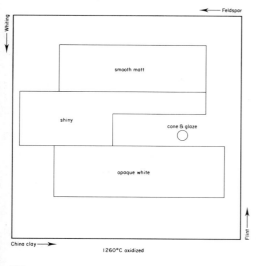

Diagram 9

9 Stoneware tile. Blend of four materials – whiting, china clay, flint, feldspar. Diagram 9 gives an analysis of the results for 121 tests.

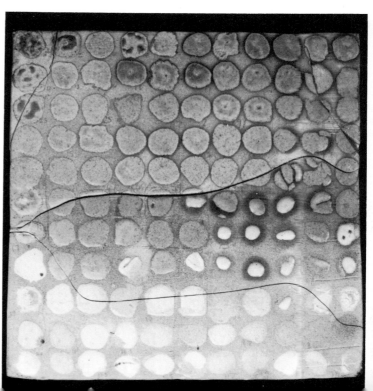

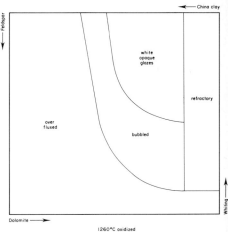

10 *Stoneware tile – blend of four materials – feldspar, whiting, dolomite and china clay.*

Diagram 10

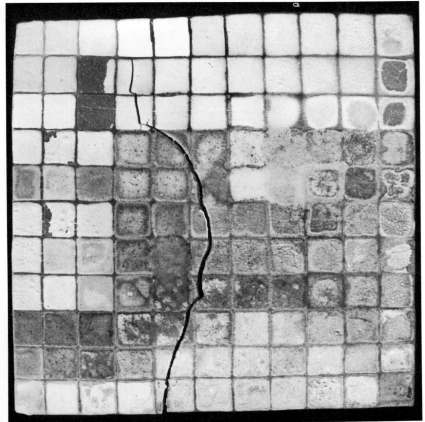

Diagram 11

11 *Stoneware tile – blend of four materials – barium carbonate, feldspar, whiting, china clay.*

26

Material D → (columns): 0, 10, 20, 30, 40, 50

Material A ↓ (rows): 50, 40, 30, 20, 10, 0

Material A	D=0	D=10	D=20	D=30	D=40	D=50	Material C
50	1) A50 B50 C0 D0	2) A50 B40 C0 D10	3) A50 B30 C0 D20	4) A50 B20 C D30	5) A50 B10 C0 D40	6) A50 B0 C0 D50	0
40	7) A40 B50 C10 D0	8) A40 B40 C10 D10	9) A40 B30 C10 D20	10) A40 B20 C10 D30	11) A40 B10 C10 D40	12) A40 B0 C10 D50	10
30	13) A30 B50 C20 D0	14) A30 B40 C20 D10	15) A30 B30 C20 D20	16) A30 B20 C20 D30	17) A30 B10 C20 D40	18) A30 B20 C20 D50	20
20	19) A20 B50 C30 D0	20) A20 B40 C30 D10	21) A20 B30 C30 D20	22) A20 B20 C30 D30	23) A20 B10 C30 D40	24) A20 B0 C30 D50	30
10	25) A10 B50 C40 D0	26) A10 B40 C40 D10	27) A10 B30 C40 D20	28) A10 B20 C40 D30	29) A10 B10 C40 D40	30) A10 B0 C40 D50	40
0	31) A0 B50 C50 D0	32) A0 B40 C50 D10	33) A0 B30 C50 D20	34) A0 B20 C50 D30	35) A0 B10 C50 D40	36) A0 B0 C50 D50	50

Material B → (bottom): 50, 40, 30, 20, 10, 0

Table 2

A blend of four materials, 36 tests.

Material D → (columns %): 0, 5, 10, 15, 20, 25, 30, 35, 40, 45, 50

Material A ↓ (rows %): 50, 45, 40, 35, 30, 25, 20, 15, 10, 5, 0

Material A	0	5	10	15	20	25	30	35	40	45	50	Material C %
50	1	2	3	4	5	6	7	8	9	10	11	0
45	12	13	14	15	16	17	18	19	20	21	22	5
40	23	24	25	26	27	28	29	30	31	32	33	10
35	34	35	36	37	38	39	40	41	42	43	44	15
30	45	46	47	48	49	50	51	52	53	54	55	20
25	56	57	58	59	60	61	62	63	64	65	66	25
20	67	68	69	70	71	72	73	74	75	76	77	30
15	78	79	80	81	82	83	84	85	86	87	88	35
10	89	90	91	92	93	94	95	96	97	98	99	40
5	100	101	102	103	104	105	106	107	108	109	110	45
0	111	112	113	114	115	116	117	118	119	120	121	50

Material B → (bottom %): 50, 45, 40, 35, 30, 25, 20, 15, 10, 5, 0

Table 3

A blend of four materials, 121 tests.

Test no.	% A	% B	% C	% D
1	50	50	—	—
2	50	45	—	5
3	50	40	—	10
4	50	35	—	15
5	50	30	—	20
6	50	25	—	25
7	50	20	—	30
8	50	15	—	35
9	50	10	—	40
10	50	5	—	45
11	50	—	—	50
12	45	50	5	—
13	45	45	5	5
14	45	40	5	10
15	45	35	5	15
16	45	30	5	20
17	45	25	5	25
18	45	20	5	30
19	45	15	5	35
20	45	10	5	40
21	45	5	5	45
22	45	—	5	50
23	40	50	10	—
24	40	45	10	5
25	40	40	10	10
26	40	35	10	15
27	40	30	10	20
28	40	25	10	25
29	40	20	10	30
30	40	15	10	35
31	40	10	10	40
32	40	5	10	45
33	40	—	10	50
34	35	50	15	—
35	35	45	15	5
36	35	40	15	10
37	35	35	15	15
38	35	30	15	20
39	35	25	15	25
40	35	20	15	30
41	35	15	15	35
42	35	10	15	40
43	35	5	15	45
44	35	—	15	50
45	30	50	20	—
46	30	45	20	5
47	30	40	20	10
48	30	35	20	15
49	30	30	20	20
50	30	25	20	25
51	30	20	20	30
52	30	15	20	35
53	30	10	20	40
54	30	5	20	45
55	30	—	20	50
56	25	50	25	—
57	25	45	25	5
58	25	40	25	10
59	25	35	25	15
60	25	30	25	20
61	25	25	25	25
62	25	20	25	30
63	25	15	25	35
64	25	10	25	40
65	25	5	25	45
66	25	—	25	50
67	20	50	30	—
68	20	45	30	5
69	20	40	30	10
70	20	35	30	15
71	20	30	30	20
72	20	25	30	25
73	20	20	30	30
74	20	15	30	35
75	20	10	30	40
76	20	5	30	45
77	20	—	30	50
78	15	50	35	—
79	15	45	35	5
80	15	40	35	10
81	15	35	35	15
82	15	30	35	20
83	15	25	35	25
84	15	20	35	30
85	15	15	35	35
86	15	10	35	40
87	15	5	35	45
88	15	—	35	50
89	10	50	40	—
90	10	45	40	5
91	10	40	40	10
92	10	35	40	15
93	10	30	40	20
94	10	25	40	25
95	10	20	40	30
96	10	15	40	35
97	10	10	40	40
98	10	5	40	45
99	10	—	40	50
100	5	50	45	—
101	5	45	45	5
102	5	40	45	10
103	5	35	45	15
104	5	30	45	20
105	5	25	45	25
106	5	20	45	30
107	5	15	45	35
108	5	10	45	40
109	5	5	45	45
110	5	—	45	50
111	—	50	50	—
112	—	45	50	5
113	—	40	50	10
114	—	35	50	15
115	—	30	50	20
116	—	25	50	25
117	—	20	50	30
118	—	15	50	35
119	—	10	50	40
120	—	5	50	45
121	—	—	50	50

Table 4
A blend of four materials, 121 tests.

Using the results

A quick look at a tile with a great many individual results cannot be interpreted instantly. Certainly some areas will seem more promising than others, and some glazes may stand out as real possibilities, but usually more careful scrutiny is necessary. It is often helpful to cover up many of the tests so that each can be looked at with greater care. What often appears to be a suitable glaze on a small area of tile may not be so successful on a pot, and a second test of selected results needs to be made to check this. Tests at this stage give most satisfactory results used on small test pots or bowls rather than on test tiles, though if these are fired upright they are a better guide to the workability of the glaze.

Once a few standard glazes have been obtained they can form the basis for further tests. Good, useful basic glazes are:

A smooth transparent glaze.
A matt glaze.
A semi-matt glaze.

NATURAL MATERIALS

Materials which were put into section two, and called natural glaze materials, have no definite chemical formula, and are used empirically in glazes. These materials can be defined as occurring in nature and can be used in glazes with a minimum of preparation. The advantages of such materials, apart from the fact that they are probably available free of charge, is that they contain traces of 'impurities' which cannot without great difficulty be chemically identified. The presence of these impurities enables many unique glaze effects to be obtained. It is almost impossible to reproduce these effects using chemically 'pure' ingredients A second point of interest is that these impurities, often present in large numbers in small quantities, can act as a powerful flux.

However, such materials also have certain disadvantages; for example, the regular reproductibility of particular effects is limited by the amount of the materials in stock, since two separate lots of the same material do not necessarily react in the same way. Further supplies of what may nominally be similar materials may not produce the same effect. Some materials need careful preparation to eliminate unwanted effects, such as the washing away of soluble salts present in ash: the sieving of material to remove stones. Most natural materials are only really effective at stoneware temperatures. Below this, their effects are not particularly noticeable.

Wood ash

The use of wood and plant ash as a glaze ingredient dates far back in antiquity and it was the Chinese who discovered that at higher temperatures the ash from wood used to fire the kiln settled on the surface of clays to form fairly simple, but often attractively mottled, glaze. Ashes contain, in a fine state of division, large proportions of silica, some potassium and sodium salts, alkaline earths, iron and often phosphate salts. The amounts and varieties of these minerals vary considerably from plant to plant, soil to soil and, with the same plant, season to season. The colour of ashes, either before or after washing, varies from white to grey brown and black, and while some of this colour is due to fine particles of charcoal (carbon), which burns out from the glaze, some is due to the presence of iron, which affects the colour of the glaze, though some potters think that small quantities of copper may be present in certain ashes – for example, those of the cupressus.

When combined with feldspar or clay, wood or plant ash will form richly textured and coloured glazes at temperatures about 1200°C (2192°F). The romantic appeal of using ash makes it a favourite material for the stoneware potter. Various analyses of ashes have been carried out but are relevant only for that particular batch. The same sort of wood grown on different ground will inevitably yield a different analysis.

Ashes can be classified by several means. The useful classification is hard, soft and medium ashes. A more precise classification identifies each ash by its name. Generally speaking, the quicker the growth, the higher the proportion of silica and the harder the ash. The longer the growth, the softer the ash; as a result the hard woods, which have taken many years to grow, yield low silica and high flux content, such as potassium and calcium, and give soft ash. Quickly grown plants, such as bracken, give ash with a high silica content and a hard ash. However, the silica content of ash is often intimately combined with the other ingredients and does not act as a refractory material in the way that flint or quartz acts.

12 Cross section of ash glaze on stoneware. Transmitted light (crossed polars) × 160. Notice how integrated the glaze and body have become.

13 Eric James Mellon. Ash glazed bowl 'Europa and the Bull – the Journey to Crete' 35 cm (14 in.). A slip glaze (Apple ash 20, whiting 10, feldspar 10, iron oxide 6, ball clay (Pikes) 57) was brushed onto the raw clay and the design scratched through with a sharpened stick. After the bisque firing the design was painted using colouring oxides of iron, cobalt and copper mixed with water. The whiting in the slip glaze turns the iron to yellows and red and gives warmth to the cobalt. An ash glaze (Elm ash 40, body clay 5, china clay 25, feldspar 40, flint 10) was applied over the decoration to give a soft pale grey in the firing, the thickness of application affects the intensity of the colouring oxides. The kiln was packed as tightly as possible and fired to 1300°C (2372°F) over 20–24 hours. Photograph by Michael Moore.

Classical combinations of materials in glazes with ash include feldspar, clay and flint. Small quantities of calcium carbonate (whiting) or dolomite are often added. Ash is usually considered to be a fluxing material falling into group one materials.

Preparing ash: Ash can be collected from several sources, but tests are only economically worthwhile on sizable batches. Ash burnt in the hearth, if collected over a period, can provide a good supply, as can bonfires. Wood and plants specially collected for burning to provide named species should be burnt on a fire-brick base in the open on a calm day; the bricks prevent contamination from iron (present in soil), enable a good supply of oxygen so that thorough burning can take place and the lack of wind helps to prevent the fine ash particles from being blown away. As soon as the ashes are cold – this takes some time as ash is an efficient insulating material – put them into water; the unburnt black carbon will float to the top and can be removed, the water will begin to dissolve the soluble salts of sodium and as a result will appear yellow and feel soapy to touch. The water should be changed several times until it stays clear and tasteless – about three changes are usually sufficient. The ash can now be passed through an 80 mesh sieve and allowed to dry. The method of preparation used for the ash should, as far as possible, be the same for all similar batches. Some potters prefer to use unwashed ash after passing it dry through a fairly coarse sieve. This will render the glaze produced less reliable as it will gradually change as the soluble sodium salts are dissolved out of the ash.

Testing the ash: The first test is to mix the ash with water, paint it on a test tile, and fire it on its own. At 1250°C (2282°F) most ashes will melt readily, while others will be much less fluid; some will be dark, while others will be white opaque. From these tests combinations with other materials can begin – either in line blends with feldspar, nepheline syenite or clay (because of their low alumina content ashes need stiffening), or in triaxial blends with such materials as feldspar and clay. Two classical ash recipes are:

ash 2 feldspar 2 china clay 1.
ash 2 feldspar 2 ball clay 1.

Useful line blends of ash with feldspar, nepheline syenite, cornish stone or clay, etc., will yield interesting results. Different ashes will, of course, in similar combinations, give different results. Small amounts of flint added to the glaze will tend to make it more glassy.

Some ash glazes only develop their full qualities at higher temperatures than those reached in the average stoneware firing. Such glazes can be rendered more fusible, without greatly affecting the glaze composition by the addition of 5% alkaline frit. Ash glazes respond very well to small additions of colouring oxides and painted oxide decoration. Iron oxide seems to look particularly well on or in ash glazes where it breaks and forms bright reds to dull yellows.

Local clays and soils
Generally speaking, clay only differs from soil by its lack of vegetable or organic materials. This causes soil to crumble rather than enabling it to be moulded and modelled. However, in the kiln, organic material burns away and the soil can be used as a sort of clay for use in glazes. Soil usually contains iron in varying amounts and this will always have the effect of colouring the glaze.

Clay, as dug, varies enormously in composition from area to area. Outcrops of clay, which have a fairly consistent composition, are mined and sold commercially in the UK in Staffordshire, Devon and Cornwall. These clays, for the purpose of special effects in glazes, are usually too pure. Also for special glaze effects, the finer the clay particles, the more integrated they become in the glaze mix. Red, brown and yellow clays indicate varying amounts of iron and/or manganese present in different forms. Sometimes the lighter coloured clays contain the higher amounts of iron. 'London' clay found approximately at a depth of two feet in the London area, is yellow ochre in colour and can form the basis of many iron glazes. At stoneware temperatures it vitrifies to a dull brown or red colour. Another rich source of clay is a local brick works. Any local clay gives better results in a glaze if the particles are fine; in the case of US materials Albany and Barnard clay this is no problem. UK clays are much improved if they are first milled for 2–4 hours in a ball mill.

Preparation of clay: collect from a depth of at least 4 feet if possible, as this helps to eliminate vegetable matter and stones.

1 Dry out clay, break into small pieces and soak in plenty of water.
2 Skim off any floating material, pass remainder through 80 mesh sieve.
3 Dry out clay, stirring regularly to create a homogeneous mix and to prevent large particles from remaining at the bottom.

Testing

1   Test alone on the tile – painted at various thicknesses and, depending upon the result (i.e. hard, medium, soft), use in line blends with such materials as whiting, ash, cryolite, dolomite.
2   Test in triaxial blends, e.g. clay, ash, feldspar; clay, whiting, feldspar.

Occasionally recipes call for quite large amounts of clay – up to and over 30% for example – and this presents certain problems of application. Such high proportions of raw clay may cause the glaze to crawl on biscuit fired ware. If raw glazing is impractical, a proportion of the clay to be used in the glaze can be crushed, calcined at ordinary biscuit temperature, crushed again and then added to the glaze mix. Most glazes benefit from the presence of a reasonable proportion of raw clay so a combination of calcined and raw clay will enable the glaze to be successfully applied to a biscuited pot.

Mud

The fine mud found in streams, rivers and ponds, will often make a good vitrified dark glaze used alone or in combination with other materials at high temperature. Famous examples are Albany Slip and Barnard Slip from the USA. No direct equivalents are known in the UK except those which may be discovered locally. Line blends with feldspar, whiting and ash, may again produce successful results. Red Fremington clay has an analysis which approximates nearest to Albany Slip and can be used as the nearest British equivalent.

Granite and other rocks

Outcrops of granite occur in the UK in Devon, Cornwall and Scotland (The Grampians), and in County Wicklow, Ireland. Granite varies in colour according to the amount of iron present. In polished granite the three ingredients present can be recognized by their separate colour and shape – feldspar, mica and quartz. Granite dust will melt at stoneware temperature to form a stiff glass. In glazes it can be substituted for feldspar. Accessible sources are monumental masons, quarries and road building materials. Some suppliers of raw materials supply granite dust and will provide analysis of named stones. Hornblende, a ferro-magnesium alumino-silicate rock, quarried at Helsbury Quarry, Camborne, Cornwall (UK), can be used in a glaze to replace some or all of the feldspar. It approximates to the formula $(MgFe)_2.SiO_4$. Other similar materials are the basalts, pumice and volcanic ash, all of which are general terms rather than specific types. All can be used in a glaze to replace feldspar. Pumice can be used in glazes and has recently come into use to replace feldspar. Its high iron content makes it unsuitable for transparent or white glazes. Analyses are given as follows:

	European	*American*
SiO_2	55.28	72.51
Al_2O_3	21.90	11.55
Fe_2O_3	2.66	1.21
K_2O	6.21	7.84
Na_2O	5.10	1.79
TiO_2	0.28	0.54
CaO	1.88	0.68
MgO	0.37	0.07
H_2O	5.64	3.81
	99.32	100.00

Having the molecular formulae:

European
$0.429\ Na_2O$
$0.346\ K_2O$ $1.126\ Al_2O_3$ $4.822\ SiO_2$
$0.047\ MgO$ $0.089\ Fe_2O_3$
$0.178\ CaO$ $0.021\ TiO_2$

American
$0.230\ Na_2O$
$0.659\ K_2O$ $0.897\ Al_2O_3$ $9.596\ SiO_2$
$0.016\ MgO$ $0.063\ Fe_2O_3$
$0.095\ CaO$ $0.056\ TiO_2$

Other materials

It is surprising how many materials can be used by the glaze maker, though most are either too expensive or too difficult to acquire to be used for other than experimental purposes. Furnace slag has been used successfully in glazes. It melts at 1250°C (2282°F) to form a glaze. A similar material is basic slag (steelworks flue sweepings) which is often used as garden fertiliser, and can be obtained from a garden supplier. The material has a complex molecular formula ($Ca_3P_2O_1$, $CaSiO_2$, C, Fe_2O_3) and is a useful source of phosphorous. When basic slag is used, adjustments to the alkaline earth content of any glaze must be made because of the high calcium content.

Iron rust can also be used as an impure iron pigment after grinding the scales in a pestle and mortar. Coal and coke, when burnt, render an ash which seems to have a high portion of iron. Coal ash contains a large amount of silica and can be successfully introduced into the glaze by substituting it for flint.

THE 'IMPOSSIBLE' MATERIALS

Into this section come those materials which are soluble in water and cannot be used with any degree of accuracy in normal glaze compositions, but are usually incorporated into frit compositions, which are then used as ordinary glaze ingredients. However, these soluble materials can be used as ingredients for dry glazing, and have their own particular features

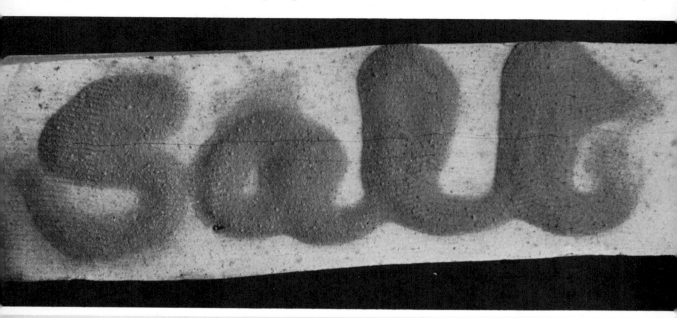

which are useful to the potter. The use of such materials is largely restricted to flat surfaces where they will melt to form glassy surfaces which are relatively soft and susceptible to acid attack. For this reason, such effects are best used on decorative pieces not intended for use with food.

The chief quality of these materials is firstly their ability to melt and form clear glazes (which are inevitably crazed) and secondly their response to additions of colouring oxides. The alkaline nature of the materials is particularly responsive to certain colours, and here there is much experimenting the studio potter can do to discover the wide variety of colours available from the use of these materials.

Materials involved:

Borax ($Na_2.B_4O_7$) (i.e. dehydrated).
Boric acid (H_3BO_3).
Potassium carbonate (K_2CO_3) Pearl ash.
Potassium nitrate (KNO_3) Nitre.
Potassium bicarbonate ($KHCO_3$).
Sodium carbonate (Na_2CO_3).

Tests with each material on its own will give some workable results, others will need to be combined with flint to give glassy surfaces. Additions of 1–2% colouring oxides will usually be sufficient to give a rich colour response, especially from copper, manganese and nickel; less cobalt is required for good colour.

14 'Salt' written in ordinary table salt and fired on a flat tile to stoneware temperature (oxidized).

15 Stoneware bowl thrown from clay to which has been added a small percentage of ordinary salt. During drying the salt migrated to the surface and in the firing caused this turbulent volcanic surface (oxidized).

16 Pestle and mortar. Photograph – Harrison Mayer Ltd.

The usual method is to weigh the ingredients in the normal way, then grind them well in a pestle and mortar; the colour is best developed if the powder is sprinkled on top of white slip which acts as a reflector to bring out the richness of the colour, though the powder can be used on top of a white glaze. The amount of powder required is difficult to estimate, but usually it seems that more rather than less is needed for a good covering. From a practical point of view, it is safer to restrict the colour to limited areas which are recessed by a pattern, or place the powder in the bottom of a bowl or flat dish to prevent it from running onto the kiln shelves.

Results obtained at earthenware temperatures
Few materials fired on their own below 1150°C (2100°F) will have melted sufficiently to form a usable glaze; the most important materials around which glazes can be built are the lead and alkaline frits which avoid problems of solubility and poison.

The following lists materials which are useful to the earthenware glazer, and the groups in which they fall.

Classification of materials fired alone at 1100°C (2012°F)
Group one (melted)
Cryolite, colemanite, fluorspar, alkaline frit, lead frit, lithium carbonate.
Group two (affected)
Yellow ochre, petalite, cornish stone, whiting, Fremington clay, local clay, zinc oxide.
Group three (unaffected)
Nepheline syenite, dolomite, talc, feldspar, bone ash, china clay.

This list does not include such natural materials as wood ash which are of little use in glazes at this temperature as they are too refractory.
Successful pairs of materials for testing are:

Any frit with any clay.
Any frit with any feldspar.
Colemanite with feldspar or clay.

Triaxial blends could include:

Any frit, any clay, any feldspar;
or frit, clay and fluorspar.

A careful selection will enable many unusual glazes to be formed.

Useful basic transparent glazes with a wide firing range which are relatively craze-free can be made from a mixture of lead bisilicate, borax frit, cornish stone and flint. Blends of these four materials will produce a wide range of glaze textures. A transparent glaze with the following recipe is a good starting point:

Lead bisilicate	25	Flint	10	
Borax frit	50	China clay	5	for suspension
Cornish stone	10	(or bentonite	2)	

Experiments can be made with this glaze base; additions of other materials will give rich and interesting results.

Zinc oxide is a useful material for the earthenware glazer. It is the major flux in Bristol glazes which were developed in the nineteenth century to replace glazes which contained lead. Zinc is a flux with a wider operating range than lead and also has an effect on the quality of the glaze as well as affecting the colours of added metal oxides. Zinc has the advantage over lead of being non-piosonous. A useful starting point for Bristol glazes are mixtures of four materials – zinc oxide, nepheline syenite, whiting and flint. A high proportion of zinc oxide will result in crystalline glazes.

Colemanite or gerstley borate (or calcium borate frit) is also a useful basis for earthenware glazes, with up to 60%–70% in a mixture, with the remainder made up of equal parts china clay and flint. Increased amounts of flint will harden the glaze. Glazes based on colemanite will respond well to small additions of copper and cobalt.

For highly textured earthenware glazes cryolite and fluorspar are useful materials. When combined with china clay and flint in roughly equal proportions mottled textured glazes result. Likewise, fine silicon carbide, added in small amounts of 1–1.5%, will give textured surfaces and all can be combined with the usual colouring oxides to give rich decorative effects.

For making glazes opaque the usual additions of tin or zirconium are effective; for matt effects combinations of zinc and china clay are suitable. Titanium dioxide is a usual addition to earthenware glazes: in small amounts (4–7%) it gives a pleasant satin vellum matt which responds well to small amounts of colouring oxides. For example it tends to produce green blues with cobalt, and yellows with nickel. An attractive vellum glaze for 1050°C (1922°F) which responds well to added colouring oxides:

Lead bisilicate	60
Borax frit	15
China clay	15
Zinc oxide	5
Titanium oxide	5
+ Tin oxide 4%	

Testing the effects of introducing single materials to a basic glaze
Once a basic glaze has been discovered, by any of the empirical methods outlined, the effect of adding increasing amounts of another glaze material can be observed. The simplest way is to blend by the wet line method the basic glaze with the basic glaze plus, say, 20%, 40% or 60% of the new materials. This additional amount depends to some extent on the likely effect which will be produced.

In the tests illustrated, using a semi-transparent basic glaze with the recipe Feldspar 30, Whiting 25, China clay 20 Flint 25 fired to 1260°C (2300°F), proportions of raw materials were added by the wet blend method using as A the basic glaze blended with B – the basic glaze plus either 20% or 40% of the material tested; oxidized firing.

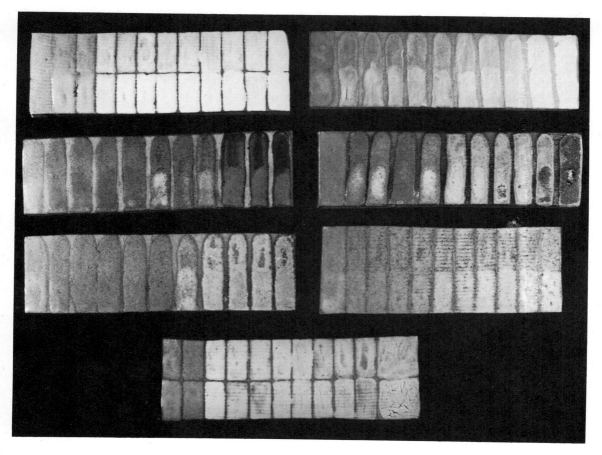

17 Tiles showing the effects of adding increasing amounts of one material to a basic milky/clear stoneware glaze – feldspar 25, whiting 20, china clay 25, flint 30. The glaze on its own is at the left of each tile, the largest addition is at the right. Additions are:
Top left – china clay
Second row left – dolomite
Third row left – magnesium carbonate
Bottom – titanium oxide
Top right – tin oxide
Second row right – cryolite
Third row right – talc

1 Feldspar (20%) glaze became more opaque and stiffer with a tendency to pinhole.

2 Whiting (40%) initially gave a clearer, more transparent glaze. At the maximum additions, it gave opaque effects with crystallization.

3 China clay (40%). About 15% addition gave a dull opaque matt; 40% gave a dry white.

4 Flint (40%). The glaze gave progressively shinier and more opaque results, each with a very hard surface.

5 Dolomite (40%). Initial additions gave a transparent glaze which gradually changed to a matt white opaque which at 30–40% broke the glaze surface with crystal formations.

6 Talc (40%). Small additions gave a clearer glaze which became more opaque; 25–35% additions gave a dark green matt; 40% gave pinholing.

7 Magnesium carbonate (4%) gave progressively brighter and whiter glazes which reacted with the body to give an attractive speckled effect; 40% gave a crawled white opaque glaze with orange speckles.

8 Colemanite (40%). 5% gave a rich transparent glaze which as amounts increased ran freely and boiled at 40% addition to give a rough bubbled surface.

9   Borocalcite (40%). Results almost identical to those of colemanite additions.

10 Barium carbonate (40%). Additions of 5–10% gave a clear glaze with some air bubbles; 25–30% gave a matt glaze with a crystalline surface; 35–40% gave a very rough dry surface.

11 Fluorspar (40%). 10–15% gave a bright clear glaze with a hard surface; 25–30% gave a semi-matt surface and 35–40% gave a whitish crystalline glaze with a crazed surface.

12 Cryolite (40%). 5–20% gave a white opaque glaze with a pleasant blue colour; 20–30% gave a dry matt glaze which broke with crystals on the surface; 35–40% gave a runny treacle glaze with heavy crazing.

13 Zinc oxide (40%). 5–15% additions gave a white opaque semi-matt glaze. Greater quantities gave a drier and more opaque glaze.

14 Amblygonite. 5–15% gave a semi-matt opaque speckled glaze; 20–30% gave a clear runny glaze with opaque patches; 30–40% peeled and flaked off the surface of the clay.

15 Titanium (40%). Additions of 5–10% gave matt white, which progressively became more matt and yellow/cream, and where thin red; 40% gave a thick crawled glaze.

16 Tin oxide (40%) gave a rich, thick white glaze. In increasing amounts, glazes became drier and showed less tendency to smooth out.

17 Zircon (40%). Opacity was gradually increased but with a creamy colour.

18 Bone ash (40%). Gradually induced a pleasant sugary greyish matt whiteness which at quantities above 20% was dry.

19 Luxulyan stone (40%). Little effect, a tendency towards dryness as the amounts increased.

20 Wood ash (40%). Additions of 10–20% gave a more transparent glaze with a delicate yellow tinge. Greater amounts were more matt, especially where thin.

21 Yellow ochre (40%). Small additions gave a transparent glaze coloured pale cream. The colour intensified as the amounts increased and 40% gave a dark brown matt glaze.

22 London clay (40%). Matt glazes resulted which were coloured beige or stone. Amounts above 20% became stiff and full of pinholes. Additions of iron oxide may render it rather attractive in glazes.

3
Colour in Ceramics

There are five different ways of obtaining colour in ceramics (though they do not all come under the strict classification of glazes, they do all affect the final glaze colour) and two methods of glaze firing which affect colour (chapter 10). Various metal oxides are the sources of colour and they can be used in any of five ways:

1   Mixed into the clay body.
2   Mixed into the engobe or slip and applied onto the surface of the clay body.
3   Painted or sprayed onto the pot as underglaze colours.
4   Painted on top of or mixed into the raw (i.e. unfired) glaze as in glaze colours.
5   Applied on to the fired glaze as on-glaze colours in the form of enamels or as transfer decorations.

All colours, by whatever method they are employed, are affected to some extent by the conditions under which they are fired in the kiln, by the composition of the glaze with which they are used, and by the temperature to which they are fired. In other words, from a small number of colouring oxides a great range of shades is available to the studio potter who is prepared to experiment and search for the effects and qualities available, without being discouraged by early failures.

The potter seeking colour at stoneware temperatures in an electric kiln is faced with certain problems of subtlety and softness not immediately facing the potter firing in a reducing atmosphere. A good example is that of iron oxide present in small quantities in the body and glaze which, under reducing conditions, gives soft blues and pale green which are typical effects found in many classical Chinese glazes. Such small quantities of iron oxide in the electric kiln will, however, have little effect, other than to give a pale yellow colour irrespective on the glaze composition. Under reducing kiln conditions, certain other effects can be achieved which are denied the potter working with an oxidized kiln atmosphere; of particular significance in this respect are copper and iron, both of which behave very differently in the two conditions and this must be borne in mind.

Generally, the higher the temperature the more limited the range of colouring oxides becomes. For instance certain colours, such as signal red, cannot be obtained at temperatures much in excess of 1100°C (2012°F). At high temperatures, too, the interaction which occurs between the body and the glaze tends to soften colours and render them less brilliant. This is in contrast to the typical earthenware colours which are likely to be bright and clear. To the stoneware potter a different palette is available in which softness, depth and richness of colour are the chief qualities. The range of tones and effects is almost limitless with all the variations which are possible and it is useful to consider all the five different methods by which the colour can be applied before looking individually at the effects of each colouring oxide.

BODY COLOUR

Most people are familiar with the commonest example of this technique, that is Wedgwood's Black Basalt and Blue and Green Jasper ware. By compounding special clay into which were added various colouring oxides, coloured bodies were made. Glazing was not always necessary to complete the effect. On a more general level most potters will have found that at stoneware temperatures a white glaze will react differently when fired over a light coloured body from when it is fired over a darker body in which there is a proportion of iron. Often the effect is startlingly different.

18 Paul Philp. Pressmould bowl, made of earthenware clay coloured with body stains and partially mixed together. Transparent earthenware glaze 10 cm (4 in.) across.

The colouring of clay bodies can be achieved by using either metal oxides or prepared body stains. Such stains are prepared commercially from intimate mixtures of metal oxides and raw materials heated together until they sinter to form the calcined colour required. This calcining process removes the volatile impurities, develops the colour and renders it inert at temperatures below the calcination temperature. Most manufacturers offer a wide range of such prepared stains which can be added to a light firing clay body in quantities up to a maximum of 20% depending upon the strength of colour required. Some stains withstand stoneware temperatures, whilst others may become dull or virtually disappear.

Large additions of stain added to the body affect its composition and therefore its firing possibilities and also the working qualities of the clay may be affected. The addition of metal oxides, in particular to the body may cause it to bloat and blister in the firing by the action of the oxide causing the clay to fuse. This can be overcome to some extent by adding refractory materials such as high-temperature grog to the body to strengthen the clay and reduce the shrinkage. Little can be done about the reduced working qualities of the clay to which a large proportion of non-plastic materials such as grog or body stain has been added. This mainly results in loss of plasticity.

Colouring metal oxides are weight-for-weight much more powerful than body stains and 5% or 10% present in the body is often sufficient to give very strong effects. On the whole, glazes need to be applied more thickly over coloured bodies to develop a rich effect and careful trials with selected glazes are necessary.

ENGOBES OR SLIPS

Slips can serve one of three main purposes: they can be used to cover over a body to provide either a suitable base for a particular glaze or a layer of colour, in which instance they are then known as underslips; they can provide a coloured decorative layer which will react positively with the glaze to give particular effects, an example is an iron bearing slip; they can be used as a decorative technique in their own right and if covered with a transparent glaze are known as slipware. Coloured slips painted or sprayed onto greenware and then fired without glaze can also give beautiful and subtle results.

19 Emmanuel Cooper. Stoneware bowl. White opaque glaze, with an addition of 3% bone ash, over black slip which breaks through to give a richly textured but practical surface; 25 cm (10 in.) across 1260°C (2300°F).

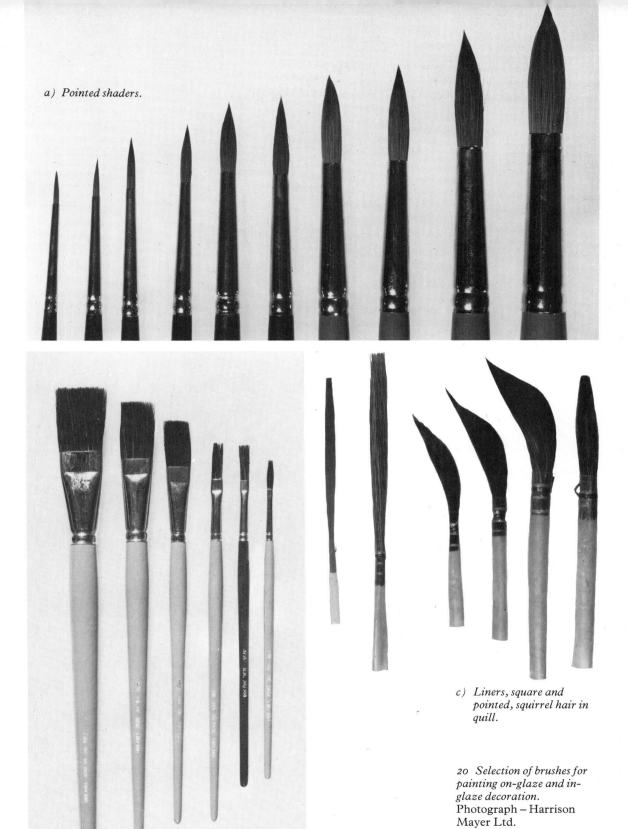

a) Pointed shaders.

b) Flat ox-hair brushes.

c) Liners, square and pointed, squirrel hair in quill.

20 Selection of brushes for painting on-glaze and in-glaze decoration. Photograph – Harrison Mayer Ltd.

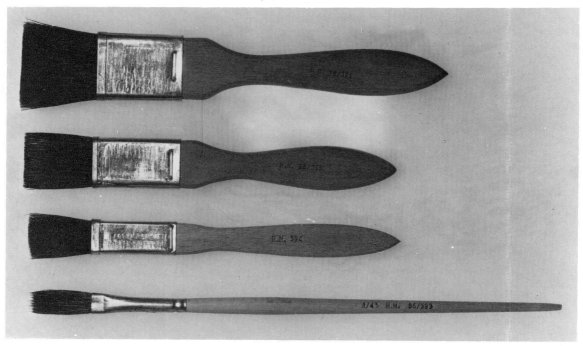

d) Flat lacquer brushes for broad strokes.

e) Japanese brushes.

Slips must physically adhere to the body both before and after firing. Coloured slips can most easily be made from softened body clay with the addition of colouring oxides, usually up to a maximum of 10%. White slips which will adhere well are, however, not so easily made. The basic problem is to get an equal shrinkage between slip and body without losing whiteness or opacity. A good basis is a mixture of china clay, ball clay, feldspar and flint in equal proportions which gives a creamy white slip which fits most bodies well. For a whiter slip the quantity of ball clay is reduced and the china clay increased. Some potters recommend the addition of tin oxide or zirconium silicate to improve opacity. Slips can be coloured by the addition of body stains, the depth of colour required determining the amount added. A typical black slip would be made by adding iron 5%, cobalt oxide 3%, and manganese dioxide 3% to a basic slip made from the body of the pot. Blue slips can be made by adding cobalt oxide or prepared blue body stains.

UNDERGLAZE COLOURS

Metal oxides or commercially prepared underglaze colours are used in this way. The major difference between them is strength and colour indication. The oxides are pure and therefore much more powerful. Because the underglaze colours have already been fired during manufacture, their colour is a good indication of the fired result.

21 John Maltby – reduced stoneware bowl. Tenmoku glaze inside, white outside, with attractive iron and cobalt brush decoration on outside rim; 15 cm (6 in.) diameter.

Underglaze colours can be applied by either painting or spraying onto the raw or biscuit fired pot; the applied glaze develops the full colour in the firing. Three points need to be noted: designs tend to be softened by the glaze and some may even lose definition; the type of glaze will affect the development of colour; and too thick an application of colour may cause the glaze to crawl on the powdery surface of the colour. This can be overcome by mixing a little glaze into the colour. Ten parts colour to one part glaze is a useful starting point.

IN-GLAZE COLOURS

This is the main method of the glazer – as opposed to the decorator – and it is here that the widest range is possible. Again, prepared glaze stains (often very similar to body stains, or underglaze colours) or metal oxides can serve, though studio potters often choose the basic metal oxides from which to concoct their effects. In-glaze colour can be applied either by painting or spraying the colour onto the surface of the raw (unfired) glaze or by mixing the colour into the glaze batch. Painting colour on top of the unfired glaze is the traditional technique used by the Hispano-Moresque and Italian Maiolica potters and because of the absorbent nature of the glaze it demands speed of execution and sureness of touch. Mixing colours in the glaze batch, however, is a technique almost as old as glaze itself.

Some colouring metal oxides added in quantities over 5% act to lower the melting point of the glaze and this needs to be considered. A rule of thumb method to combat this is to add the same quantity of china clay as oxide to the glaze; alternatively the major flux in the glaze (i.e. whiting or dolomite etc.) can be reduced by the corresponding amount.

The development of the glaze colour will depend on the oxide or oxides chosen, the amount added, the composition of the glazes and the type and temperature of firing. The following general points will prove useful:

1. Oxides commonly available are listed on pages 48 ff and how they react one with the other is indicated, but these effects are dependent on all the other factors.

2. The particular amount of oxide added to glazes is often crucial in the development of certain colours. For example in an oxidized stoneware firing a 2% addition of iron in a feldspathic/whiting glaze may give a pale green whereas a 3% will give a honey brown. In some types of glaze 1% of copper oxide gives a salmon pink while the same quantity in a different glaze gives turquoise green. In another example 1% of cobalt gives a deep blue, while 3% in the same glaze gives pale mauve. Only comparatively slight differences in quantity of oxide added can seem large in terms of effect.

Colour testing to establish these slight differences can be carried out by blending together mixtures of the same glaze each with additions of the oxides. Useful pairs are cobalt and iron oxides, cobalt and nickel, cobalt and rutile, and all are examples in which a small difference in quantity will be important. For a single oxide a line blend of the glaze with added oxide of say 10% or 15%, is blended with the glaze without oxide, as explained on page 18. For working out suitable additions of two oxides to a single glaze a triaxial blend will be useful. Two corners of the triangle have,

say, 10% or 15% of one oxide added to the glaze and in the third corner
the glaze is left without oxide. These are blended as suggested on page 19
and will provide a full picture of possible combinations. This is a more
involved method of carrying out colour tests but will provide a useful
range of results in a suitable base glaze, that is, one in which response to
oxides is sensitive.

A second method of blending where more than two oxides are involved
is to mix up each glaze test with a percentage of oxide and blend the
mixtures in 50–50 proportions. With four oxides the following chart
could be used; the same glaze base is used with oxides added:

Glaze + oxide A	*Glaze + oxide B*	*Glaze + oxide C*	*Glaze + oxide D*
A	B	C	D
	AB	AC	AD
		BC	BD
			CD

For a more detailed chart using the same oxides in varying proportions:

A+5%	*A+10%*	*B+5%*	*B+10%*	*C+5%*	*C+10%*	*D+5%*	*D+10%*
A5/A10	A5/B5	A5/B10	A5/C5	A5/C10	A5/D5	A5/D10	
	A10/B5	A10/B10	A10/C5	A10/C10	A10/D5	A10/D10	
		B5/B10	B5/C5	B5/C10	B5/D5	B5/D10	
			B10/C5	B10/C10	B10/D5	B10/D10	
				C5/C10	C5/D5	C5/D10	
					C10/D5	C10/D10	
						D5/D10	

(30 tests)

Carried out by the wet blend method such tests can be done reasonably
quickly. Glaze stains can be substituted for colouring oxides.

ON-GLAZE COLOURS

Often known as enamels, on-glaze colours are basically low temperature
glazes which are applied on the fired glaze and fixed in a third (low
temperature) firing. They are the least permanent of glazes and are likely
to suffer from attack by acids and alkaline detergents. Such glazes are
made from about 25% colour with 75% glaze, usually in the form of a frit
made up of equal proportions of lead, borax, and flint. While some on-
glaze colours can easily be made in the studio, the potters' suppliers
prepare a very wide variety of colours, most of which are intermixable.
These colours can be applied on to the fired glaze by painting or spraying
or in the form of transfer decoration. On-glaze colours used in the
production of transfers are mixed with a suitable medium.

Prepared on-glaze colours are usually supplied in powder form and are
mixed with a suitable stiffening medium for applying to a glazed surface.
A fat oil or specially prepared medium can be bought and a small quantity
can be mixed with the powdered glaze to the required consistency.
Occasionally the powdered on-glaze colour is more workable after being
ground in a pestle and mortar and then mixed on a glass slab with the oil.
Some oils may be more suitable for certain purposes. For example a thin

solution for painting fine lines can be made by using aniseed or lavender oil. Water is rarely satisfactory as it does not allow the glaze to be applied thinly without it running down the pot. With oil mediums brushes need to be washed in turpentine which can also be used to wipe off any unfired and unwanted decoration.

Firing temperatures for on-glaze colours depend to some degree on the glaze. A porcelain glaze which contains a large amount of feldspar, for example, will have a softening temperature higher than a lead or borax glaze used on earthenware, and the difference may be as much as 80°C (176°F). As a general guide, on-glaze colours are fired within the range of 720–780°C (1328–1436°F). At this temperature the glaze underneath softens, the on-glaze vitrifies, and the colour is at its richest. A dry effect in the fired piece indicates too high (or low) a firing temperature. During the early part of the firing the temperature should not be too rapid or cracking of the pieces will result; an increase in temperature of 1°C (1.8°F) per minute is usually reliable. Full ventilation should be allowed in the kiln to enable the burning oil fumes to escape and so avoid affecting the heating elements. Ideally, the on-glaze mixed with oil should be allowed to dry completely before it is fired. Drying takes about 12–24 hours in the atmosphere and a couple of hours in a heated drying cabinet.

THE COLOURING OXIDES

Iron Oxide

Perhaps the most useful, the most common, and yet the most unreliable of the metal oxides used by the studio potter is iron oxide. It occurs as an impurity in most of the potter's raw materials, in particular the clay, and can be added to glaze in its 'pure' form or in one of its naturally occurring states where it is always in combination with other materials. Its effect upon the glaze is mainly one of colour but in quantities above 5% it acts as a flux. Iron oxide is very much affected by the atmosphere of the kiln. In a high temperature reduced atmosphere it will produce a range of colours from pale blue to black, depending on the quantity used, while similar quantities in a neutral or oxidizing kiln will give pale yellows to browns. As far as the glaze ingredients are concerned magnesia inhibits the development of colour while barium oxide and alumina improve the colour. Rich honey browns or tenmoku glazes can only be obtained from iron in shiny glazes. The recipes on page 164 will usually work Iron oxide is commonly sold either in its red state known as ferric oxide (Fe_2O_3) or its black state, ferrous oxide (FeO) which is coarser in particle size though, weight for weight, is more powerful than the ferric oxide. Some potters prefer the magnetic iron sold as iron spangles which has the formula Fe_3O_4.

The ancient Chinese potters used iron as the major colouring oxide and achieved a rich variety of colours and effects in their glazes. In an oxidizing stoneware kiln, 2% will give pale yellow in a clear feldspathic glaze while the same quantity in a magnesia glaze which includes dolomite or talc will give an opaque banana yellow. Between 8% and 10% will give brown; higher amounts tend to give crystalline red effects which can be attractive. In the reducing kiln atmosphere $\frac{1}{2}$–1% will give pale blue grey, 2%–5% pale green to dark blue green, 8%–10% gives black, and in some glazes the characteristic tenmoku associated with the Sung wares of China. A true tenmoku glaze has light red brown rims and ridges contrasting with a dark brown or black glaze, the surface of which is often dotted with a textured effect similar to that of orange peel. Other effects obtained from iron in this sort of quantity are the oil spot glaze, in which dots of iridescent colour contrast with a darker background and the hare's fur glaze which is characterized by a striped effect resembling that of a hare. Greater quantities of iron give the khaki glazes which are lighter and more even in colour. Up to 12% of iron oxide in some glazes will give a more opaque glaze with gold spangle.

Small quantities of iron oxide are often used in combination with other oxides to soften the colour. It is particularly useful for rendering the crudeness of cobalt oxide into the more subtle shades of grey blues.

As well as in the chemically pure oxide state, iron can be used with great advantage by the studio potter in one of its impure and naturally occurring states when the presence of small quantities of other oxides give rich and subtle effects. For example, red clay contains about 8% iron oxide and some red clays, if blended with borax frit (roughly 50–50) and extra iron oxide, give rich brown glazes. Albany slip is a type of clay found in the vicinity of Albany, New York, which on its own becomes a deep brown colour at 1200–1250°C (2192–2282°F) and if mixed with other materials is an excellent base for iron coloured glazes. A suggested mixture is:

Albany slip	50
Feldspar	40
Borax frit	6
Iron oxide	4

Karl Lagenbeck in *The Chemistry of Pottery* gives the following formula for Albany slip:

$$0.195 K_2O \qquad 0.608\ Al_2O_3 \qquad 3.965\ SiO_2$$
$$0.459 CaO \qquad 0.081\ Fe_2O_3$$
$$0.345 MgO$$

One percentage analysis of Albany slip:

SiO_2	59.48
Al_2O_3	10.60
TiO_2	0.90
Fe_2O_3	4.13
MnO	0.08
CaO	6.28
MgO	3.35
Na_2O	0.40
K_2O	2.75
Loss on ignition	10.40

Such an analysis reveals how complex many natural substances are and why many cannot adequately be made up. Certain local red clays such as Fremington clay (England) are similar in composition to Albany slip and can be substituted with considerable success.

Ochres are another popular source of naturally-occurring iron oxide commonly available, and vary in composition and in colour from red to yellow to brown. Essentially they are mixtures of hydrated ferric oxide, clay, sand and occasionally lime. The variation in the composition of ochres means that each batch must be checked before using as a glaze ingredient for a known recipe. Some ochres melt and flow at 1250°C (2282°F) while others are more refractory. On average, ochres contain some 35%–40% of oxide by weight. Umbers are similar in composition but always contain a percentage of manganese oxide. Raw umber is the newly dug material and, when calcined, it takes on a more reddish colour and is called burnt umber. Lignite (crude coal) is the source of some of these materials. Crocus martis is a prepared purple-red oxide of iron made by heating the mineral pyrites and gives a bright range of yellows and reds when either painted onto or mixed in a glaze. The viers earth, sometimes called Armenian bole, forms the basis of jeweller's rouge, used for cleaning and polishing gold. It gives a good Japanese red pigment because of its low alumina content. When combined with nepheline syenite and quartz it gives a very rich, bright salmon red pigment.

Iron rust, iron scales and iron filings can all be used as impure sources of iron and will give results which may well have a richness lacking in the more pure oxides.

Copper Oxide

Of all the metal oxides, copper oxide is the most versatile and is almost as unreliable as iron oxide. Though it commonly gives shades of green at earthenware temperatures, its use for this purpose has largely ceased because of the unwanted and often dangerous effect it has upon any lead present in the glaze. If iron was the main colouring oxide used by the Chinese, copper served in much the same way for the Ancient Egyptians and later, the Islamic potters of Persia. In a glaze with a high alkaline content, copper gives the beautiful shades of turquoise commonly seen on such objects as the small moulded figures, 'Ushabis', from Egypt. Later, the turquoise glazes, which often crazed over the light coloured clay bodies or slips, achieved their effect by the presence of small quantities of copper present in the highly alkaline glazes (which usually contained sodium).

Copper oxide not only has strong colouring power in a glaze but also, in quantities in excess of 3%, it will lower the melting point of a glaze; in increased amounts the copper will give the glaze a metallic 'pewter' effect. This ability of copper to cause melting can be simply demonstrated by painting a thin mixture of copper oxide 5, cobalt oxide 2, and manganese oxide 3 on a tile and firing to stoneware temperatures. It will be found that the oxides have eaten into the clay surface and a gold bronze effect has been deposited.

Copper is available in three main forms. Cupric oxide (CuO), which is black in colour, has the least fine particle size and weight for weight has the most copper and is therefore the most powerful. Cuprous oxide (Cu_2O), which is red in colour, is copper in its reduced state and is preferred by some potters for high temperature firings. Copper carbonate is often pale purple or green in colour and has the finest particles but is, weight for weight, the least strong form of copper.

Copper oxide on its own begins to volatilize at around 1050°C (1922°F) though in a glaze the ingredients will affect this volatilization; for example a glaze which is well fused at this temperature 'traps' the copper in and prevents its escape into the atmosphere. At stoneware temperature, however, particularly under reducing conditions, this tendency to volatilize can have an effect on the inside of the kiln, and on the kiln furniture which, in subsequent firings, will release the copper which may react with glazed ware to cause unwanted shades of pinks or greens. Volatilizing copper may also 'strike' surrounding pots in a stoneware kiln causing unwanted and unpleasant effects. In oxidizing atmospheres, however, copper does not seem to be quite so unstable – though it will strike pots which are immediately adjacent, particularly if the glaze is highly reactive to small amounts of copper, such as those which contain barium carbonate. At earthenware temperatures, in a lead glaze, copper gives shades of green. In alkaline glazes over the whole temperature range, 1% or 2% gives turquoise. Most turquoise glazes, however, craze over normal bodies and are only completely craze-free when used over a highly siliceous body which contains 80–85% silica. With such a body cooling must be slow between 620–550°C (1148–1022°F) to prevent dunting. Ideally the body and glaze should be separated by a silica engobe made up of 90% quartz, 5% bentonite and 5% low-temperature flux (melting at around 720°C (1328°F)). To achieve a successful colour the glaze must be high in the alkaline fluxes potassium and sodium which can be incorporated in either fritted or natural form. A proportion of lead does not hinder the colour but the presence of calcium, barium, strontium or zinc will give green rather than turquoise. At high temperatures a glaze high in nepheline syenite will give a pleasant matt glaze and a rich turquoise colour over a white slip or light coloured body, though it will usually craze. A small amount of copper, i.e. 1.5%, in a magnesium or calcium glaze will give a salmon pink. Increased amounts give a rich grey colour and it is in this versatility of the oxide that much of its interest lies. A slight excess of copper in the glaze will cause very attractive tiny black spots to form in the green background. Occasionally these spots will have yellow centres and give a very pleasant mottled glaze. When copper is rubbed into the surface of a green or a biscuited pot a pleasant metallic black colour results after firing to stoneware temperature which enhances the surface texture.

The other major characteristic of copper is to produce rich red colours in glazes fired in a reduced atmosphere and in glaze in which a small percentage of silicon carbide (which causes local reducing conditions in the glaze) had been added. Both of these phenomena are fully explained in chapter 9 page 112.

Cobalt

Black cobalt oxide is one of the most powerful colouring oxides known and if present in glazes even in such amounts as 0.25% will give a blue shade. It is also a remarkably reliable colouring oxide which is not affected by the atmosphere in the kiln. Used alone, 1% cobalt oxide will give a strong blue and if the quantity is increased to 3% in a magnesium glaze it will give a pinkish lavender colour. In glazes which contain no alumina or a very low percentage of alumina rose-pink glazes may be obtained from the addition of small quantities of cobalt.

Most studio potters find cobalt is best used in conjunction with other oxides which soften the rather strident blue colour. Most people are familiar with cobalt decoration on the famous blue and white wares of Ming China, or, more commonly, on the Willow Pattern plates so popular in Britain in the nineteenth century. In Ming China an impure form of cobalt was painted on to fine porcelain pieces and the resulting colours varied from greyish blue to midnight blue. Today cobalt oxide purchased from the suppliers has few if any impurities and subtle effects are only achieved by adding small quantities of such oxides as iron, manganese, copper or rutile. It is claimed that impure arsenious cobalt can be found in the chimneys of the old tin smelting works in Cornwall. Cobalt carbonate is a less strong and more finely ground form of cobalt which is easier to use in small quantities and disperses more easily in the glaze without causing specking of the colour. Specks can often only be completely avoided by ball milling a portion of the glaze with the cobalt added.

Manganese

In glazes manganese (either as the oxide which is the most powerful form, or as the less powerful carbonate) is used to give red, brown, purple and black, though it is chiefly and reliably used for shades of brown depending on the amount used. On it own, manganese oxide vitrifies to form a smooth dark brown pigment at stoneware temperature and when mixed with an equal part of red clay can be painted on pots to give a pleasant matt black pigment glaze. In highly alkaline glazes manganese gives a purple brown colour, though this can be a pinker purple in certain conditions, but at high temperatures these colours tend to be more muted. Manganese in combination with iron gives richer and more interesting results than when it is used alone and is the basis of the classic Rockingham brown glaze. A typical addition to achieve this effect is 7% iron and 3% manganese in a shiny feldspathic glaze. At stoneware temperature in a feldspar glaze this addition gives a dark brown glaze breaking black with a rich surface quality. Manganese is used as an oxide in a black glaze and a typical addition is iron 4%, manganese 2%, cobalt 4%. In some alkaline glazes, where a broken, slightly speckled colour is required, manganese carbonate should be well mixed, but not sieved, in the glaze.

Chromium

Chromium oxide is the main source of green colours in glaze though, being a highly refractory material, it cannot be added in large quantities; 2–3% is considered a maximum. Only $1\frac{1}{2}$% will dissolve in the glaze and amounts above this will cause opacity. Soluble forms of chromium, such as potassium dichromate, are useful for obtaining softer effects with an oxide which, unless carefully used, is completely opaque. In most glazes 1–2% of chromium oxide will give an opaque green, however, in certain combinations, other colours will be produced. In a glaze containing tin oxide fired in an oxidizing atmosphere, small amounts of chromium, $\frac{1}{2}$–$1\frac{1}{2}$%, will give pink. Chrome fired at temperatures above 1100°C (2012°F) is often picked up in the kiln by glazes rich in tin and unpleasant pink shades result. To achieve pink, though not always with great reliability, glaze fluxes should be mainly alkaline earths such as calcium and strontium with silica and up to 10% tin oxide. A Chinese red colour with a crystalline texture can be obtained from chrome in a high lead, low alumina glaze fired to around 800–900°C (1472–1652°F). Because of the low amount of alumina such glazes tend to run easily and are most easily used on flat surfaces. Because of the high lead content these glazes are likely to be poisonous and are therefore never used on domestic wares. As a decorative effect, however, they can be attractive.

When zinc oxide is present in the glaze, chrome will give a brown colour, and in a high lead earthenware glaze, a yellow colour. A basic green underglaze colour can be made up of chrome 30, feldspar 25 and flint 50. With a small amount of cobalt added pleasant shades of jade green can be obtained, for example chrome 15, cobalt 10, feldspar 15, and flint 60.

Nickel

Because of its relative erratic and unpredictable behaviour, the use of nickel alone as a colouring oxide is rare; it is more commonly used in combination with other oxides to modify colour. For example, browns and greys are the commonly obtainable colours but greens, blues, yellows and purple can also be obtained. With varying proportions of zinc oxide in the glaze, nickel with zinc gives dark blue with a high quantity of zinc, and with lower proportions reddish purple and brown. Like chromium, nickel is a highly refractory oxide and more than 2% or 3% can cause glazes to go rough and powdery. In a glaze with equal quantities of barium carbonate and feldspar 0.25–1% nickel will produce quite strong purples and violets. In glazes containing barium carbonate and zinc oxide small quantities of nickel will give rich pinks and mauves.

Vanadium

Yellow brown in colour and coarse in texture, vanadium gives various shades of yellow and brown depending on the amount introduced in the glaze. Having relatively weak colouring powers, quantities of at least 5% are required to give yellow. An excess of vanadium will give a matt opaque brown which often breaks with rich effects. In combination with zirconium and silica, vanadium will give a rich turquoise blue colour, though this is not a reliable method of getting this colour. Rich reddish brown matt effect can be obtained by adding 10% vanadium. When used in conjunction with tin, brighter yellow colours will result.

Ilmenite

Available in various grain sizes from coarse to fine, ilmenite is a naturally occurring ore containing titanium and iron. When added to a glaze it can cause rich surface break-ups of colour with spotted effects resulting from the iron. It is also used in engobes and bodies to give spotting and speckling of the body.

Rutile

An impure ore which contains small quantities of mainly iron oxide, chromium oxide and vanadium oxide; rutile has a low colouring effect and the chief interest is in the surface textures resulting from the titanium which is present. In conjunction with other oxides, broken colour and pleasant mottled effects can be obtained, and 1 or 2% of rutile added with other oxides often gives softer, richer effects.

Uranium oxide

A refractory colouring oxide, this produces reds in earthenware temperatures. At stoneware temperatures in oxidizing atmospheres uranium can be used to produce yellows and yellow/greens. Occasionally the colour can be bright and rich, though it can equally be garish. Recently the use of uranium has virtually ceased due to its slight radio activity and its cost. It is not normally marketed by potters' suppliers though it can be obtained from chemical suppliers. For the glazer it is a colouring oxide which is well worth experimenting with.

4
Clear, Matt and Opaque Glazes

An 'ideal' glaze is one in which all the necessary practical qualities of a glaze are fulfilled, and all the ingredients are in balance one with the other. The resulting glaze is usually an even, regular covering, clear or transparent with a smooth shiny surface free from blemishes, bubbles and crazing. During the firing the glaze does not flow off rims and edges, but has the ability of staying evenly over the surface of the pot. This ideal glaze does not craze because it is under a slight compression but it is not compressed so hard that the glaze peels or shells from the rim. Other aspects of a 'perfect' glaze are not apparent on examination but involve qualities such as ease of application and handling, wide and tolerant firing range, and so on. These features are discussed in greater detail in chapter 11.

CLEAR GLAZES

From the empirical tests explained in chapter 2, it will be seen that clear stoneware glazes can be made from mixtures of two materials (e.g. cornish stone and whiting); three materials (e.g. cornish stone, whiting and ball clay) and four materials (e.g. feldspar, flint, whiting and china clay). Needless to say, numerous other materials can also be used to formulate clear glazes. Depending on the sort of clear glaze required, e.g. one which has a calcium/feldspar base, or other major fluxes such as colemanite or lithium present, additions to the clear glaze will be affected. A useful clear stoneware glaze is cornish stone 60, whiting 20, and china clay or ball clay 20.

Frits are also useful materials with which to form a glaze, at either stoneware or earthenware temperature. First test the frit on a flat tile and, depending on the degree of melt and/or crazing, add other ingredients to this. Lead bisilicate frit with 20–30% clay will give earthenware glazes at 1080–1100°C (1976–2012°F). Alkaline or borax frits will work well in glazes at all temperatures, and are useful for obtaining various colour effects.

A good clear glaze is one which has a wide temperature tolerance and has a well balanced anti-craze tendency. For studio potters this sort of 'ideal' glaze is rarely of sufficient interest: as individualists, they want their own 'ideal' glazes which may incorporate these practical qualities but must also be satisfying to look at and to handle. Too clear and too smooth a glaze surface often lacks the visual qualities which the studio potter regards as vital. However, the perfect glaze outlined above is often an ideal basis from which numerous other glazes with different qualities can be made. Of these, the two most common types are the opaque and the matt glaze.

OPAQUE GLAZES

A transparent glaze allows light to pass through it to be reflected by the surface of the pot. A clear glaze can be made opaque by the reflection, refraction and diffraction of light by particles suspended in the matrix of the glaze. The surface of an opaque glaze remains smooth and shows no sign of crystallization. Such effects can be obtained by various means.

1   The most common method is by the addition of a material which is undissolved in the glaze and remains suspended in it. A typical example is the addition of up to 10% tin oxide to give the milky white smooth shiny surfaces of the majolica, or maiolica, glazes. The finer the grain size of the opacifier the greater the degree of opacification. With tin this is particularly important; the finer, low density variety gives best results; the high density sort is used in coloured glazes. Too great an addition of such a refractory material can cause the glaze to crawl as it raises the viscosity and surface tension of the solution and prevents the glaze levelling out. During the firing about 2% of tin is soluble in the glaze (though this depends upon the glaze ingredients) and this amount can impart high lustre, fluidity, and improved gloss to the glaze. Additions of 2–8% make a glaze opaque, though alkaline glazes may need as much as 15% to give full opacity. In stoneware glaze, 4% has a marked effect on opacity without preventing any iron in the body from giving colours and speckle to the glaze in an attractive way. In fact, the presence in the glaze of 1–3% of tin oxide will often give a pleasant orange speckle effect. Zirconium oxide is a good, effective and cheaper alternative to tin oxide and with very much the same properties of making the glaze opaque. Opacification begins with 4–5% additions with a 10–15% maximum. Zircon is useful, not only as an opacifier, but will also effectively control crazing resistance and colour stability. It is particularly good for producing greens from chrome where the presence of tin may give pinks or crimsons.

Titanium in the glaze in quantities over 5% will affect opacity and texture though at stoneware temperatures it often gives yellow cream colours which are not always pleasant. Titanium in stoneware glazes is also likely to affect the surface and may render it matt rather than smooth and shiny. The chief value of titanium as an opacifier is in earthenware glazes where 4% will give rich vellum type glazes which can be coloured by oxides or stains. Under certain conditions zinc oxide will cause opacity at medium to high temperatures, though its function in the glaze varies according to the particular composition in which it is included. When combined with alumina, zinc oxide gives opacity and whiteness provided the lime content is low. However, the main effects of zinc in the glaze are detailed in chapter 5 page 71.

2 Certain opaque effects are caused by materials dissolved in the glaze crystallizing out during cooling. Typical of these are the so called opalescent chun glazes containing calcium borate which separates out as fine droplets to give a pleasant milky quality. Lime and boric oxide give milkiness and opalescence in a glaze but the alumina oxide must be kept low so as to prevent crystallization. Such glazes work particularly well over black slips. Two natural forms of calcium borate are available: colemanite, which is relatively pure and gerstley borate, an ore containing the minerals colemanite and ulexite, which is a sodium calcium borate. Both materials, however, can cause trouble in the glaze by crawling and spitting off during firing. An adequate substitute is calcium borate frit. Bone ash (calcium phosphate) will also produce opacity which can be considered in this group, though the colour is likely to lack brightness and if added in too great a proportion can cause dryness and pinholing.

3 Fine bubbles of gas, if trapped in the glaze in sufficient quantity, will cause opacity. Unfortunately such effects, though pleasant, are unreliable and can largely be discounted as a useful method.

4 The addition of colouring oxides which are not soluble in the glaze result in opaque effects. Amounts of chromium oxide over $1\frac{1}{2}\%$ will cause opacity as will large amounts of vanadium oxide and nickel oxide.

MATT GLAZES

In contrast to opaque glazes, matt glazes are not in the 'ideal' well-balanced state, but have one or more materials in excess which form a mass of tiny crystals in the glaze. Unlike a typical opaque glaze, the surface of a matt glaze is comparatively rough to touch and has a crystalline texture. Matt glazes are always opaque and have a dull surface which, while it may often be aesthetically pleasing, is rarely satisfactory for use on tableware because of its tendency to stain and the noise made by metal eating utensils. It should be possible to write on a matt glaze with an ordinary pencil and then to rub off the mark without leaving a stain. A matt effect can be achieved in the glaze by adding one or more materials from three different groups – zinc oxide, alumina or the alkaline earths (calcium, strontium, and barium are the common ones).

Zinc oxide

An excellent matting agent can be made by calcining together at 950°C (1742°F) a mixture of equal proportions of zinc oxide and china clay. Added to a suitable glaze, attractive matt effects result. Used on its own, zinc oxide causes the formation of large crystals. When it is combined with china clay the growth of large crystals is inhibited and smaller crystals result. The china clay makes the glaze more viscous and also widens the firing range. A small quantity of whiting added to the glaze reduces the amount of matting agent required. Large proportions of zinc may render a glaze susceptible to organic acid attack from such liquids as succinic acid found in coffee and whisky, citric acid found in fruit juice and acetic acid in vinegar. For this reason high zinc glazes are not recommended for use on pots intended for domestic use, but can be used for decorative or sculptural objects.

Alumina matt glazes

In many ways, alumina matts can be considered as immature glazes and give the driest looking effects. They are simply made by adding quantities of either china clay, ball clay, alumina or alumina hydrate to a glaze until the desired effect is obtained. Alumina or alumina hydrate may be rejected as too expensive. While a certain proportion of plastic material is essential in a glaze mix, too great a quantity can cause crawling. This can be remedied by substituting part of the clay by calcined china clay (molochite) or by ground pitchers. A simple demonstration of an alumina matt is to add up to 20% of china clay to a clear glaze recipe which can be found on page 163.

The alkaline earths

The oxides of barium, calcium and strontium are the true alkaline earths, though it is customary to include magnesium in this group. This group of metal oxides, in certain proportions in high temperature glazes, will act as fluxes; that is they cause the glaze to melt and flow. However, if used in excess they form small crystals in the glaze which gives it a matt appearance. 20–30% calcium oxide, added in the form of whiting will give a smooth matt effect in certain circumstances, though the minimum possible amount should be used as the resistance to acid and water attack is lowered as the proportion of whiting is increased. Mattness, in this instance, is caused by the formation of calcium silicate crystals and for this reason, the boric oxide in the glaze should be kept as low as possible. Barium oxide, added to the glaze as barium carbonate gives matt effects in proportions greater than about 10%. This is an especially useful sort of glaze to the stoneware potter and provides a particularly good base for rich colour effects and broken textures, especially those obtainable from copper. In barium glazes small amounts of copper (1–2%) will give rich blue greens and will often break to give a pleasant textured pattern. Nickel oxide (1–2%) in a barium glaze may give pleasant pink hues. Magnesium oxide is not such a reliable matting agent as barium or calcium, but in excess gives its own quality to the glaze. These glazes are characterized by a smooth silky satiny surface, milky white colour and their ability to break over edges and rims to show the body colour. Unfortunately such glazes often have a limited firing range and if over fired produce an unpleasant transparent colour. Magnesium can be added to the glaze in one of several forms. The purest form is magnesium carbonate, which has two disadvantages for glazes: it is very slightly soluble in water and has a tendency to make the glaze crawl, although this

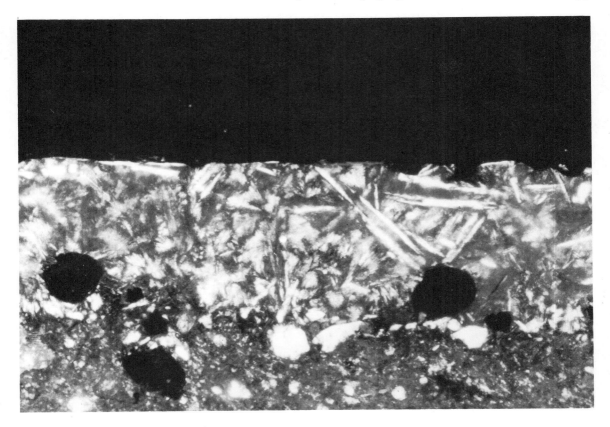

can be overcome to some extent by first calcining the material to 900°C (1652°F).

Talc and dolomite are naturally occurring minerals which contain magnesium in conjunction with other elements and, when added to the glaze, achieve much the same effect as pure magnesium carbonate. Obviously when using these materials, the other elements which they contain have to be taken into consideration. It should also be noted that high quantities of magnesia in a glaze will affect the colour of various pigments. Iron is turned to coffee brown and cobalt tends to produce grey mauve blues rather than inky blues. Strontium oxide acts in a similar way to calcium and barium and gives an effect about halfway between the two.

22 Cross section of magnesia matt glaze (No. 2B) on stoneware. Transmitted light (crossed polars) × 10.

Part Two
UNDERSTANDING THE GLAZE

5
Raw Materials

Most of the raw materials used by the potter and supplied by the pottery supplier are ground beautifully fine and have a very similar appearance, yet they behave very differently in the glaze. All the raw materials originate from rocks of one sort or another. Rocks are aggregates of minerals, which are natural chemical compounds, and the term 'rock' is a broad one which describes any compacted earth whatever its physical state. Some rocks occur as a hard solid mass, whilst others occur as small-sized, loose and broken pieces. Clay is included in this broad definition.

There are three main types of rock and all play a part in providing the potter's raw materials. These are igneous, sedimentary, and metamorphic. It is generally thought by geologists that igneous rocks were the first rocks to have been formed on the earth, and from igneous rocks the other two rock types – sedimentary and metamorphic – developed. The word igneous comes from a Latin word meaning fire, and the rocks are formed by the cooling and solidifying of extremely hot molten material. Igneous rocks constitute the oldest and newest rocks – for they are still being formed. Magma, which is the name given to hot molten rock, breaks through the earth's crust and cools to form solid igneous rocks, which are hard and tough, and consist of a small number of minerals fused together.

There are basically three fundamental igneous rock groups. One is an acid type, rich in silicon and alumina, and gives rocks which have an abundance of quartz and feldspar minerals. Examples are granite, quartz and obsidian. The second type is composed largely of feldspar, with only small amounts of quartz, and is known as intermediate igneous rock. The third type is known as basic igneous rock, rich in iron and magnesium. Such minerals are usually black or dark green in colour and include olivine and hornblende. Basalt, which is the most abundant rock on the earth's surface, is a basic igneous rock.

In Britain examples of such rocks are the granite outcrops in Cornwall and the basalt outcrops in Scotland. Such rock, if crushed, finely ground and prepared as a glaze material, may be found to have a melting point around 1200°C (2192°F) and will often prove to be an excellent glaze material. Such materials suffer from the disadvantages of being variable in composition and of having no fixed chemical formula.

The following is the percentage composition of Luxulyan granite, supplied by English China Clays (UK):

SiO_2	69.8	CaO	1.1
Al_2O_3	15.8	MgO	0.7
Fe_2O_3	2.3	K_2O	5.9
TiO_2	0.3	Na_2O	3.1
		L.O.I.	0.7

Sedimentary rocks are formed, very much as their name implies, from deposits of sediment. Some are formed from the debris which has come about as a result of the breaking down and consolidation of already existing rocks; clay is an example of this type. Others derive from the collection of material derived from organic material – the remains of plant and animal life. A third group of sedimentary rocks is formed by a process of mineral collection by precipitation from water saturated with a particular mineral.

Most sedimentary rocks have complex origins. The action of wind, water and ice denudes and erodes existing rocks over millions of years and involves quite complex chemical changes. Examples are sandstone, shale and mudstone. Coal, lignite and jet are types of sedimentary rocks formed from plant life. Limestone, rock salt, chert and flint are sedimentary rocks precipitated as mineral accumulates.

Metamorphic rocks form the third and last major group of rocks present in the earth's outer layers. These are formed from rocks which already exist, being subjected to extreme heating, fluid infiltration, or high pressure. Under intense heat and pressure, existing rocks undergo physical and chemical changes. Known as metamorphism, this process usually happens deep inside the earth's outer layers. Slate, a metamorphic rock, is derived from sedimentary shales and mudstones. Marble is the metamorphosized form of sedimentary limestone. Metamorphic rocks derived from igneous rocks include schist, gneiss, serpentine and soapstone.

RAW MATERIALS IN THE POTTERY

Rocks are raw materials and it is necessary to consider what minerals they contain and in what amounts, and to explain their use to the potter.

Silica (SiO_2)

Next to oxygen (O) (60%), silicon (Si) is the most abundant element found in nature (25%). The potter uses silica in two forms, both of which behave in a similar way in glazes. Silica in its crystalline form includes quartz, tridymite and cristobalite; in its cryptocrystalline (i.e. tiny or minutely crystalline) form it includes flint and chalcedony. Silica occurs in combination with other oxides, e.g. as clay or feldspar; as a single but impure material; and as the pure mineral. In combination with various other materials, silica forms the large group of minerals known as the silicates. The potter uses silica in the form of sand, silica sand, flint, and quartz.

Deposits of flints, which are derived from the remains of sponge siliceous sea animals, are found, in conjunction with chalk, especially in the coastal areas of Normandy in France and Norfolk in Britain. Flints are concentrated to economically interesting amounts on the seashore as coarse pebbles with the limestone coatings removed by attrition. The dark colour of a flint stone is due to the presence of traces of carbonaceous matter. Flint stones break with a characteristic conchoical fracture (a property utilized with great success in the production of arrow heads in the Stone Age). Flints are now largely produced as a by-product of the cement industry. They are extracted from the chalk deposits and cleaned with water. The preparation of flint for ceramic use involves calcination to a temperature of 900°C (1652°F), when the flints shatter, which enables it to be ground. This process also removes all organic matter and reduces slightly the specific gravity of the flint. Calcination takes place in a modern rotary kiln though traditionally flint was layered with coal and fired in up-draught kilns. Jaw crushers break down the calcined flint and finally it is ground in water, to keep down the dust and prevent workers contracting silicosis. The graded powder is supplied with a moisture content of 5–10% which prevents the dust rising and reduces the risk of breathing in the fine particles.

Flint has a melting point of 1650–1730°C (3002–3146°F) and good flint has a composition of approximately 99.9% silica and 0.01% iron. Most flint will contain a small proportion (less than 0.5%) of lime. Its use in clay bodies is vital for reliable behaviour and it generally helps to prevent crazing of the glaze. For this reason, and due to the expansion and contraction flint undergoes on heating, the size of the particles is of particular importance. Its first use as an ingredient in the body is attributed to Astbury around 1720 who experimented with many materials in his search for a strong and workable white body.

Silica is used in glazes as the chief, and often the only, acid radical. The amount used can be adjusted to alter the melting point of the glaze. Generally, the higher the proportion of silica in a glaze, the higher the melting point and the greater the acid resistance.

Alumina (Al_2O_3)

This is one of the most refractory of the glazer's materials, with a melting point of 2040°C (3704°F). Single crystals of alumina occur naturally as corundum, ruby and sapphire. Corundum is a clear, transparent crystal of high purity; sapphire and ruby owe their colour to the presence of very small amounts of impurities, titanium and chromium respectively. Alumina occurs only very rarely in nature as a separate material, and the main source of purified alumina and hydrated alumina is bauxite. Pure alumina is rarely used in glaze batches: hydrated aluminas are fine white powders which are useful to the potter in several ways: they can be mixed with clays to increase their refractory powers, reduce shrinkage and improve their working qualities; they form the basis of batt wash (a

1 Press moulded red earthenware dish by Geoffrey Eastop, with selenium/cadmium glazes and painted oxide decoration; length 50cm (20 in).

2 Test tiles with commercially produced cadmium/selenium glazes fired in a temperature gradient kiln – top 720°C (1328°F), bottom 1080°C (1976°F) – to show the dramatic effects of different temperatures.

3   Porcelain bowls by
Emmanuel Cooper. Left:
*Uranium glaze, yellow
with green speckles (see
page 165)*.
Right: *A matt glaze which
developed crystals in the
glaze slop on standing for a
few weeks, nepheline
syenite 80, whiting 10,
china clay 10 + bone ash
2, vanadium 5, zirconium
5, fired at 1260°C
(2300°F)*.

4   Stoneware bowl by
Emmanuel Cooper.
*Barium carbonate glaze
with copper carbonate
(soda feldspar 25,
dolomite 15, china clay 25,
bone ash 10, flint 25 +
1.5% copper carbonate),
fired at 1260°C
(2300°F)*.

typical recipe would be alumina hydrate 60–70, china clay 40). Alumina hydrate (often sold commercially as 'placing sand') is also useful for dusting on kiln shelves during the placing of various ceramic products when there is a high risk of the ware and the support or setter sticking together. This is particularly important for firing bone china when the alumina hydrate supports the wares and so prevents warping. In the production of commercial bone china, calcined alumina is used as a 'bedding material'.

Alumina is usually incorporated in glazes in combination with other materials, such as china clay, feldspar, cornwall stone and nepheline syenite. Generally speaking, alumina increases glaze viscosity, refractoriness and opacity, and also affects mattness and brilliance. Alumina also increases resistance to both chemical attack and impact. It improves tensile strength and weathering qualities.

Some glazes will work without the presence of alumina, but such glazes have little temperature toleration and consequently a very short melt and flow period. However, low alumina glazes, while still highly unreliable in use, are capable of unique and very pleasant effects. The presence of alumina aids the development of pink colours from chrome oxide and from manganese oxide. Some colours, however, are hindered by the presence of alumina which has a tendency to form minute crystals in the glaze. For this reason alumina is used for alumina matt glazes where a slight excess of alumina gives pleasant matt qualities.

Feldspar ($R_2O.Al_2O_3.6SiO$)

If there is one single glazing material which can be considered as 'potter's gold', it is the group classified as the feldspars. On their own, most feldspars start to melt around 1180°C (2156°F) and by 1300°C (2372°F) their appearance and melt has only slightly changed. Feldspar is a cheap, easily available material and is the basis of many of the stoneware potter's glazes. With small additions of whiting it can be made to form a fluid melted glass at 1200°C (2192°F) and can constitute up to 70% of a normal glaze recipe.

Feldspar is an alkali alumino-silicate. The three main sorts of feldspars most commonly used by the studio potter are, in their order of importance: orthoclase, which contains potash and has the formula $K_2O.Al_2O_3.6SiO_2$; albite, which contains soda, $Na_2O.Al_2O_3.6SiO_2$; and anorthorite, which contains calcium and has the formula $CaO.Al_2O_3.2SiO_2$. Potash feldspar, sometimes referred to as K feldspar gives the hardest and more durable glaze with the widest maturing range. Soda feldspar gives a softer glaze, a lower melting point, and its chief advantage lies in its effect on various colouring oxides used in the glaze. Soda has a higher expansion rate than potassium and therefore has more tendency to make a glaze craze. Anorthorite, a much rarer feldspar, little used by studio potters, has a much higher melting point. Because feldspar is a natural material, no particular batch corresponds exactly to a theoretically ideal chemical formula and all will contain a small percentage of other feldspars and iron – which is expressed in an analysis of each batch, but not necessarily in the chemical formula.

Nepheline syenite $(K_2O.3Na_2O.4Al_2O_3.8SiO_2)$

This has only come into general use by the studio potter in the last 30 years or so. Like feldspar, it is a good reliable glaze base and is, in fact, feldspar with another soda alumino-silicate nepheline $Na_2O.Al_2O_3.2SiO_2$. It is a material which has certain attractive qualities which true feldspars do not have. Generally it has a higher proportion of alumina, a lower proportion of silica and more alkali. The melting point is lower than that of ordinary feldspar which extends the working range. The high proportion of soda and potash present in relation to its silica content also encourages the development of typical alkaline colour effects, though such glazes often craze under normal conditions.

Nepheline syenite is found in Ontario, Canada and milled in the USA; it is also produced in North Cape, Norway. Two typical analyses:

	North Cape	*USA*
Silica	56.3	60.4
Alumina	24.9	23.6
Soda	8.1	4.6
Potash	9.0	9.8
Other	1.7	0.7

Nepheline syenite is particularly useful for glazes in which small quantities of copper (1–2%) are present; delicate turquoise colours sometimes broken by tiny dots can be obtained. It also reacts well to produce good iron coloured glazes and pale purple colours from manganese.

China clay $(Al_2O_3.2SiO_2.2H_2O)$

This is a clay mineral added to the glaze to provide both alumina and silica. After winning, kaolinized granite contains virtually no impurities. China clay is found in huge deposits in Cornwall where it is excavated for the paper and cosmetic industries as well as the ceramic industry. Large amounts are exported. Other deposits of china clay are found throughout the world, some, especially in the USA, having a comparatively high level of plasticity. From a practical point of view, most glazes are easier to apply if they contain a proportion of plastic clay which acts as a binder. Twenty per cent is considered to be the maximum amount possible though quantities in excess of this can be introduced as molochite. China clay has a low level of plasticity and ball clay is usually used in the glaze because of its plastic qualities which act as a suspender in the glaze batch and as a binder in the dried glaze powder. Even 5–10% of ball clay makes a useful addition. Though ball clays add alumina and silica to the glaze they cannot be considered such a refractory glaze material as china clay. In white glazes and slips china clay, which has the theoretically pure formula $Al_2O_3.2SiO_2.2H_2O$, is used because of its iron-free composition. In contrast, ball clays have no such theoretically pure formula and a typical analysis shows the presence of considerable quantities of iron and other impurities which tend to give glazes a creamy colour, and weight for weight are far less refractory than china clay. Various sorts of white ball clays can be substituted for china clay in the glaze and, though for convenience the theoretical chemical formula for china clay can be used for any calculations, the effect in the glaze will not be the same. Red clays and local clays, which usually contain 3–8% of iron oxide as well as fluxes, will have a greater effect in the glaze recipe than white ball clays. Such clays can often form the basis of attractive, darker coloured glazes, though they will usually be discovered by empirical means rather than through calculation.

Cornish stone (or china stone or cornwall stone) $(K_2O.Al_2O_3.8SiO_2)$
This rock clearly belongs to the feldspar family and is in fact halfway between unaltered granite and china clay rock. It has a greatly increased proportion of quartz which renders it a harder and slightly more refractory material. In the USA, Carolina stone is marketed as a viable alternative to the British material. Three sorts of cornish stone are sold: hard purple, which contains about 8.5% alkali and has the lowest melting point; mild purple, which has 7.5% alkali; and dry white, which is the most refractory with only 5% alkali. The colour of the first two varieties is attributed to the presence of small quantities of fluorspar which can cause pitting and pinholing of the glaze surface due to volatilization. Cornwall stone is useful in white slips (engobes) where it increases the adhesion of the slip and body during and after firing. It is also useful for converting the silica content without radically changing the basic glaze construction.

On its own, cornwall stone can satisfactorily make up to 70% of a stoneware glaze with 15% additions of whiting and china clay. Unfortunately the major supplier of cornwall stone has ceased production and as the supply becomes more limited this has resulted in the virtual elimination of the different sorts of stone from the market. Instead a synthetic stone 'mixture' with the name Mineral Flux 4 (Harrison Mayer Ltd) is being sold. A typical analysis of such a material is SiO_2 80.6, Al_2O_3 11.4, $(KNa)_2O$ 6.10, CaO 1.01, rest 0.89. There are several other blends available to suit most specific requirements.

THE FLUXES

So far, this chapter has examined the potter's raw materials which largely fall into the groups two and three originally listed on page 14–15. It is now time to look at the materials in group one (page 14) most of which melt readily on their own at stoneware temperature and are generally known as fluxes. A flux is any material which lowers the fusion point of any mixtures in which it is present. There are few 'pure' fluxes which occur naturally; the most important exception is limestone in the pure fired formula CaO, and used by the potter in the form of whiting ($CaCO_3$, calcium carbonate). Calcium, along with barium and strontium, form the group of materials known as the alkaline earths; and some authorities also include magnesium. All behave in similar ways in the glaze and are intermediate in their properties between the true alkalies, i.e. potassium and sodium, and the earths proper.

Whiting ($CaCO_3$)

Of all the stoneware fluxes, whiting is the cheapest and most useful; depending on the proportion present, it can render a glaze smooth and transparent or silky, matt and opaque. In small quantities, whiting gives hardness and durability to the glaze. In larger quantities it encourages gloss and when combined with a lower proportion of alumina and silica, will give matt effects. It is extremely cheap to buy and is prepared by the grinding in water and drying, of chalk dug from cliffs in England, France and Belgium. British whiting is 97–98% pure. Whiting is extremely useful under reducing conditions when the presence of small quantities of iron encourage rich pale blue and celadon effects and reduced red from copper. In low temperature (earthenware) glazes the carbon dioxide liberated from whiting can cause bubbling. This can be overcome by using fluorspar (CaF_2) instead of whiting. Fluorspar decomposes at a much higher temperature.

Barium carbonate ($BaCO_3$)

This occurs naturally as the mineral witherite which is mined in England and California. Ceramists use precipitated barium carbonate obtained from barytes; it is insoluble in water, melts around 1360°C (2480°F) and in its raw state is poisonous.

Barium carbonate is particularly useful to the stoneware potter for its remarkable results with colouring oxides and its matting effect on the glaze when used in quantities in excess of 15–20%. Up to 20% can be used in a glaze but amounts over this are difficult to handle as they usually produce rough unattractive surfaces, though 50% barium carbonate and 50% feldspar will give rich turquoise blues from 1% copper and purples from 1% nickel. The flocculating effect (i.e. thickening) of barium carbonate in the glaze batch must be taken into account when applying the glaze and such glazes are best applied more thickly than would seem necessary: again, this may give rise to crawling problems during the firing though these can be overcome to an extent by the addition of a natural binder such as gum arabic to the glaze batch.

Strontium carbonate ($SrCO_3$)

Most of the strontium carbonate is prepared from the mineral celestite which occurs in England, Germany and Sicily. Strontium still remains for potters in the west a rare and expensive material, little used or understood in glazes, though recent experiments in the USSR suggest it is a practical and non-poisonous alternative to lead in earthenware glazes. Experiments with strontium at higher temperatures suggest that when it replaces calcium and, or, barium improved glaze fit results. Additions of strontium to such glazes should increase the hardness of the glaze and scratch resistance should also be improved, due in part to the earlier reaction of strontia enabling the glaze to clear with a minimum of pits. On the whole, this is a material which as yet has many unexplored possibilities.

Magnesium carbonate (MgCO$_3$)

In low temperature glazes, magnesium carbonate acts as a refractory material though at stoneware temperature it can be a powerful flux. Suppliers usually offer two forms – light and heavy; both have similar compositions though the latter is slightly less soluble in water. The mineral magnesite, from which magnesium carbonate is obtained, is quarried throughout the world. When present in the glaze, magnesium silicate is formed; this has excellent elastic properties and at the same time develops glazes of rather low expansion co-efficient. It is often used in crystalline glazes to check fluidity, and it also improves adherence between glaze and body. In combination with barium carbonate good matt effects are produced, though in fairly large quantities, magnesium will give attractive silky matt surfaces. Magnesium in the glaze is particularly effective for obtaining cobalt purples and pinks and nickel green.

Because of the slight solubility of magnesium carbonate potters usually add it to the glaze in the form of dolomite or talc where it is in combination with other materials. Dolomite and talc are discussed on page 72.

Sodium (Na) and potassium (K)

These are the two true alkali materials, though the term is often extended to include lithium when the group is known as the alkaline metals. All these metals are soft and highly reactive. Most pure forms of sodium and potassium are soluble in water to which their hydroxides give a soapy feel and taste – a property which was utilized for washing clothes when wood ash, which contains sodium and potassium, was added to the washing water. Sodium and potassium are present in different types of feldspar and are added to the glaze in this or the fritted form. Wood ash is also a useful source of these two alkalis though, as the proportions vary, no pure chemical composition can be calculated. Potassium and sodium have a high co-efficient of expansion which can cause crazing in a glaze and lowers resistance to attack; both are particularly useful for obtaining typical alkali response from colouring metal oxides. The pure salts of sodium and potassium are useful for the decorative glaze effects when they can be applied as dry powder on flat surfaces. Rich colours and textures can be obtained in this way.

Lithium (Li)

This is similar in behaviour to potassium and sodium but has the advantage of being extremely powerful in very small quantities, especially when used in conjunction with potash and soda feldspars. Lithium carbonate is the purest form available and contains about 40% lithium, and is slightly soluble in water. However, in the glaze, lithia heightens alkali colour response, extends firing range and brightens glazes.

Lithium is usually added to the glaze by means of one of the natural ores such as lepidolite which contains about 3% lithia, petalite, with about 4% lithia, spodumene with about 7.2% lithia though it also contains a small amount of iron, amblygonite with about 10.1% of lithia. (See separate entries, page 73–4).

Lead (Pb)

Lead and its oxides are derived from the mineral, galena, which is mined in the USA, Mexico, Australia, Canada, Germany and Peru. Two types of lead oxide are used in ceramics: the first is litharge or lead monoxide (PbO) which is insoluble in water but soluble in alkalies, and certain acids; the second is red lead (Pb_3O_4) which is insoluble in water but soluble in some acids. As a glaze ingredient, lead has many advantages which results in its continued use despite of its hazard to the factory worker. Lead is a cumulative poison in the body when absorbed. The introduction of lead silicate frits has virtually eliminated the health risks with regard to handling the unfired glaze material but still leaves the problem of devising a well-balanced fired lead glaze which will not release lead when used on domestic table or cooking ware.

The superiority of lead glazes lies in their brilliance, lustre and smoothness, which are due to low fusion point and viscosity. Such glazes are, in general, resistant to chipping and scratching and form strong body and glaze bonds. Of the lead silicates the bisilicate ($PbO.2SiO_2$) is much less soluble than sequisilicate ($2PbO.SiO_2$) or monosilicate ($PbO.SiO_2$).

Because of the greater awareness of the dangers of handling and using raw lead compounds more and more studio potters are turning their attention to alternative fluxes. The qualities of a lead glaze are hard to equal from the point of view of the working and fired qualities in terms of brilliance and reliability though lead is confined to glaze temperatures maturing below 1150°C (2102°F). Above this volatilization occurs, though small quantities of lead in high fired glazes will often increase brilliance. A carefully constructed earthenware lead glaze, fired under the correct conditions and temperature is perfectly safe to use. If, however, colouring metal oxides, especially copper, are added the balance of the glaze will be affected, the lead released and rendered dangerous. For this reason studio potters usually follow this advice:

1   Never use any form of lead oxide, only the lead silicates; lead bisilicate has the lowest level of solubility.
2   Always handle lead compounds with care. Avoid breathing in the dust, never eat in the workshop and scrub hands after handling glaze materials.
3   Restrict the use of homemade lead glazes to decorative wares unless the glaze has been tested and passed for lead solubility by an established and reputable laboratory. (Addresses page 180)
4   Use a manufacturer's lead glaze for domestic wares. Fire it exactly to the specified temperature; do not add any material to the glaze, do not use it over a slip containing oxides or paint either underglaze colours or metal oxides on to the glaze. (Should potters desire to add to a manufacturer's glaze or paint on to it, they would be well advised to have the pots tested as per B.S. 4860.)

Borax (sodium tetraborate)

Borax is a mineral and prepared chemical compound which contains about 16% sodium oxide, 36% boric oxide and 48% water. It is soluble in water, soluble in acid, and melts around 200°C (392°F). Anhydrous or dehydrated borax is less soluble in water than borax and, weight for weight, 53 lbs is the equivalent of 100 lbs of borax.

Borax is widely used as a powerful flux for glazes though the problem of water solubility of the raw material means that the glaze batch must be used immediately. Alternatively borax can be added to the batch in the form of a frit or as a natural mineral such as colemanite in which case solubility is not a problem. The effects of sodium oxide in the glaze have already been referred to on page 69: boric oxide contains boron which is an element with properties similar to those of silicon. Boron, however, becomes active at a much lower temperature though the resulting glaze is not so strong as that formed by silicon. In earthenware glazes boron has a useful role in providing an excellent alternative to lead and is used in the fritted form of borosilicate. The stoneware potter also finds borax in some forms a useful addition. In small quantities it promotes gloss and fusion and, in the presence of lime, will cause milky blue white opalescence due to precipitation which can be very attractive, though the effects cannot be accurately predicted. This opalescent quality can often be heightened by placing the glaze over an iron-bearing slip.

Zinc oxide (ZnO)

Zinc oxide is used in many types of glazes where its function depends on the glaze composition and the quantity included. Generally, zinc can be considered to be a flux, especially at high temperatures; also it reduces expansion and helps to prevent crazing. Zinc forms the basis of the American Bristol glaze which was an early attempt to provide opaque glazes and eliminate the use of lead. In combination with alumina and with a low lime content opacity and whiteness result. Zinc has no opacifying power when used in borosilicate glazes, this is in marked contrast to feldspathic glazes where it helps to form opaque silicates. In high temperature glazes zinc extends the firing range and generally makes the glaze more flexible.

In coloured glazes zinc has a powerful effect on colouring oxides, altering some of the colours obtained with underglaze decorations, destroying some and improving others; it lightens strong blues and greens and renders copper colours more brilliant. Chrome is turned brown in the presence of zinc.

However, it is in the forming of crystalline glazes that zinc is particularly useful. Zinc compounds crystallize when the melted solution reaches critical fluidity and, if then cooled rapidly, the crystals are held in suspension. A super saturation of the glaze by zinc will promote the formation of crystals which will absorb any pigment present. The more homogenous a zinc crystalline glaze, the more perfectly will the crystals separate out. Full notes on crystalline glazes are found on page 112. It should be noted that light zinc will be more effective than the denser form of zinc which tends to suspend itself in glazes, and give unpleasant porridge-like effects.

Other natural minerals

Dolomite ($CaCO_3 . MgCO_3$) is a rock intermediate in composition between limestone and magnesite. It contains about 56% calcium carbonate and 44% magnesium carbonate and it is used in stoneware glazes as a powerful flux. Commercial deposits of dolomite are found in many countries, with major deposits in the USA, England, and Germany. All have similar compositions. In its raw state dolomite may be light buff, pink, yellow to brown and grey to blue. Dolomite acts as a flux and, in excess, will give smooth matt glazes which will turn cream in the presence of small amounts of iron, mauve in the presence of cobalt and pink in the presence of copper.

Talc ($3MgO.4SiO_2.H_2O$) (Magnesium silicate, French chalk) is used in stoneware glazes to add magnesite and silica and a typical talc glaze has a smooth satin white opaque matt surface. Too great a quantity in the glaze will render it refractory. Talc improves body and glaze fit because of its low expansion. Some talcs contain small quantities of iron which is likely to affect the glaze colour. Talc is a useful anti-craze ingredient in the glaze. Both magnesia and silica will reduce crazing.

Fluorspar (CaF_2) (Fluorite). In low temperature glazes fluorspar has two useful functions; it gives opacity and also acts as a flux. The opacity results from the formation of fluoride crystals, and while it is not completely opaque, a cloudy effect is obtained which decreases the amounts required of other more costly opacifiers. In higher temperature glazes fluorspar is used as a flux where it promotes more fusible glazes and lessens the tendency to craze. During the firing process fluorspar seems to dissociate to form a gas which can attack kiln refractories. It can also cause boiling and bubbling in the glaze which may or may not be desirable. Fluorspar is useful for making chrome green pigments and renders a very pleasant colour.

Wollastonite ($CaSiO_3$) is a naturally occurring calcium silicate used as a replacement for flint and limestone. It is mined in the USA and its most outstanding characteristics are its brilliant whiteness and its chemical and physical uniformity. Its use in ceramics is relatively new but already it is a material which is claimed to give higher fired strength, improved heat shock and better bonding. A typical analysis shows SiO_2 50.90%; and CaO 46.90%.

Bone ash ($Ca_3(PO_4)_2$) (Calcium phosphate) is used by the English ceramic industry for the production of bone china, the ideal composition would be bone ash 50, china clay 25, and cornish stone 25. For the stoneware glazer quantities used are very much smaller and the use of bone ash is confined to creating opalescent effects in the glaze by the presence of phosphorus. Bone ash is prepared from the calcined bones of ox, cow, sheep, donkey or horse. First, all the fat is removed with benzine, then the gelatine is removed by steam under pressure (and used for glue); slow calcination then takes place to 700°C (1292°F) to remove organic matter. The bone is then hand picked, wet ground in an open pan and washed to remove soluble alkalies before being dried. In stoneware glazes up to 4% is used and pleasant frosty effects can be obtained. Amounts over this tend to act as a refractory with unpleasant results.

Cryolite (Na_3AlF_6) (Sodium aluminium fluoride) is colourless and translucent and a typical composition shows sodium 32.9, aluminium 54.3, fluoride 54.3%. Huge deposits occur in Greenland, and smaller deposits in the USA and the USSR. Cryolite makes sodium oxide available to the glazer in a natural and powerful form and is useful in preparing alkaline glazes. Cryolite melts at 1000°C (1832°F) and the strong volatilization that occurs subsequently can be observed on the test tile. On porcelain, cryolite volatilizes to give rich orange halos which become more subdued on stoneware.

Colemanite ($2CaO.3B_2O_3.5H_2O$) is a natural hydrated calcium borate which occurs in the USA and is useful to the studio potter as a natural material which contains boron in an almost insoluble form. Gerstley borate and ulexite are similar in behaviour to colemanite. It is an extremely powerful flux and has a brightening effect on most colouring oxides. By forming borates in the glaze it reduces thermal expansion and so increases resistance to crazing. Colemanite is found in the USA and Turkey and each differs in composition. Because of the slight solubility of colemanite different parts of the same batch can differ in composition. This necessitates testing each particular batch before use.

Colemanite is not a reliable glaze material in use; it has a tendency to make the glaze crawl and fly off during firing, with disastrous effect on the kiln shelves, due partly to the large amount of water in colemanite. To overcome this problem manufacturers sell a boro-calcite frit which in most respects behaves in a similar way to colemanite, roughly weight for weight, without any of the firing disadvantages.

Amblygonite ($2LiF.Al_2O_3.P_2O_5$) is a material found in the USA, Brazil and Africa. It is the least expensive source of alumina phosphate and is the highest lithia containing material. A typical analysis shows the major ingredients as alumina 34.43, phosphorus pentoxide 46.75, lithia 8.48. It is used in the glaze to introduce lithium and phosphorus.

Lepidolite ($LiF.KF.Al_2O_3.3SiO_2$) is chiefly found in the USA and Africa. Commonly called lithium mica, it is a compound of lithium-potassium-aluminium fluosilicate. A typical analysis shows the major ingredients as silica 55, alumina 25, lithium 4 and potassium (plus Rb_2O) 9, fluorine 5. In the glaze lepidolite gives all the advantages of lithium bearing minerals but the fluoride can cause boiling and blistering. It may be added with flint at the expense of feldspar on a balanced alumino-silica ratio basis.

Petalite ($Li_2O.Al_2O_3.8SiO_2$) is a lithium-aluminium silicate which contains about 77% silica, 17.5% aluminium and 4.3% lithium. Up to

40% can be added to glaze batches as its low content of other alkalies gives it good body glaze bonding properties.

Spodumene ($Li_2O.Al_2O_3.4SiO_2$) is lithium-aluminium silicate, similar to petalite but with a higher proportion of lithium as well as other alkalies. A typical analysis shows silica 63%, alumina 28.40%, lithia 6.3% and 3% other alkalies. It is found chiefly in the USA and Canada. In glazes weight for weight reduction of feldspar by spodumene (or any lithia bearing mineral) materially reduces the vitrification temperature.

6
Glaze Formulae and Calculations

Results obtained from the tests of heating single materials in section one, listed on page 14 chapter 2, enabled the materials to be divided into three groups according to the degree of melt which had occurred. Very few glazes are made up of one material and so the way a material reacts on its own is not always an indication of the way the material will behave in the glaze. However, the testing of materials on their own is a useful starting point and from the tests the degree of reaction which takes place between the material and the clay surface is also a good indication of the way the material will behave in the kiln.

The three groups formed according to the effect of the heat at 1260°C (2300°F):

One: colemanite, cryolite, dolomite, fluorspar, barium carbonate, whiting.
Two: nepheline syenite, cornish stone, lepidolite, potash feldspar, soda feldspar, petalite.
Three: talc, china clay, ball clay, red clay, bone ash, flint.

By experiment, the behaviour of these materials when fired alone in the kiln has been found; little else is known. The names of the materials listed above give no indication of any similarities of behaviour, however, there are other facts about these materials which may give some indication as to how they will behave. For example, the chemical formulae of the materials, if compared, may give an indication of their behaviour when heated. All the materials in this section were chosen because all have known chemical formulae, and though the given formula is often for theoretically pure materials, each is sufficiently accurate to enable useful comparison to be made.

But before comparing the chemical formulae, it is necessary to explain exactly what a chemical formula is and how it arose. Briefly, all materials as well as having a common name have a Latin name which provides a universal language for all scientists. A look at the history of science and how this common language evolved will help to understand the present situation. The Ancients believed that there were four elements, earth, fire water and air: that is, four elements which could not be made, and from which all matter was made. Not one of these is an element in the accepted modern sense, yet all four were accepted as the elements until the late eighteenth century. In 1789, Lavoisier listed about 33 substances which, as far as it was known then, could not be split into any simpler substances; nor could they be made from other substances. By the end of the nineteenth century there were believed to be about 90 elements, but today this number has been extended to 103 and includes elements which do not occur in nature, but are produced by nuclear reactions. These materials, called elements, were given Latin names from which single or double letter abbreviations were made; this formed a universal language for chemists which is still in use today. Hence, the material known in the West as lead has the chemical symbol Pb which is the abbreviated form of the Latin for lead (plumbum). Only about 30 of the elements are used by the potter who soon becomes familiar with the chemical symbols and the elements they represent. A list of these elements can be found in the Appendix 4 on page 169. From the elements an infinite variety of substances, known as compounds, can be made.

Further discoveries were made in the nineteenth century when Mendeleev first began classifying elements according to their atomic weights; he arranged the elements in a table according to their atomic number and discovered that their chemical properties repeated periodically. It is on this information that the Periodic Table of Elements was first drawn up and here Science first played a major part in glaze chemistry. For the table to have any significance some understanding of the construction of an element is necessary.

The atom

An atom is the smallest part of an element which can retain the characteristic properties of the element and enter into a chemical reaction. Atoms of all elements are made up of three sub-atomic units: the proton, the neutron, and the electron. Protons and neutrons together form the central mass, or nucleus, of an atom. Electrons are outside the nucleus and are in constant motion in orbit around it. A proton is a particle with a mass measured as one. Each proton carries a single electrical charge which is positive. A neutron has the same mass as a proton, that is, one, but it is electrically neutral. An electron is of insignificant mass compared with the mass of a proton or a neutron and can be ignored. The weight of an atom is therefore taken as the weight of the nucleus. An electron is a charge of negative electricity, equal in magnitude, but opposite to, the positive electrical charge on the proton.

The lightest element, hydrogen, has a nucleus which consists of a single proton and a single orbiting electron. This is the only element with a nucleus which does not contain neutrons. The *atomic weight* of an element is the sum of the weights of the protons and neutrons contained in the nucleus of one of its atoms. The atomic weight of hydrogen (no neutron) is therefore one. The *atomic number* of an element is the number of electrons in one of its atoms (or the number of protons in the atom). The atomic number of hydrogen is therefore also one. When calculating the amount of any particular atom required, it is the atomic weight, not the physical weight, which is used. It is this which indicates the amount required.

Helium is second to hydrogen in order of weight. An atom of helium has two electrons orbiting the nucleus which consists of two protons and two neutrons. So the atomic number of helium is two and the atomic weight is four. Naturally, the atomic weights do not increase evenly but it is not necessary to go into great detail here. The table on page 169 gives the atomic number and atomic weight of all the elements with which the potter has contact.

Because of the nature of the structure of the atom with electrons orbiting around the nucleus, very few elements have atoms which can exist on their own and they combine with other atoms of that material to form molecules. The ability of atoms to combine with other atoms is known as valency, valency electrons are only available in the outermost electron shell which are incomplete. Elements whose atoms have the same number of valency electrons have similar chemical properties. For example, lithium, sodium and potassium react with other elements to form similar chemical compounds.

When atoms link together they form molecules. Whenever more than one atom is present, whether the atoms are the same or different elements, a molecule is formed. In this case, it is not the atomic weight but the molecular weight which is necessary for calculations, and this is the sum of the atomic weights of the atoms which constitute the molecule.

Clay, one of the most common of the potter's materials, serves as a general example. This has the chemical formula $Al_2O_3.2SiO_2.2H_2O$. This formula represents in theory one molecule of clay. What does such a formula mean, first, to a chemist, and then to the potter? To the chemist it means that two atoms of aluminium (Al) are combined with three atoms of oxygen (O), that two atoms of silicon (Si) are combined with four of oxygen, and that four atoms of hydrogen (H) are combined with two atoms of oxygen, and together all form one molecule of the material known to the potter as clay – and to the chemist as hydrated aluminium silicate. The chemical formula, with its precise meaning, enables an experienced chemist to estimate how it will behave when heated. Looking at all the separate materials which constitute clay, the chemist will know that, on the whole, it is a material fairly resistant to the effects of heat and one which is probably white in colour. The chemist will have no idea how this material can be worked by hand (as a potter needs to know).

Without the chemist's knowledge, the potter knows from his experience a great deal about the clay. He will know about its working qualities and how it withstands the effect of heat. Using the information gained from heating this material on the test tile, it will have been observed that clay, when used as a material is, on the whole, only partially affected by the stoneware temperatures and can be classified as a group three, refractory stable material unless it is a low-firing local red clay (i.e. Albany slip or Fremington clay). A simple test plus practical experience teaches the potter much, but from the chemical formula he can gain different information. Bearing in mind the two major ingredients, aluminium oxide (Al_2O_3) and silica (SiO_2) and discounting the water (H_2O), which is driven off as steam as the temperature increases sufficiently, and knowing how china clay behaves when heated, the chemical formulae of other materials can now be examined.

CHEMICAL FORMULAE

Group one materials

To begin, a comparison of the chemical formulae of the materials tested in group one may prove some help in determining why they behave as they do.

Colemanite　$2CaO.3B_2O_3.5H_2O$
Cryolite　Na_3AlF_6
Dolomite　$CaCO_3.MgCO_3$
Fluorspar　CaF_2
Barium carbonate　$BaCO_3$
Whiting　$CaCO_3$

At first sight, such a list seems to confuse rather than clarify, and it is only when a simplification has been made that meaning can be found. In this list all the materials are given in formulae of the prefired state, that is, as they are when incorporated in the glaze recipe; from the example of china clay, used earlier, it was pointed out that the water combined in the formula was released as steam during the firing process. So what started off as a formula with three ingredients was left with only two after firing. Most materials do not contain water, but do contain materials which form gases which are driven off during the firing, leaving behind the materials which affect the glaze. The lists opposite show materials affected by heat, and give the formulae before and after firing. The most common gas liberated during firing is carbon dioxide (CO_2), which is given off from dolomite, barium carbonate and whiting and plays no part in the formation of the glaze. The fact that carbon dioxide is liberated as gas during the heating must be taken into account when calculations are made for the glaze recipe, for example, 100 pounds of whiting would not produce 100 pounds of the material needed, calcium oxide (CaO). To find the percentage composition present, calculation must be made from the known chemical formula.

For example, to find the calcium oxide in $CaCO_3$, the molecular weight of calcium carbonate (the chemist's name for whiting) must be calculated. As explained earlier, the molecular weight is the sum total of all the atomic weights (listed on page 169) of the elements combined to make one molecule, calculated by this method:

	No. of atoms present		*atomic weight*	*total weight*
(Ca) Calcium	1	×	40	40
(C)　Carbon	1	×	12	12
(O)　Oxygen	3	×	16	48

Molecular Weight = 100

Percentage of calcium oxide in calcium carbonate is given by:

$$\frac{\text{Molecular weight of CaO}}{\text{Molecular weight of CaCO}_3} \times 100$$

that is:

$$\tfrac{56}{100} \times 100 = 56\%$$

Therefore whiting is 56% by weight calcium oxide, and one pound of whiting would yield about nine ounces of calcium oxide.

When the carbon dioxide is removed from all the formulae above we are left with:

        CaO MgO   (Dolomite)
        BaO   (Barium oxide)
        CaO   (Calcium oxide)

which leave chemical formulae which are all very similar in structure in that each of the elements is combined with one atom of oxygen.

The list of chemical formulae for other materials in group one shows other materials present which are released during the firing so leaving behind the elements which combine in the glaze. Colemanite contains water (which is liberated early in the firing), calcium and boron. Cryolite, which is particularly reactive on its own, contains Na which is sodium, Al, which is aluminium, and F, which is the gas fluorine (liberated in the firing). Fluorspar contains calcium and the gas fluorine. All these materials from group one listed together showing the chemical formulae of the fired materials show a remarkable similarity in structure.

Formula of fired material	*Name of original material*
CaO	whiting
CaO.MgO	dolomite
BaO	barium carbonate
$CaO.B_2O_3$	colemanite
$Na_2O.Al_2O_3$	cryolite
CaO	fluorspar

All show the same sort of structure, with each material combining with one atom of oxygen.

Group two materials
In the second group of materials which all behave in a similiar way the chemical formulae are on the whole more complex:

Nepheline syenite	$K_2O.3NaO.4Al_2O_3.8SiO_2$
Cornish Stone	$\left.\begin{array}{l} 0.030MgO \\ 0.180CaO \\ 0.315\,K_2O \\ 0.143Na_2O \end{array}\right\} Al_2O_3 . 7.15SiO_2$
Lepidolite	$LiF.KF.Al_2O_3.3SiO_2$
Potash Feldspar	$K_2O.Al_2O_3.6SiO_2$
Soda Feldspar	$Na_2O.Al_2O_3.6SiO_2$
Petalite	$Li_2O.Al_2O_3.8SiO_2$

This list shows far more complex materials than those found in group one, but again reveals important similarities of structure. Alumina and silica occur in each material, though in different proportions. Combined with the alumina and silica are other materials, one of which has occurred already – sodium (Na) and the other two potassium (K), lithium (Li) are in combination with oxygen in the ratio two to one. Generally, each material can be said to have three main components two of which, alumina and silica, occur in each.

Group three materials
Materials which form the third group (omitting bone ash) again show a marked similarity of structure:

Quartz	SiO_2
Flint	SiO_2
China Clay	$Al_2O_3 2SiO_2 . 2H_2O$
Talc	$3MgO 4SiO_2 . H_2O$

Silica (SiO_2) is present in all the materials. Flint and quartz, which are both pure silicon oxide, can for the purpose of a glaze material be considered identical in terms of their effect in the glaze. In large quantities, talc acts as a refractory material, but in smaller quantities it will act as a flux.

Of all the three groups, it is the middle group which produces a melt nearest in effect to that of the glaze. And, more significantly from the point of view of making glazes, it is the middle group which contains materials from group one and group three. It is in the formulae for this middle group of materials that the three parts of a glaze are found.

This point will be better understood if the letter R, meaning root or radical, is substituted for each of the chemical symbols for each element that is combined with oxygen. Such a list reads:

Group one		
Dolomite	RO	RO
Barium	RO	
Calcium	RO	

Group two			
Potash Feldspar	R_2O	R_2O_3	$6RO_2$
Petalite	R_2O	R_2O_3	$8RO_2$

Group three		
Flint	RO_2	
China Clay	R_2O_3	RO_2

What seems to determine how a material behaves in the glaze is the ratio between the radical R and O (oxygen). In group one, there is either a 2–1, i.e. Li_2O, or 1–1, i.e. BaO. In group two, it is 2–3, i.e. Al_2O_3 and in group three, 1–2, i.e. SiO_2. In the glaze all these sorts of materials from the three groups are present. The proportions of each group to each other vary according to the maturing temperature of the desired glaze. A higher temperature glaze has a lower proportion of fluxes, and so on. The method of expressing the proportions of each group present in the glaze are by means of the Seger formula, which is explained in detail later.

Group one: known as the RO or R_2O group; called the bases, they activate or flux the other materials to melt at the desired temperature.

Group two: known as the R_2O_3 group and called the amphoteric oxides; these materials can work partly in group one and partly in group three.

Group three: known as the RO_2 or acid group. These materials, of which silica plays the major part, are the glass formers; they are fluxed by the bases to melt at the desired temperature to give the necessary glasses. No single group will work alone, but all must be used in conjunction. This is why materials falling into the middle group, in which all three groups are represented, melt to form the basis of useful glazes, and why these materials constitute a large part of the glaze recipe. In contradiction to this general idea of the three groups, B_2O_3 (boric oxide) is placed in the acidic or RO_2 group, as it behaves more like silica than alumina.

The Seger Formula

In the nineteenth century, the German Hermann Seger (1839–94), was one of the first to apply scientific knowledge to the understanding and construction of glazes. He conceived the idea of representing glazes as chemical formulae expressed in certain ways which enable easy comparisons to be made between glazes. It is interesting to note that the testing of single materials of more or less mysterious ingredients, and the mixtures made as a result of these tests, follow, as we have seen, certain well-defined laws and rules. Seger first observed from the chemical formulae, that the oxides used in glazes fall into three separate groups: RO and R_2O; R_2O_3; and RO_2.

Under these groups the following oxides fall:

RO/R_2O	R_2O_3	RO_2
PbO	Al_2O_3	SiO_2
Na_2O		TiO_2
K_2O		B_2O_3
ZnO		
CaO		
MgO		
BaO		
SrO		
Li_2O		

He then expressed the glaze in a formula which presented the three separate groups and went on to make the formula even more useful. He noticed that almost any glaze contains more than one base (RO or R_2O)

and up to five or six are not unusual. On the other hand, it is usual to have only one material each in the R_2O_3 and RO_2 group. To enable one glaze to be compared with another, he made the sum of the RO R$_2$O group total one or unity, and calculated the rest of the glaze formula accordingly. This procedure, known as the Seger formula, is still commonly used for the representation of the composition of a ceramic glaze and is still one of the most useful and logical ways to compare glazes. From the Seger delineation of glazes, it is obvious that the proportions of R_2O_3 to the RO_2 give some indication of the sort of glaze which will result, and that the proportion of the bases to the other two groups gives an indication of the maturing temperature of the glazes. Maximum and minimum limits of each oxide can be worked out by practical tests. These are referred to on page 91.

Seger also devised a set of rules for the prevention of crazing and peeling in the glaze, and these are dealt with in chapter 7 The Seger formula is used for all ceramic materials however complex, and two useful examples are those of clay and feldspar.

China clay: $Al_2O_3.2SiO_2.2H_2O$ (the H_2O represents chemically combined water which is driven off as steam during the firing).
Potash feldspar: $K_2O.Al_2O_3.6SiO_2$.

With some knowledge of the behaviour of the three groups defined by Seger, it is possible to recognize in the feldspar formula that the presence of K_2O will tend to lower the melting point. In the example of china clay, the absence of any materials from the RO/R_2O group will indicate a refractory material with a fairly high melting point. From the fired test of china clay as a single material, we know this is correct. On the test tile of single materials, feldspar melted to form a stiff glass, and on the test pot, feldspar gave a stiff crackly glaze. Line blends of feldspar with a material from the RO/R_2O group produced a reasonably clear glaze with the mixture feldspar 80 and whiting 20. Such a mixture can be represented in the Seger formula by a mathematical calculation.

Calculations in ceramics can involve figures expressed to three decimal points or can be simplified by a more approximate method in which the sums are taken to only one decimal point: for practical purposes this gives sufficient accuracy. It is also usual to place zero before a decimal point in quantities less than one and to put the quantities of all chemical formulae in front of the symbol. Before looking at how this calculation is worked out, the relevance of the molecular weight of a material needs an explanation.

The formulae for feldspar and whiting shows the presence of four elements in addition to oxygen (O) and carbon (C). Each of the two materials has a known molecular weight which refers to the chemical and not the physical weight. The purpose of the calculation is to express the physical weight of the two glaze ingredients in terms of the different chemical proportions present, and this is done using the molecular weight.

Reference has been made earlier to molecular weight and how this is calculated and the full list of M.W. (molecular weight) can be found on page 171. To calculate the formula for the glaze recipe feldspar 80 and whiting 20:

Recipe	*Formula*	*Molecular Weight*
Feldspar 80	$K_2O.Al_2O_3.6SiO_2$	556
Whiting 20	$CaCO_3$	100

1 To find the proportion of the molecules of each ingredient present in a glaze, divide each quantity by its molecular weight:

$$\frac{\text{pts by wt.}}{\text{mol wt.}} = \text{mol. parts.}$$

Feldspar $\frac{80}{556} = 0.144$ mol. parts

Whiting $\frac{20}{100} = 0.200$ mol. parts

2 To find the proportion of each oxide present in each material, multiply the molecular parts by the number of molecules present in the formula:

	K_2O	Al_2O_3	SiO_2		CaO
Feldspar	0.144	0.144	0.864 (0.144×6)		—
Whiting	—	—	—		0.20
Totals	0.144	0.144	0.861		0.20

This may now be expressed in the formula:

$$0.144\, K_2O \qquad 0.144\, Al_2O_3 \qquad 0.864\, SiO_2$$
$$0.200\, CaO$$

This formula can more easily be compared with other glaze formulae if the total of all the RO/R_2O column is one or unity. This is simply achieved by dividing all the figures in the formula by the sum of the RO/R_2O (i.e. 0.344). The formula now reads:

$$0.42\, K_2O \qquad 0.42\, Al_2O_3 \qquad 2.5\, SiO_2$$
$$0.58\, CaO$$

The interpretation of such a glaze formula is limited largely by experience. Only by calculating formulae from many working glazes can a store of interpretative knowledge result. It is possible, however, to generalize. For example, the high proportion of K_2O (0.42) in this glaze will tend to induce crazing and weaken the resistance of the glaze to acids. From the amount of calcium present a good response to iron can be expected. From a practical point of view, the recipe contains no clay and this gives a glaze batch in which the solid materials will settle quickly, and, when dried on the surface of the pot in the raw state, will be very powdery and difficult to handle. Calculations from recipes to formulae were simplified to a large extent in the example shown above, by regarding each material present in the glaze recipe as a single material with its own molecular weight. This method ignores the fact that each ingredient has a specific analysis and though this may not always be available, most suppliers of raw material will provide such an analysis. Typical analyses are listed on page 176. Calculations which take these analyses into account involve much greater detail and the same example is used to illustrate this point.

Recipe: Feldspar 80

Whiting 20

1   Obtain the correct percentage composition of each ingredient. Examples of materials supplied by Harrison Mayer Ltd are listed on page 173.

	K_2O	Na_2O	CaO	Al_2O_3	SiO_2
Feldspar	11.1	2.5	—	19.45	66.00
Whiting	—	—	55.34	0.12	0.19

2   Calculate the amount of each oxide in the glaze from the recipe. Multiply the percentage of oxide given in the analysis by the quantity of the ingredient in the glaze and divide by 100.

Feldspar

K_2O $\dfrac{11.1 \times 80}{100} = 8.88$ Na_2O $\dfrac{2.5 \times 80}{100} = 2.0$

Al_2O_3 $\dfrac{19.45 \times 80}{100} = 15.56$ SiO_2 $\dfrac{66 \times 80}{100} = 52.8$

Whiting

CaO $\dfrac{55.34 \times 20}{100} = 11.07$ Al_2O_3 $\dfrac{0.12 \times 20}{100} = 0.02$

SiO_2 $\dfrac{0.19 \times 20}{100} = 0.4$

3   Total up the amounts of each oxide.

	K_2O	Na_2O	CaO	Al_2O_3	SiO_2
Feldspar	8.88	2.0	—	15.56	52.8
Whiting	—	—	11.07	0.02	0.4
	8.88	2.0	11.07	15.58	53.2

4   Each total is divided by its molecular weight to convert physical weights into comparative number of molecules.

K_2O $\dfrac{8.88}{94} = 0.09$ Na_2O $\dfrac{2.0}{62} = 0.3$ CaO $\dfrac{11.07}{56} = 0.2$

Al_2O_3 $\dfrac{15.58}{102} = 0.15$ SiO_2 $\dfrac{53.2}{60} = 0.9$

The formula can now be assembled and written as:

$$0.09 \quad K_2O \qquad 0.15 \quad Al_2O_3 \qquad 0.9 \quad SiO_2$$
$$0.03 \quad NaO$$
$$0.2 \quad CaO$$

5 To reduce the bases to unity, divide the sum of the bases into the molecular parts of each of the oxides in the formula.

$$0.09 \quad K_2O$$
$$0.03 \quad Na_2O$$
$$0.20 \quad CaO$$
$$\overline{}$$
$$0.32 = \text{sum of mol. parts of bases}$$

$$K_2O \quad \frac{0.09}{0.32} = 0.28 \qquad Na_2O \quad \frac{0.03}{0.32} = 0.09 \qquad CaO \quad \frac{0.20}{0.32} = 0.63$$

$$Al_2O_3 \quad \frac{0.15}{0.32} = 1.47 \qquad SiO_2 \quad \frac{0.9}{0.32} = 2.81$$

6. The Seger formula, with bases totalling unity, can now be written:

$$0.28 \quad K_2O \qquad 0.47 \quad Al_2O_3 \qquad 2.81 \quad SiO_2$$
$$0.09 \quad NaO$$
$$\underline{0.63} \quad CaO$$
$$1.00$$

It is interesting to compare this formula with the formula calculated by the simplified method used on page 83.

Calculations are made easier if charts are prepared which outline the various steps of the calculation; for example, like the one illustrated on page 20. With the aid of either a slide rule, (see Appendix 3 for method of working) or an electronic calculator the arithmetic of these calculations presents no problems and the results can provide useful interpretative information. If, for example, a full 121 test blend was made of the four materials – feldspar, china clay, whiting and flint; from the results achieved, calculations to find the chemical formula of each glaze produced will point out certain facts.

Test no.	CaO	K_2O	Al_2O_3	SiO_2	Ratio Al_2O_3/SiO_2
47	0.96	0.04	0.5	2.2	1 − 4
49	0.90	0.10	0.45	2.3	1 − 5
51	0.84	0.16	0.35	2.2	1 − 6
53	0.8	0.2	0.29	2.2	1 − 7
57	0.96	0.04	0.45	2.2	1 − 6
59	0.9	0.1	0.6	2.4	1 − 4
69	0.95	0.05	0.88	3.8	1 − 4
71	0.86	0.14	1.49	6.5	1 − 4

CaO } 0.9 K_2O } 0.1 Al_2O_3 } 0.62 SiO_2 } 3.0   Ratio } 5

Table 5

Formulae which produced shining glazes in the blend of four materials – feldspar, whiting, china clay, and flint.

Test no.	CaO	K_2O	Al_2O_3	SiO_2	Ratio Al_2O_3/SiO_2
15	0.94	0.06	0.34	0.98	1 – 3
17	0.9	0.1	0.27	1.0	1 – 4
19	0.88	0.12	0.23	1.1	1 – 5
21	0.84	0.12	0.18	1.13	1 – 6
25	0.95	0.05	0.41	1.38	1 – 3
27	0.93	0.07	0.32	1.3	1 – 4
29	0.88	0.12	0.26	1.33	1 – 5
31	0.85	0.15	0.26	1.4	1 – 6
35	0.99	0.01	0.2	0.74	1 – 4
37	0.94	0.06	0.4	1.7	1 – 4
39	0.89	0.11	0.33	1.7	1 – 4
41	0.85	0.15	0.28	1.7	1 – 6
	0.9	0.09	0.28	1.2	4.5

Table 6
Formulae which produce smooth matt glazes.

Test no.	CaO	K_2O	Al_2O_3	SiO_2	Ratio Al_2O_3/SiO_2
10	0.45	0.55	1.13	10.2	1 – 9
77	0.71	0.29	0.28	3.5	1 – 12
103	0.7	0.3	2.4	16.7	1 – 7
81	0.88	0.12	1	5.8	1 – 6
99	0.58	0.42	0.42	4.8	1 – 11
83	0.78	0.22	0.78	5.4	1 – 7
97	0.58	0.42	0.64	6.8	1 – 11
91	0.9	0.1	1.68	9.7	1 – 6
95	0.66	0.34	0.86	7.4	1 – 7
93	0.76	0.24	1.2	8.4	1 – 7
	0.7	0.3	1.0	8.41	8

Table 7
Formulae which give opaque white matt glazes.

GLAZE FORMULA TO GLAZE RECIPE

From these formulae it could be estimated by averaging out the results that a shiny glaze has the formula:

$$\left. \begin{array}{l} 0.9 \quad CaO \\ 0.1 \quad K_2O \end{array} \right\} \quad 0.62Al_2O_3 \quad 3.0SiO_2$$

This can now be translated into a recipe, using the reverse procedure, by the following method.

1. Choose materials which will give the required oxides. In this example the materials are known – feldspar, whiting, china clay and flint.
2. Draw up a table showing the raw material and the quantity of each oxide required.

Raw material with formula	CaO	K_2O	Al_2O_3	SiO_2
	0.90	0.10	0.62	3.0

3. Fill in the chart, one material at a time. First whiting ($CaCO_3$). 0.9 CaO is called for in the formula and as whiting contains only calcium, the

ratio of whiting required is 1 (the number of molecules of CaO in whiting) $\times$ 0.90 = 0.90. This is written in the chart as indicated, and a line is drawn underneath the CaO column as this requirement is satisfied.

4   The next material, feldspar, is more complex; it contains three materials present in different proportions. Each molecule of feldspar contained one molecule of K_2O, therefore the ratio of feldspar required is 1 $\times$ 0.10 = 0.10 which is put in the K_2O column. As feldspar contains the one molecule of Al_2O_3, the same amount (0.10) goes in the Al_2O_3 column, and is subtracted from the total Al_2O_3 required (0.62) which leaves 0.52 still required. As a molecule of feldspar contains not one but six molecules of SiO_2, the ratio of feldspar required (0.10) will give 6 $\times$ 0.10 of SiO_2 = 0.60. This sum is put in the SiO_2 column and subtracted from the total required.

The chart will now look like this:

Raw materials with formula	Ratio required	CaO 0.90	K_2O 0.10	Al_2O_3 0.62	SiO_2 3.0
Whiting $CaCO_3$	0.90	0.90			
Feldspar $K_2O.Al_2O_3.6SiO_2$	0.10		0.10	0.10	0.60
				0.52	2.40

5   This leaves 0.52 Al_2O_3 and 2.40 SiO_2 to be satisfied. The remainder of the chart is now completed using china clay and flint, with the same method, noting that china clay gives one molecule of Al_2O_3 and two of SiO_2. The completed chart now looks like this:

Raw materials with formula	Ratio required	CaO 0.90	K_2O 0.10	Al_2O_3 0.62	SiO_2 3.0
Whiting $CaCO_3$	0.90	0.90			
Feldspar $K_2O.Al_2O_3.6SiO_2$	0.10		0.10	0.10	0.60
				0.52	2.40
China clay $Al_2O_3.2SiO_2.2H_2O$	0.52			0.52	1.04
					1.36
Flint SiO_2	1.36				1.36

6   The ratio of the molecules of the raw materials has now been found and has to be converted into the physical weight of each material by multiplying each ratio by its molecular weight:

Whiting	$0.90 \times 100 =$	90.0
Feldspar	$0.10 \times 558 =$	55.8
China Clay	$0.52 \times 258 =$	134.2
Flint	$1.36 \times 60 =$	81.6

Total 361.6

7   The recipe is converted into a percentage by dividing each amount by the sum total of the amounts (346) and multiplying by 100 to give the following recipe in whole numbers:

Whiting $= 25$
Feldspar $= 15.4$
China Clay $= 37$
Flint $= 22.6$

Calculations from formula to recipe are made easier by the use of a chart such as the one illustrated on page 182. Similar calculations based on the test blend of four material gave the following glazes.

	Shiny glaze	*opaque matt white*	*matt smooth*
Whiting	25	15	45
Feldspar	15	21	28
China Clay	35	22	20
Flint	25	42	7

Using this method of blending materials, many combinations can be tested; by calculation it will be found that certain broad types of glazes, for example, shiny and clear, have similar sorts of chemical formulae. All materials depend for their effect on the proportion present in the glaze, as well as the other materials in the glaze.

5 *Six pots, each with a different oxidized tenmoku glaze (see page 164) fired at 1260°C
(2300°F). Left to right: (1) Feldspar 50, quartz 15, whiting 10, borax frit 25 + iron 10.
(2) Blue/black. (3) Black. (4) China stone 75, china clay 10, whiting 10, calcium borate
frit 5 + iron 9. (5) Matt. (6) Shiny black.*

6 *Stoneware bowls with ash glazes by Emmanuel Cooper. Left: White/yellow. Centre:
Orange/yellow/white. Right: Glaze made only of mixed medium, unsieved ash, fired at
1250°C (2282°F) – 1260°C (2300°F).*

7 *Lidded porcelain boxes by Eileen Lewenstein, fired at about 1250°C (2282°F). Varying
proportions of colouring oxides and carbonates were added to a base glaze of feldspar 4,
whiting 31, china clay 40, flint 18, dolomite 7. Left to right: (1) plus 0.7% cobalt carbonate;
(2) plus 2.5% copper oxide and 2.5% red iron oxide; (3) plus 1.5% rutile and 0.5% cobalt
carbonate; (4) plus 1% cobalt carbonate and 1% iron oxide; (5) plus 2.5% copper oxide
and 2.5% red iron oxide fired in cool part of kiln.*

8 *Flat bowls with dry glaze mixtures (see page 33).*

9 *Three tiles oxidized stoneware, with mixtures of three materials.* Left: *Feldspar, china clay and whiting.* Centre: *Whiting, granite and wood ash.* Right: *London clay, feldspar and wood ash.*

7
Adapting, Formulating and Correcting Glazes

From the practical tests described in chapter 2 certain facts will have been discovered. The information learned can be made even more useful by applying it to the problems of glaze construction. The empirical method of evolving glazes – ably demonstrated by mixtures of two, three or four materials, is a lengthy, though informative, method of discovering what happens when certain materials are mixed together. Likewise, the practical knowledge gained by adding increments of one material to a basic glaze until the point of excess is reached is also a lengthy method of acquiring information. From all these practical tests, good useful glazes will have been discovered which will form a wide repertoire of glazes and effects upon which more experiments can be based.

However, with a knowledge of the molecular formulae of glazes explained in the last chapter it is not always necessary to carry out so many tests to discover that some mixtures will not work as glazes – they may just refuse to melt at all, or conversely, melt to such a degree as to be of no use. If the molecular formulae of all these glazes were to be calculated, and the results set down along side a description of the sort of glaze which had been produced, a useful guide would be produced which would enable the experienced glazer to work out from the molecular formula of the glaze the probable appearance of the fired glaze. Such knowledge is far from being 100% accurate, yet it is a practical method of determining glaze construction.

The work of Seger has already been mentioned in connection with the delineation and formation of glaze formula. When he was formulating the construction of his temperature indicating cones, he evolved a whole series of formulae for the different temperatures he required. At the calculated temperature, the cone was so formulated to soften and fall over, but not to actually melt. Seger cones actually melt at temperatures of 100–150°C (212–302°F) above their bending temperature.

Typical molecular compositions of cones:

Bending point	Molecular proportions					
	K_2O	CaO	Al_2O_3	SiO_2	B_2O_3	Fe_2O_3
1060°C (1940°F)	0.3	0.7	0.3	3.9	0.1	0.2
1100°C (2021°F)	0.3	0.7	0.3	4.0	—	0.2

Understanding the glaze

1140°C (2084°F)	0.3	0.7	0.45	4.0	—	0.5
1180°C (2156°F)	0.3	0.7	0.5	5.0	—	—
1230°C (2246°F)	0.3	0.7	0.7	7.0	—	—

If calculated as glazes, the formulae would provide mixtures which give a fairly clear melt at temperatures 100–150°C (212–302°F) above the bending temperature of the cone. A recipe for the 1100°C (2012°F) cone would be:

Feldspar   40
Whiting   20
Flint   30
Iron   8

which at 1260°C (2300°F) gives a shiny brown glaze with blue streaks. This is a good working glaze which can be made even more useful with the addition of china clay.

From the blends of three materials, it can be seen that towards the corners of the triangle diagram (page 19), as one material forms a larger part of the glaze, various effects are found. In the blend of feldspar, china clay and whiting, an increasing amount of china clay will tend to give a matt glaze which, at maximum, is almost unaffected by the heat. An excess of whiting causes excessive melting, boiling and bubbling. Too much feldspar will give a stiff melt which will tend to trap bubbles and the glaze will tend to craze. From this series of tests the following glazes gave good results, and their molecular formulae were found to be

No. 4

Feldspar	80	A good clear glaze			
Whiting	20		0.4	K_2O	Al_2O_3	SiO_2
			0.6	CaO	0.4	2.4

No. 39

Whiting	20	A pleasant dry white matt			
Feldspar	60		0.67	CaO	Al_2O_3	SiO_2
China Clay	20		0.33	K_2O	0.6	2.5

No. 27

Whiting	40	A dry yellow speckled matt glaze			
Feldspar	10		0.95	CaO	Al_2O_3	SiO_2
China Clay	50		0.05	K_2O	0.58	1.3

No. 48

Whiting	10	A shiny stiff white opaque			
Feldspar	70		0.44	CaO	Al_2O_3	SiO_2
China Clay	20		0.56	K_2O	0.95	4.15

No. 4 and no. 39 were the most 'practical' glazes, and, though the appearance of each glaze is different, their molecular formulae are very similar. Glazes no. 27 and 40 have very different formulae, especially no. 27 which has a high proportion of calcium and alumina, and low potash and silica. By firing these glazes, the relationships between fired appearance and the molecular formula can be seen. Much useful research has been carried out by glaze chemists, usually working within the ceramics industry towards trying to formulate well balanced glazes. A chart has been drawn up showing that at specific temperatures maximum and minimum amounts of oxide present in the molecular formula will yield particular sorts of results. If the results obtained from practical tests are compared with this information, useful knowledge will be gained.

(a) The fluxes RO/R_2O—maximum proportions present in the glaze formula.

Temperature	MgO	BaO	ZnO	CaO	B_2O_3	KNa
1200°C (2192°F)	0.325	0.400	0.300	0.550	0.350	0.375
1225°C (2237°F)	0.330	0.425	0.320	0.600	0.300	0.350
1250°C (2282°F)	0.335	0.450	0.340	0.650	0.250	0.325
1275°C (2327°F)	0.340	0.475	0.360	0.700	0.225	0.300
1300°C (2372°F)	0.345	0.500	0.380	0.750	0.210	0.275

(b) The amphoteric and acid oxides:

Temperature	Al_2O_3	SiO_2
1200°C (2192°F)	0.275–0.650	2.400–4.700
1225°C (2237°F)	0.325–0.700	2.600–5.150
1250°C (2282°F)	0.375–0.750	3.000–5.750
1275°C (2327°F)	0.450–0.825	3.500–6.400
1300°C (2372°F)	0.500–0.900	4.000–7.200

Table 8
The maximum and minimum amounts of materials used in glaze.

The ratio between the R_2O_3 and RO_2 group. As a general guide to the alumina/silica ratio, it has been found that for a transparent glaze, the ratio is 1–10 and for a matt glaze 1–5.

It must always be remembered, however, that the value of such limits is restricted to indicating fired effects of a glaze in a general way. Outside these limits it is possible to construct unusual and richly textured glazes which do not possess a 'balanced' formula.

CONSTRUCTING GLAZES FROM MOLECULAR FORMULAE

With a practical knowledge of how materials behave in the glaze and how to use the chemical formulae to work out calculations, it is possible to construct glazes on paper and to predict to some extent how they will behave in the kiln. To work out such a formula, the fluxes chosen will determine many of the sort of effects which will result; the details of the materials listed on page 67 give their effects in glaze batches with regard to fluxing ability and to the likely response to colour. Matt and opaque glazes have already been discussed (chapter 4) and inclusion in the glaze composition of suitable fluxes or opacifiers will give these effects. There are two other factors affecting the glaze which need consideration; the expansion and the strength of the fluxes.

Expansion

Research has found that the expansion and contraction rate for all glaze materials is not the same. At the top end of the scale with maximum expansion is sodium and at the bottom is boron with almost no expansion and contraction rate.

The following list shows the diminishing order of expansion.

High expansion	Sodium	Na
	Potassium	K
	Calcium	Ca
	Barium	Ba
	Titanium	Ti
	Lead	Pb
	Antimony	Sb
	Lithium	Li
	Zinc	Zn
	Magnesium	Mg
	Zirconium	Zr
	Tin	Sn
	Aluminium	Al
	Silicon	Si
Low expansion	Boron	B

A glaze with a high proportion of sodium will tend to give a crazed surface and this can be changed by the substitution of part of the sodium for a flux with less high expansion, such as lithium. Alternatively, the addition of a small amount of boron, found in colemanite or calcium borate will, because of its low expansion, be able to counteract much of the expansion effect of the sodium and render a non-crazed glaze.

STRENGTH OF GLAZES AND BODIES

A glaze which is well fitting gives greater mechanical strength to the ceramic body it covers. This is an important consideration for any functional sort of ware. Conversely, a badly fitting glaze can lower the mechanical strength of the ceramic body and make it more liable to chipping and breakage. An analogy can be drawn between a glazed body and plywood; in both cases the combined surfaces act together to produce a material which has a far greater strength than the mere total of each separate layer. To give greatest strength, the ideal situation occurs where on heating the glaze expands slightly less than the body. On cooling the body contracts just slightly more than the glaze. This leaves the glaze under very slight compression resulting in an increased mechanical strength. Too great a compression can result in the glaze being forced to flake or peel off the body surface. A glaze under tension will develop hairline craze lines which, depending upon one viewpoint, can be either a pleasant decorative feature, or unsightly and undesirable. Both of these glaze faults, crazing and shelling, will be dealt with in detail later in this chapter.

In addition to consideration of the mechanical strength of the ceramic body for useful pots the glaze should also be made to be as scratch-proof as possible. It is known that glazes high in soda are less resistant to attack from acids and they give surfaces which are softer. Substitution of part of the soda by potash will increase this resistance and it will also improve the scratch resistance of the glaze surface. However, many glazes which lack surface strength have often other specific qualities with regard to colour and texture which make adjustment more difficult and tests to improve strength can usually only be made by empirical methods such as adding 5% of various materials in turn. Calcium in the glaze increases both its resistance to abrasion and its tensile strength. Glazes high in alumina have a high surface strength, but too great an amount of alumina will give a glaze surface which will not be sufficiently smooth for practical use. Boron, in small quantities, is also said to increase the surface strength of glazes.

The fluxing power of components have been listed by Seger who gives the following as the order of strength of various fluxes and colouring oxides in the glaze:

Fluxes in glazes in order of activity	*Fluxing power of colouring oxides in order of activity*
Lead oxide	Manganese oxide
Barium oxide	Cobalt oxide
Sodium oxide	Iron oxide
Potassium oxide	Uranium oxide
Zinc oxide	Chromium oxide
Magnesia	Nickel oxide
Alumina	

GLAZE FAULTS

One potter's fault is another potter's 'effect' and it is difficult to estimate how these so-called faults can be corrected when so few studio potters want the perfect, well-balanced glaze, which is the assumption on which all industrial development work on glazes has been based. The difficulties of producing perfect glazes should, in any case, never be underestimated. The pioneering work on glazes carried out by Seger has not yet been superseded and still forms the basis of most advice given; and much of his advice is useful because there is a difference between undesirable effects – such as shelling or peeling, which no potter wants – and effects like crazing, which can be attractive, though not necessarily on domestic pottery. Crawling too can be either a persistent problem or a source of exciting effects. Many of the basic problems of the glaze fitting the body have been dealt with in general. This section deals specifically with how to cope with the common problems, and it is assumed that the glaze rather than the body will be adjusted.

Crazing
The formation of a network of surface cracks is known as either crazing or crackling, and is caused by tensile stresses greater than the glaze is able to

23 Transparent crackle glaze.

withstand. In other words, the glaze is stretched to the point where it literally cracks or crazes apart on the surface of the pot. Crazing may be present when the ware is taken from the kiln or may develop days or months after firing. It was explained earlier that for the body and glaze to provide the greatest mechanical strength, they must expand and contract to almost the same extent – with the body contracting slightly more than the glaze to leave it in a state of compression. Crazing occurs when the reverse has happened and the glaze has contracted more than the body. One of the side effects of crazing on a pot is that it will not 'ring' when tapped and thus one of the qualities of stoneware is lost. Crazed pots may also be insanitary and if the body is porous will permit leaking or seepage of liquids. The remedy lies in adjusting the glaze to reduce the amount of expansion and contraction. This can be done in several ways.

1 Increase the amount of silica in the glaze thus reducing slightly the proportion of fluxes and alumina.
2 Adjust the glaze fluxes by substituting part of the alkalies with magnesia. This can be done empirically by adding small amounts of talc ($3MgO.4SiO_2.H_2O$).
3 Apply a thinner coating of glaze.
4 Decrease the amount of feldspar in the glaze.

5 Increase the proportion of boron.
6 Try increasing or lowering the glost firing temperature.

With earthenware bodies, the problems are slightly different because the degree of bonding which takes place between the glaze and body is considerably less at earthenware temperatures than at stoneware temperatures. There is also the fact that earthenware bodies are usually porous and will absorb moisture. After a period of time this moisture brings about a slight increase in body volume which may be sufficient to neutralize the initial compression in the glaze and make it craze. The remedy here is to fire the ware to a higher temperature to reduce the porosity of the body or reduce the expansion of the glaze still further to increase the compression in the glaze.

Peeling or shelling or shivering
Glaze which flakes off edges or rims or handles is known by any of these terms. In extreme circumstances spiral cracking or splitting of the pot may occur; this is where the bonding of the glaze and body is so firm that the glaze does not break away from the body surface but breaks the whole pot. The condition is a relatively common problem, and is basically the opposite of crazing. The glaze has too low a level of expansion and therefore contraction: as the body cools the glaze is left in a state of too great a compression. This particularly weakens pots glazed only on one side. Frequently such pots lack mechanical strength and are unable to withstand any sort of thermal shock – as one potter discovered to his cost when a number of teapots shattered when boiling water was poured into them. On subsequent pots, this was overcome by glazing on the inside and on the outside so that a balance was set up. The remedies for peeling lie in increasing the high expansion oxides and decreasing the low expansion oxides in the glaze. This means changing the composition of the glaze by one or more of the following methods:

1 Decreasing the silica.
2 Increasing the feldspar or substituting soda feldspar for potash feldspar.
3 Increasing the alkaline oxides, for example, by the addition of a suitable frit.
4 Decreasing the magnesia.

24 Peeling or shelling on the rim of a bowl.

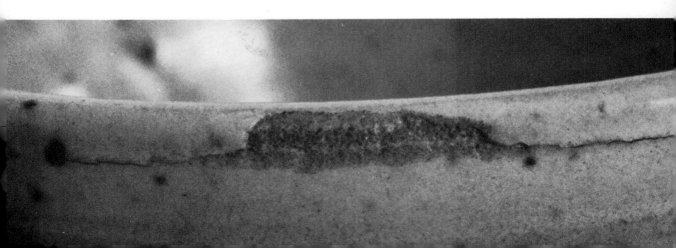

Pitting and pinholing

Of all the faults in glazes, tiny pinhole sized marks are the most difficult to eliminate. A glaze will develop pinholes on one sort of body and not on another, and this too makes it difficult to alter or adjust the glaze without involving radical changes. Pinholes are unsightly and unhygienic on tableware, though volcanic and pitted glazes use this particular feature for their effect. The cause of the pinholing can lie with the body, the composition of the glaze, and the firing cycle. During the firing, the glaze ingredients go through a long slow period of melting, when volatile gasses are released accompanied by bubbling and turbulence; there is also interaction and reaction with the body. A refractory body will tend to 'absorb' more of the glaze, giving a drier surface and one which is more likely to have pinholes. Occasionally, some glazes break through and burst as gases from the body push their way through the glaze layer. If such glazes have a shiny surface, the pinholing is a particularly unsightly flaw. Matt glazes too can be marred by pinholing, and on such a glaze the remedy is even more difficult.

25 Dark blue zinc/feldspar stoneware glaze showing pinholed surface.

It is often better to avoid the particular combination of glaze and body, rather than try to cure pinholing. However, there are several possible solutions:

1　Increase the firing temperature slightly to bring about a better glaze melt.
2　Soak the kiln at top temperature to allow time for bubbles to burst and glaze to flow over.
3　Add a small quantity of frit to the glaze to lower its melting point.
4　Decrease the amount of alumina in the glaze.

Blistered surface
A surface which is blistered with sharp edged craters is usually the result of overfiring. During the firing the glaze goes through a first period when it is melting when bubbling and turbulence occur, followed by the maturing period when the glaze, as a stiff viscous layer, evens out to give a smooth and regular covering. When the glaze has melted and evened out, the firing is terminated. If the firing is continued, reactions continue and the glaze becomes less viscous and begins to flow down the pot. Blistering and bubbling occur as further reactions take place. The remedy here lies in either an increase in the alumina and silica content of the glaze or a lowering of the firing temperature, or a mixture of both.

Crawling
This can be attributed to three different sources – cracking of the glaze during drying, storing the glazed biscuit for a long time before firing, and thirdly, by the presence in the glaze of materials which increase viscosity and surface tension.

26 Emmanuel Cooper. Stoneware bowl with a thickly applied layer of clay matt glaze (plus cobalt and rutile) which crawled in the firing to give a rich decorative effect; 12 cm (5 in.) across.

If the unfired glaze layer cracks on drying, or in the early stages of firing, the 'islands' of the glaze will draw themselves up into heaps. Excessive contraction of the glaze will have weakened the bond between glaze and body. This condition is likely to arise if the glaze contains high proportions of plastic clay resulting in a high wet to dry contraction. A thick layer of glaze is more likely to crack than a thin layer. The use of overground glaze materials is also likely to give rise to this sort of cracking, though this is not a problem the studio potter is likely to face. Dusty or greasy body surfaces are also likely to cause poor adhesion between body and glaze.

High surface tension and viscosity of the glaze may be due to the presence in the glaze of too high a proportion of refractory materials such as matting agents or opacifiers such as tin oxide or, more particularly, zirconium silicate. Raw clay content of such glazes must also be carefully controlled.

A special type of crawling may occur on once-fired ware which is allowed to stand for a long period after glazing. The exact mechanism of the fault is by no means fully understood, but is associated with the re-absorption of water vapour by the glaze layer, from the surrounding atmosphere. The fault is simply avoided by firing the ware soon after glazing or by storing in warm, dry conditions.

To avoid crawling:

1   Keep the plastic clay content of the glaze low; if necessary, replace some of the raw clay with calcined clay or molochite (calcined china clay).
2   Keep opacifiers to a minimum and use tin rather than zirconium.
3   Keep the surface to be glazed clean and dust free.
4   Paint on glaze mixed with gum tragacanth if flaking or cracking occurs.
5   Avoid thick application of glaze.

Under and over firing
These are not faults in the sense described so far, but are particular conditions which, if recognized, are simple to avoid and can occasionally be remedied. Underfired glazes, especially if they are matt, are usually dry, dull and rough, and occasionally the surface has hard blobs; a tenmoku glaze, if underfired will appear as a flat pale olive or dark honey colour, but in other respects appears to be a mature glaze. Increasing the firing temperature in the case of this glaze will lower the viscosity and the glaze will flow slightly to become much darker and therefore the glaze gets thinner on the edges which will show a lighter colour. Some glazes appear cloudy and crazed if underfired with both conditions disappearing at increased temperature. Most pots which have been underfired can safely be refired, especially if the glaze is matt; shiny glazes often present a more difficult problem as the stiff glaze layer traps in any volatile gases released in a second glaze firing with the result that bloating and blistering of the glaze may occur. This is often a particular problem with

porcelain fired a second time. Some glazes, however, change on being refired. This is particularly the case with some ash glazes which go much drier when fired a second time. Glazes which tend to develop crystals will also change when fired a second or even third time – often with very pleasant results.

Overfiring cannot easily be remedied, and it is not always easy to recognize from the results that overfiring is to blame. Where this is the case, a temperature gradient kiln is a great asset. It consists of a long oblong firing chamber with heating elements positioned so as to cause one end of the chamber to be much hotter than the other. At top temperature readings are taken from thermocouples placed at regular intervals along the length of the firing chamber and a record is made. Small test pieces are placed on a tray which is put inside the kiln chamber and are placed so as to correspond with each thermocouple. The results will show the effects of the different temperatures.

Not all potters have, or want, such a sophisticated piece of equipment, but for the potter who has everything, it may be just what is needed! Most potters, however, are content to use the kiln they have, discovering its cool spots and its hot spots and evolving glazes to suit the arrangements.

At its worst, overfiring can result in matt glazes becoming shiny and running heavily to give a rough blistered surface. Overfired transparent glazes may run heavily and leave a streaked and unpleasant surface or boil to leave a rough blistered surface. The body may also be affected and this may show as bloating – a condition when the body swells due to bubbling of the glassy phase. Overfiring may also affect the body which may have vitrified completely; this may well cause the bottoms or feet of the pots to stick to the kiln shelf and, if pieces of the body break off, a hard glassy surface will be revealed.

Some glazes, if overfired slightly, may lose much of their subtlety. Some pale ash glazes have only a limited temperature range in which to develop their full effects; overfiring leaves them dull and bland. Certain glazes which contain small amounts of colouring oxides may also lose subtlety if slightly overfired. Glazes for special effects, discussed in chapter 9, often need carefully controlled firing conditions to fully develop the effects. An overfired copper reduction glaze, for example, will lose its spots and form streaks if the temperature is increased. Likewise the so-called 'oil spot' glaze in which bubbles burst through the glaze layer to form oil spots which level out in the glaze will disappear if the temperature is increased or maintained for too long by soaking.

Occasionally, overfiring produces brilliant glazes, though often at a cost to the kiln shelves, and general wear and tear on the kiln. For example, pleasant speckled opaque white glazes containing 3% tin oxide, if overfired, may well turn into an opalescent blue; a matt green wax glaze with 2% copper turned into a brilliant turquoise speckle when overfired; likewise a clay/feldspar/dolomite glaze with an addition of 2% iron, which usually fired a banana yellow, turned into a rich tiger skin textured matt glaze. None of the effects were easily repeatable, and in any case presented too many practical problems; a more sensible approach would be to lower the melting point of the glaze by adding a frit or reducing the alumina or silica content.

A good usable practical glaze is one which has a tolerance of at least 50°C (122°F) and within this temperature range gives interesting effects which, from a production potter's point of view, will give pots which can be matched with pots from previous firings to form sets and conform reliably with a determined effect. As most kilns have hotter and colder spots the use of such glazes also lessens the chances of loss from under and overfiring.

8
Frits

The reasons that some materials have to be made into a frit before they can be used as glaze materials has been fully explained on pages 15–37 in chapter 2. Frits extend the number of materials readily available for the glazer, yet the complex formulae of most frits present problems of calculation, and some understanding of their use in glazes is helpful when working out a glaze formula and recipe.

Most studio potters are limited in their choice of frits to those available from the major pottery suppliers who usually offer two basic types – one containing lead and the other alkali. Occasionally, however, potters may need to incorporate in their glaze particular amounts of a material which can only be done when it is in the form of a frit. If no suitable commercial frit is available, then it may be necessary to make your own and this technique is explained later in this chapter.

Most manufacturers of potters' raw materials offer several types of frits which are suitable for a wide variety of purposes. A percentage analysis or a molecular formula of the frits is supplied in the manufacturer's catalogues. Frits available in the UK and USA are listed on page 173 with their composition. Some manufacturers even provide the molecular weight. All this information can be useful for glaze calculations. Percentage analysis needs to be converted into molecular form and the same method is used for all complex materials with known percent analysis, such as granite, stone, wood ash, or in this case, a frit.

Example: The published percent analysis of Harrison Mayer alkaline leadless frit (No. 36.2.193) is:

56.1	SiO_2
8.0	B_2O_3
4.0	Al_2O_3
6.4	CaO
12.3	Na_2O
2.0	K_2O
10.9	ZnO

To find the molecular formula, each of these quantities is divided by its molecular weight to give the following results:

SiO_2	$56.1 \div 60$	$= 0.935$	Na_2O	$12.3 \div 62$	$= 0.198$
B_2O_3	$8.0 \div 70$	$= 0.114$	K_2O	$2.0 \div 94$	$= 0.021$
Al_2O_3	$4.0 \div 101.9$	$= 0.039$	ZnO	$10.9 \div 81.4$	$= 0.134$
CaO	$6.4 \div 56$	$= 0.114$			

27 *Commercial ball mills for grinding frits and raw materials*. Photograph – Harrison Mayer Ltd

which when written as a molecular formula appears as:

0.114	CaO	0.039	Al_2O_3	0.935	SiO_2
0.198	Na_2O				
0.021	K_2O			0.114	B_2O_3
0.134	ZnO				

To enable this formula to be easily compared with other formulae the total sum of the bases must be brought to total one (unity). This is done by dividing all the figures by total of bases (0.467) and the formula now reads:

0.24	CaO	0.08	Al_2O_3	2.00	SiO_2
0.42	Na_2O			0.244	B_2O_3
0.04	K_2O				
0.29	ZnO				

This for instance compares with a molecular formula given by Podmore and Sons Ltd for an alkaline frit (P2250):

0.2	CaO	0.1	Al_2O_3	1.5	SiO_2
0.5	Na_2O			0.1	B_2O_3
0.3	K_2O				

Each of these frits would comply with the limit ratio, used to determine what will be an insoluble frit, for bases to acids 1–1 to 1–3. To enable a frit to be incorporated into a glaze through calculation the molecular weight of the frit must be found by multiplying the quantity of each ingredient in the molecular formulae by its own molecular weight and the sums totalled.

e.g. with frit P2250:

CaO	0.2×56	$= 11.2$
Na_2O	0.5×62	$= 31$
K_2O	0.3×94.2	$= 28.26$
Al_2O_3	0.1×101.9	$= 10.19$
B_2O_3	0.1×69.6	$= 6.96$
SiO_2	1.5×60.1	$= 90.15$
	total	$= 177.76$

Molecular weight of frit P2250 $= 177.76$, and this figure can now be used to calculate the formula of any glaze in which it may be used.

Frits in the glaze

Frits can be used in the glaze batch as a conveniently pre-packaged base

28 *Discharging a commercial frit. Here the melted frit is pouring into water where it solidifies and shatters. The supervisor uses a metal rod to break up the frit*. Photograph – Harrison Mayer Ltd.

to which other ingredients can be added and from the test of single materials it can be seen that they melt readily at 1260°C (2300°F). There are certain empirical details which need taking into account. Lead frits are not usually suitable for use above 1150°C (2102°F) as lead volatilizes at this temperature, though small amounts of lead frit can be used as high as 1250°C (2282°F) depending upon the other glaze ingredients. Because they have already been fired, frits contribute no plasticity nor binding power to the dry glaze. They also sink rapidly in the glaze mix. From a practical point of view, it is advisable to incorporate some raw clay (preferably a plastic clay, or bentonite), into the glaze batch to aid suspension and to help bind the glaze on the pot.

It is also useful to note that a high proportion of alkalies can be incorporated in a glaze by means of a frit and the possibilities of producing crackle glazes are increased. A useful starting point is frit 50, clay 10, whiting 10, soda feldspar 25, flint 5.

Calculating frit glazes

A useful method of devising a glaze around a frit is to compare the formula of the frit with that of an 'ideal' glaze for a particular use. Such an 'ideal' glaze can be either the Seger glaze for cone 1A or can be based on the maximum and minimum limits of glaze construction suggested in the table on page 91. For example this suggests that the limits on a 1250°C (2282°F) clear glaze, the Al_2O_3 limits are between 0.375–0.750 and for SiO_2 3.000–5.750, and that the ratio for a transparent glaze is 1–10. If a clear glaze is calculated using this as the guide a suggested glaze formula would be:

0.2 CaO	0.3 Al_2O_3	3 SiO_2
0.5 Na_2O		0.2 B_2O_3
0.3 K_2O		

The amounts of Al_2O_3 and SiO_2 fall within the suggested limits and are the ratio 1–10 which is the norm for a clear glaze. Using frit P2250 with the formula:

0.2 CaO	0.1 Al_2O_3	1.5 SiO_2 (M.W. 177.76)
0.5 Na_2O		0.2 B_2O_3
0.3 K_2O		

to satisfy all the bases, all the B_2O_3 and part of the alumina and silica, the remainder can be met by china clay and flint. Using the 'formula to recipe' method of calculation chart, the receipes are found to be:

Frit P2250	60
China Clay	17
Flint	23

clear glaze 1250°C (2282°F)

Again using the tables listed on page 00, a matt glaze can be worked out and here the suggested ratio of Al_2O_3 to SiO_2 is 1–5. By doubling the amount of alumina in the theoretically correct glaze formula a matt glaze should result. It has the formula:

0.2	CaO	0.6	Al_2O_3	3	SiO_2
0.5	Na_2O			0.1	B_2O_3
0.3	K_2O				

Again the calculations are the same with the additional amounts of Al_2O_3 and SiO_2 being made up by china clay and flint. The recipe is found to be:

Frit P2250   58
China Clay   42   matt white opaque 1250°C (2282°F)
Flint   10

Both these glazes depend for their success on the theory being workable, and it is only by testing them that this will be found. For example, the matt glaze has a high proportion of raw china clay which may pose problems of crawling and so on. These may be overcome by substituting calcined china clay for raw china clay. Other points may also arise. For instance the use of a frit with such a high proportion of the alkali fluxes sodium and potassium renders the glaze liable to crazing and to attack from strong acids. Such a glaze will respond well to the colouring oxides which require a strong alkali base to give strong colour i.e. copper oxide. If required the glaze could be 'balanced' by an addition of whiting.

If 10% whiting is added to the shiny glaze recipe, it now reads:

			expressed in percentage terms is:	
	Frit	60	Frit	55
	China Clay	17	China Clay	15
	Flint	23	Flint	21
+	Whiting	10%	Whiting	9
		110		100

This recipe can be calculated on the 'recipe to formula' form to give the molecular formula:

0.38	CaO	0.24	Al_2O_3	2.33	SiO_2
0.39	Na_2O			0.16	B_2O_3
0.23	K_2O				

compared with the original:

0.2	CaO	0.30	Al_2O_3	3	SiO_2
0.5	Na_2O			0.2	B_2O_3
0.3	K_2O				

MAKING YOUR OWN FRIT

Making your own frit involves a considerable amount of preparation and quite a bit of labour breaking up the solid fired frit glass, but the actual method is not complicated. The advantages of making your own frits, apart from self-sufficiency, are that it involves seeing the entire process through from start to finish and also enables the potter to work out specific frits for special effects. This is particularly relevant for crystalline glazes where extra special mixtures are required for crystal development or copper red colours.

29 Solid frit in the bottom of flat bowl painted with a thick layer of flint, fired to 1250°C (2282°F) and removed from the kiln at 400°C (720°F); this bowl had to be broken to remove the frit which had dissolved a large amount of flint.

First, the ingredients are weighed and mixed together dry in a pestle and mortar. Ideally this mixture is placed in a crucible, heated until it melts and becomes liquid; this is then poured into cold water to shatter the glass which has formed, as this makes subsequent grinding easier. Few potters have suitable equipment for making frits by this method, and must prepare the frit in the usual biscuit kiln.

In this method the weighed frit ingredients are put into a shallow biscuited bowl which has had a thickish layer of flint mixed with water, painted on the entire inside. It is important to use a flat bowl as a thin layer of frit is easier to break up than a thick layer. The bowl, only half full of frit ingredients (for during the firing the frit ingredients boil as they melt) is fired in the biscuit kiln and allowed to cool normally. Remove the frit from the bowl, brush or wash off all the flint as, if left, it would affect the composition of the frit. Break up the melted frit into small pieces with a hammer or an iron pestle and mortar, and grind the glass into a fine powder. A ball mill makes the job of grinding very much easier. Making frits in the studio is an interesting exploration rather than a practical alternative, but it is very worthwhile.

Choosing materials suitable for fritting is not always quite as straightforward as it may seem. Rendering soluble materials completely insoluble requires a careful selection of ingredients and a number of empirical conditions have been worked out to ensure this is the case.

1   To make the frit readily fusible, the ratio of the molecular parts of base to acid oxides should be in the range 1–1 to 1–3.
2   To render the soluble ingredients completely insoluble, a second base capable of forming an insoluble glass must be introduced. For example, boric acid and alkali salts, if fused with flint, may form a frit which is still soluble. This solubility may be overcome by introducing other oxides such as calcium, lead or 1–3% alumina (as china clay).

Calculating a frit composition
In this example, the molecular formula for a frit is:

$$0.3 \ Na_2O \quad 0.3 \ K_2O \quad 0.4 \ CaO \quad 0.3 \ Al_2O_3 \quad 1.8 \ SiO_2 \quad 0.6 \ B_2O_3$$

to calculate the recipe the usual chart is used. It should be noted that borax ($Na_2O.2B_2O_3.10H_2O$) has the molecular proportions Na_2O and B_2O_3 as 1–2. This gives a frit recipe:

Borax   35.62
Feldspar   51.94
Whiting   12.43

9
Special Glaze Effects

The production potter, making a steady line of attractive and useful wares, often has little time for, or, interest in, the fascinating 'special glaze' effects that can be obtained. Effects are not reliable, do not always appear, and can be time and effort consuming. This chapter is a guide to some of the effects and will go some way to opening a few doors for the interested studio potter.

RED GLAZES

Of all the colours, red is perhaps the most difficult to obtain, yet the one which has, for hundreds of years, captured the imagination of the glaze chemist. In China, there is a traditional story of the court potter, who, having succeeded in producing a red glaze in one firing, became so desperate to repeat this success that, in despair after many failures, he threw himself into the firing box of the kiln. Though he did not live to tell the tale, his sacrifice was rewarded with brilliant red glaze. Today our efforts neither have to be so empirical nor so mysterious, though some will succeed, and some will fail. Red glazes have not yet yielded up all their secrets by any means. There are four main methods of obtaining red glazes: by using chromium, using cadmium-selenium, by firing glazes containing copper in a reducing atmosphere, and by adding a local reducing agent to a copper glaze and firing it in an electric kiln.

Chrome red glazes

Rich red glazes can be obtained from the use of small quantities of chromium oxide in low temperature, low alumina glazes fluxed by lead, and in glazes containing tin oxide. Low temperature red glazes are difficult to fire because of their narrow melting range. If overfired, they rapidly become fluxed and run off the pot; they also lose the red colour and become green. Because of this low temperature range (which must not exceed about 950–1000°C (1740–1832°F)), it is better to apply the glaze to pots which have been biscuit fired to a temperature high enough to have vitrified the body. The high proportion of lead in the glaze is quite likely to present a lead solubility problem and such glazes should *never* be used on pots to be used for food or drink. It is also a sensible precaution to restrict the use of these glazes to flat surfaces or to the insides of bowls so that glaze cannot run onto the kiln shelf to cause 'stuck ware'.

A glaze with the molecular formula $PbO. 0.1 Al_2O_3 0.7 SiO_2$, fired at 980°C (1760°F) will, with the addition of 2% chromium oxide, give a rich red glaze. As the silica content of this glaze is low, no commercially-available frit would be suitable and lead has to be incorporated in its raw (and poisonous) state. Special precautions to avoid the hazards involved in the handling of raw lead compounds should be observed, and the glaze should not be used on any ware likely to contain food and drink. The following recipe based on lead oxide is successful:

Litharge 77   Flint 10   China Clay 10   Chromium Oxide 2

Chrome-tin pink and red glazes can be obtained at both stoneware and earthenware temperatures. Almost any glaze containing tin will respond to chromium oxide applied by either painting or spraying, with a bright pink flush as the chromium flashes over the surrounding areas. This effect can be as much a problem as an advantage, especially when using commercially prepared glaze stains containing chrome. Though fairly stable in normal glazes, in the presence of tin oxide they can give a distinct, and unwelcome, pink flush.

Red and pink glazes can be made by adding either small amounts of chromium oxide or a commercially prepared red glaze stain containing chrome to a glaze base containing tin oxide. In some glazes, the amount of tin oxide can be reduced in quantity if large quantities of glaze stain is to be added. Small amounts of lead bisilicate can be added to stoneware glazes to aid melting and encourage colour response. Generally lead and high lime glazes low in alkalies give best and most reliable results. All are fired in an oxidized atmosphere. A typical basic recipe for 1150°C (210°F):

Lead bisilicate	40
Whiting	10
Feldspar	22
China clay	10
Flint	18

A matt glaze for 1260°C (2300°F):

Feldspar	40
Dolomite	7
Whiting	24
China clay	20
Flint	9
+6% tin oxide	

Experiments to achieve more delicate shades can be made by using potassium dichromate which is a form of chrome in a soluble state. Dissolved in water the solution can be either sprayed or painted onto the glaze and though the results may be slightly unpredictable, they can give soft shades.

Cadmium-selenium glazes

The brightest, reddest glazes are those obtained at earthenware temperatures from the presence of cadmium-selenium in a suitable opaque glaze mix. Both these oxides are poisonous and are not generally available in the UK as raw materials. Cadmium oxide is particularly prone to metal release in a badly balanced fired glaze. Since any glazes used on pots which are to be offered for sale should conform to any government regulations it would be wise to use only commercially-available glazes, and to treat them as indicated by the supplier – both in the thickness of application and in the specified temperature. They can be purchased in fritted glaze mixtures, prepared commercially, and if the manufacturer's firing instructions are followed, can be used safely on all types of ware. Success with these glazes depends upon an evenly thick application of colour (too thin an application will render a transparent glaze) a clean oxidizing atmosphere, and an accurate firing temperature. These glazes must also be kept free from contamination, as this will destroy their colour, they cannot usually be mixed or overlapped with other sorts of glazes though they can be used with other similar glazes. Colours ranging from orange to ruby red are usually available.

Reduction fired copper glazes

Copper red glazes rely for their effect on copper changing from one state, which has a green colour, to another, which has a red colour. Hence, they are sometimes known as transmutation glazes. The scientific explanation for this is that copper, added to the glaze as cupric oxide, CuO, is easily affected in the firing; during the reduction in the kiln, the cupric oxide is changed to cuprous oxide Cu_2O, which needs less oxygen, and also colloidal copper, Cu. This is metallic copper in the form of particles so small that their size cannot be measured; colloidal means very finely divided. Unlike crystalloids, colloids cannot form true solutions and cannot be crystallized.

Copper red glazes were first developed by Chinese potters in the Sung dynasty. The colours obtained can range from light spotted red to rich dark purple and can be produced in glazes maturing from 800°C to 1300°C (1472–2372°F). Depending on the firing conditions, the glaze composition, and the amount of copper used, various sorts of red can be obtained, some of these have been given names – sang de boeuf, oxblood, and rouge flambé. Peach bloom describes the partly reduced, partly oxidized glaze, with green red effects in the same glaze. Some potters find the colour is at its best on porcelain, others on a dark stoneware body. Most potters prefer the combination of two colours, such as red/pink, grey/pink, purple/blue etc. which depend for their success on the glaze base and the firing condition.

Any of the three states of copper can be used in the glaze, though copper carbonate, $CuCO_3$, is considered to be most suitable as it is the least stable. Only small additions of copper are necessary – 0.5–2%. Glazes need to be fairly fluid at top temperature with calcium, sodium, and potassium forming the major fluxes for stoneware glazes. Lead can be used as the flux in earthenware glazes. Additions of 2–3% zinc or tin help to disperse the colour and opacify the glaze, and 1–2% iron will darken the red, and small amounts of cobalt will make it more purple. Reduction of the kiln atmosphere needs to be started quite early in the firing – about 600°C (1112°F) for earthenware and 850°C (1562°F) for stoneware. Reduction can take place during the cooling of the kiln, and this works well for earthenware glazes 800–700°C (1472–1292°F). With stoneware glazes, reduction from top temperature down to 1100°C (2012°F) helps to prevent reoxidation, though mixtures of green and red can be obtained by alternating periods of reduction followed by periods of oxidation.

An analysis of a Sung red glaze is:

$$SiO_2 \; 73.9 \quad Al_2O_3 \; 6.0 \quad Fe_2O_3 \; 2.10 \quad CaO \; 7.30$$
$$K_2O \; 3.00 \quad Na_2O \; 3.10 \quad CuO \; 4.60$$

which has the molecular formula:

0.484	CaO	0.213	Al_2O_3	4.53	SiO_2
0.118	K_2O	0.049	Fe_2O_3		
0.185	Na_2O				
0.213	CuO				

This approximates to the recipe:

Whiting	15
K. Feldspar	20
Soda Feldspar	25
Flint	40
Copper oxide	4
Iron oxide	2

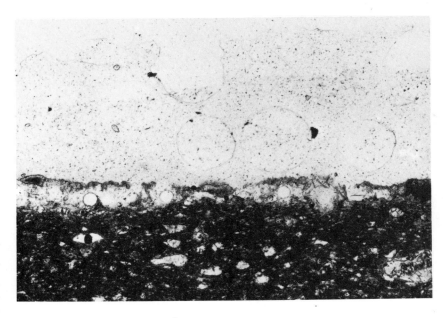

30 Cross section of cloudy pink/blue glaze (page 165) over stoneware body. The round bubbles give the glaze opalescence and the tiny black spots in glaze are silicon carbide. The reaction layer between the glaze (top) and body (bottom) can be seen. Transmitted light × 100.

Artificially reduced copper red glazes

For potters working with electric kilns, inducing a reduced atmosphere is tricky, and more important can cause excess wear upon the elements. The alternative to a reducing kiln atmosphere is to add a reducing material to the glaze. Silicon carbide (SiC), better known as Carborundum, is a suitable reducing agent. This is produced by an electric arc process and is an extremely hard refractory material from which, amongst other things, kiln shelves and props are made. When silicon carbide is fired in the glaze, the heat breaks it down into cristobolite (SiO_2) which goes into solution in the glaze and the carbon draws oxygen from its surroundings to form carbon monoxide and ultimately carbon dioxide, both of which are released as a gas. Copper, being the least stable oxide present in the glaze, is first to lose its oxygen and converts to either its colloidal or its cuprous state. Only small quantities of both copper and silicon carbide are necessary to achieve a satisfactory effect. Too large a quantity of silicon carbide results in a rough sandpaper textured glaze which looks and feels unpleasant. Glazes with a high alkaline content seem to work best, and glazes used over a smooth body seem to bring out the full colour and quality. It is also important that the silicon carbide be as finely ground as possible.

Too short a firing cycle or too low a temperature may cause the glaze to be bubbled or brown – refiring may well remove this, and may also be used to intensify colour on some pots.

31 Zinc silicate crystalline glaze, stoneware.

CRYSTALLINE GLAZES

A true crystalline glaze (macro-crystalline) is one which contains crystals of visible size to produce a decorative effect. Related to these are aventurine glazes which contain tiny crystals which can be seen suspended below the surface of the glaze. Micro-crystalline glazes contain well developed individual or clusters of crystals either fully or partly immersed in a glassy matrix. Textural qualities can vary from matt, semi-matt to shiny, and the crystals may be coloured by picking up small amounts of colouring oxides previously added to the glaze. The background may be colourless.

32 Small crystals in high clay matt glaze, stoneware with an addition of 2% cobalt and 3% rutile.

The development of crystalline glazes depends upon the nature of the glaze, temperature and length of firing, the rate of cooling, and most important of all, the basic oxide used in the glaze to form the silicate which saturates the glaze and forms the crystals on cooling.

The silicates, which crystallize out during cooling, depend for their success upon the nature of the glaze, which must act as a solvent, with a viscosity which must encourage the growth of crystals. During the firing a fluid liquid must be formed in which oxides present in the glaze can move freely. When cooling starts motion within the glaze slows down and, in this slowing down period bonds form as perfect unit cells or crystallites and these act as nuclei around which larger crystals may form. The slower the cooling rate of the glaze, the larger the crystals will be. Some oxides work better than others and it has been found that an excess of zinc, in a suitably fired glaze, will combine with silica to form large crystals of Willemite. Smaller, secondary crystals, of different shape may also occur in the same glaze.

*33 Close-up of zinc silicate
crystals in glaze with 30%
alkaline frit, stoneware, and
soaked for two hours at
1100°C (2012°F) this glaze
became very fluid and ran
freely down the pot.*

Crystals and crystal patterns vary in shape and are not predictable –
even in the same glaze in similar firings. Equally mysterious can be the
absence of crystals in a glaze which seems to conform in other ways.
Alternatives to correct this are to refire the piece as it is, or to seed the glaze
with a mixture of 70% zinc oxide and 30% flint. This mixture can be
spotted onto the fired glaze. A precaution is to dab the seeding agent
onto selected areas of the biscuited pot before applying the glaze.
Alternatively, a small amount of rutile in the glaze will act as a seeding
agent around which crystals can form and grow.

34 *Stoneware zinc silicate glaze with addition of 4% rutile and 2% cobalt.*

35 *Cross section, zinc crystalline glaze (page 163) on porcelain body.*

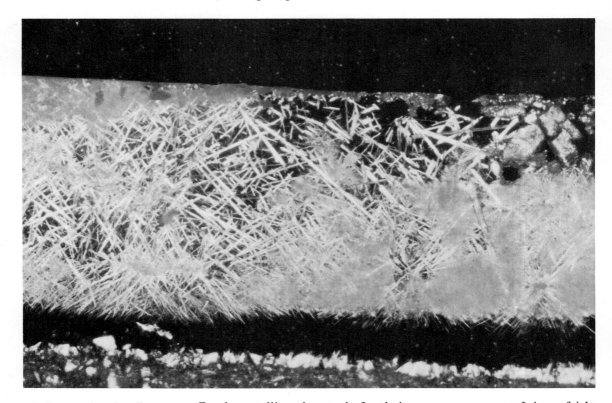

36 Cross section of rutile opaque glaze showing lifted rutile needles and good glaze body reaction layer. Transmitted light (crossed polars) × 100.

Good crystalline glazes rely for their success upon containing a fairly large amount of fritted material. These frits can either be made in the studio (see chapter 8) or can be bought from the suppliers. Commercially available alkaline and borax frits serve the stoneware potter well and, in combinations with a small amount of feldspar, flint, and calcium, form a useful base for the addition of zinc oxide and a small amount of rutile as 'seeder'. Colour is an important part of a crystalline glaze because, when added in the correct proportions, it will be preferentially absorbed by the crystals in different combinations to appear in a contrast to the colourless or beige background. Not all colouring oxides give this effect, some will colour the crystals intensely and the background lightly, and so on. Briefly, cobalt always gives blue, which may range from very light to intense. Copper gives green shades, manganese gives pale brownish mauve.

For best results the firing procedure for crystalline glazes is quite complicated. For the formation of large crystals the glaze needs to have a long slow cooling period or be allowed to cool to 1100°C (2012°F) then maintained at this temperature for up to two hours before allowing cooling to continue. Maintaining top temperature by means of a soak is likely to result in a boiled rather than a crystalline glaze. However, some crystalline glazes will form small crystal formations without any soaking period, though the crystals will never be large. Certain precautions for firing crystalline glazes need to be made. Often these glazes become very

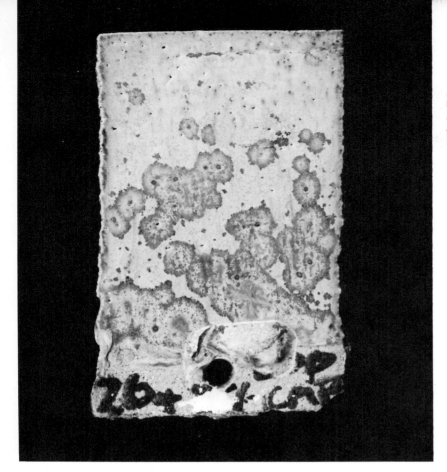

37 Green coloured crystals in cream glaze, stoneware. Zinc glaze with 4% rutile and 2% copper carbonate.

38 Zinc silicate crystalline glaze and porcelain. Creamy white crystals in white background.

fluid and are likely to run down the pot onto the kiln shelf. For this reason it is quite useful to leave a good sized bare area at the base of the pot and to stand the pot on a pad of waste clay painted with alumina, so that if the glaze does run, neither the shelf nor the pot is ruined. Another point to be borne in mind is that crystalline glazes exert a powerful force on the pot and can, in extreme cases, cause the pot to crack. For this reason, thick-walled pots are a wise precaution as well as the applying of the glaze both inside and out so that, as far as possible, the stresses are equal.

Aventurine glazes contain tiny crystals which are completely set in the glaze matrix, and, as they reflect the light, a glistening effect may be produced. Aventurine glazes are produced by saturating the glaze with a metal oxide, such as iron, which dissolves in the glaze during the firing process. As the glaze cools, the iron produces small crystals. The quantity of iron required varies, but amounts are usually 10–15%, and the effects can be obtained in low temperature as well as high temperature glazes. Good effects can be obtained by increasing the iron in a tenmoku glaze, though the problem of glaze fit may arise as such glazes often have a tendency to shell or peel off the edges. No special firing procedure is needed for aventurine glazes which seem able to form the crystals in a steadily cooling kiln.

LUSTRES

Lustre effects can be obtained by two firing methods, one is in a reducing atmosphere and the other in an oxidizing atmosphere. Traditionally lustres are made by firing metal oxides on the surface of a fired glaze in a reducing kiln atmosphere. This causes the metal to deposit as a film-like coating onto the softened glaze surface. This coating can later be burnished to a lustrous sheen when it is cool. Today, prepared lustres in an oily base in which the reducing agent is present, can be purchased from pottery suppliers: they are painted or sprayed onto the glaze surface and fired to a temperature around 720°C (1328°F). In a normal atmosphere these coatings may give a metallic, nacreous or iridescent sheen. Though it is possible to prepare these lustres, the process is complicated and it is unlikely that home-made lustres will match the excellence of the manufactured ones.

Of more interest to the studio potter are the lustres fired in the reduced atmosphere of the kiln. In this case the metal oxides are mixed with a refractory medium, such as red ochre, painted onto the fired glaze and heated to about 700–750°C (1292–1382°F) at which point the kiln is reduced for a short period. The usual method is to prepare a mixture of the dry, ground ingredients with vinegar and either gum arabic or gum tragacanth, this is then either brushed or sprayed on the fired glaze. For the firing, the kiln is heated to low red heat (700°C (1292°F)) and reduced for short periods; when reduction is effected by introducing a burning gas poker the period of reduction is kept very short as the flame is very strong; alternatively reduction can be achieved by introducing carbonaceous matter such as mothballs, wood, or sugar into the kiln. The exact temperature at which reduction is most effective will depend on the lustre and the composition of the glaze on which it is being fired. After firing the clay is brushed off and, if successful, the lustre can be burnished to its full brilliance.

Recipes for reduced lustre:

	Arabian	*Italian*	
Red ochre	65	67	50
Silver sulphate	1	—	1
Copper sulphate	34	33	25
Mercuric sulphate	—		24

Later lustres:

	green	*blue-green*
Silver carbonate	3	1
Bismuth nitrate	12	10
Red ochre	85	84
Copper oxalate	—	5

Recipe oxidized lustre:

(melt resin)   20 pts resin
              5 pts bismuth nitrate } forms resinate
           30 pts lavender oil (still hot)
Dilute with further amounts of lavender oil if necessary. Apply to fired glaze and refire to 720–730°C (1328–1346°F)

Metals and the effects they give:

Titanium — blue
Chrome — yellow green
Iron — brown
Platinum — silver
Copper — red

Commercially prepared lustres are used in a straightforward way. An even coating, not too thin, is painted onto the fired glaze, allowed to dry, and fired to the manufacturer's recommended temperature. Before firing the oil medium can only be removed with turpentine, methylated spirits or acetone. These liquids, if splashed on the painted lustre, will give attractive 'marbled' and splotch effects.

CRACKLE GLAZES

The difference between a crackle glaze and a crazed glaze is related to function and appearance. Generally, a crackle is regarded as a desirable decorative feature, while a crazed glaze is one which is considered to be a technical fault. The remedies for a crazed glaze have been dealt with in chapter 7, but recently there has been renewed interest in the crackle glaze, the most famous historical examples of which are the classic Chinese celadons.

*39 Gwyn Hanssen. Lidded
porcelain pot with
feldspathic crackle glaze,
with blue pigment banded on
top of unfired glaze.
Reduction fired ; 7.5 cm
(3 in.) tall.*

A crackle can be defined as a network of fine hairlike lines in the surface of a glaze. These are often further emphasized by rubbing colouring oxides into the glaze surface either as soon as the glazed pot comes hot from the kiln, or after it has cooled. Some of the more viscous glazes can be refired to permanently trap in the colouring oxides, and to give a second pattern network. Rate of cooling generally seems to determine the size of the crackle – rapid cooling giving a finer network – though this must ultimately depend on the glaze and body.

Crackle is caused by a glaze having an elevated thermal expansion, which, on cooling, contracts much more than the body and gives the fine network of lines. Sometimes these are squarish, other times they form long lines running vertically. The fluxes with the highest rate of expansion are the alkalies soda and potash, and these must be present in great quantity. Sources of soda are nepheline syenite and soda feldspar, but the presence of alumina and silica tends to balance out the expansion.

Excessive amounts of soda can only be introduced by means of a high expansion frit.

A useful porcelain glaze base is 80 nepheline syenite, 10 china clay, and 10 whiting, which will usually craze. Another useful starting point would be nepheline syenite with a high expansion (soda) frit; a line blend of the two materials would make a useful starting point. Small additions of copper seem to pick out the crackle in a pleasant way; in the reduction kiln, small amounts of iron have a similar effect.

40 Emmanuel Cooper – thrown porcelain eggs with nepheline syenite glaze, showing development of crackle which depends to some extent on position in kiln.

TENMOKU AND OIL SPOT GLAZES

The classic brown high fired glazes of the Chinese Sung dynasty continue to mystify and attract the modern potter. In their dark deep surface, there is an attractive simplicity for which potters continue to search. All potters have their own idea of what constitutes an attractive brown glaze; for some potters it is the shiny rich black brown glazes known as tenmokus, while others prefer the softer qualities of the 'oil spot' or 'hare's fur' glaze.

Successful tenmoku glazes have already been discussed on pages 48–50. They can be obtained in glazes using the feldspar, china clay, whiting, flint combination with an addition of 8–10% iron oxide. Rich black colours with bright red brown rims can result from these glazes, providing the body is suitable. Over dark firing bodies, the glaze tends to lose its bright edges and is at its most handsome on a light coloured, fairly dense body. In both oxidation and reduction, the colour is good, though the body colour is usually improved in reduction. Often it is difficult to distinguish the glazes fired in either oxidized or reduced firing.

41 Stoneware bowl with oil spot glaze. Recipe page 165.

Some potters have reported good tenmoku effects with the use of 20–30% borax in a glaze with little or no clay, though these glazes tend to be more spectacular with busy markings.

The 'hare's fur' and 'oil spot' glazes seem to be based very clearly on the use of natural materials to provide the necessary subtlety and variety of colour. Consequently these glazes are arrived at empirically as it is almost impossible to calculate their molecular formula. In England, Fremington red earthenware is a useful clay with which to start, while in the USA, the famous Albany clay cannot be equalled. Why these fine clays give these sorts of effects in which streaks of light brown and yellow run in a dark background, or tiny bright spots of silver show in a dark background, is difficult to say, though the presence of minute quantities of a wide variety of minerals must be a strong determining factor.

The firing also plays an important part in the development of glaze quality. Most of the quality of these clay glazes comes from the bubbling of the glaze during the maturation process. Too prolonged a firing cycle may well result in too smooth and even a glaze, while too rapid a firing

42 *Brown oil spot stoneware glaze, oxidized, made from feldspar, nepheline syenite, Fremington clay with 2% iron oxide. Larger spots developed where the glaze was applied more thickly.*

may give a surface which is bumpy and uneven. Higher temperatures seem to give the most interesting results, though the iron reds seem to respond equally well to lower temperatures ($1250°C$ ($2282°F$)).

As a starting point, the addition of colouring oxides to the basic clay material will give matt workable glazes with a remarkably wide firing range – this is a notable feature of glazes in which there is a high proportion (over 30%) of clay material. Using 70–80% of clay in the glaze the remainder can be made up to 100% with any feldspar or borax frit or a combination of similar materials. Good results have also been reported with the use of cryolite and ochre.

Rich indian red colours can be made with 20% clay and 80% nepheline syenite. This particular colour, which is quite bright, works well in both oxidation and reduction. Proportions of nepheline syenite 50, feldspar 30 and clay 20 plus 2% iron oxide will give an attractive speckled spot effect.

RAKU GLAZES

The widespread interest shown in raku has brought this comparatively unknown technique within the scope of the Western potter for the first time. Raku, in Japanese, means 'enjoyment' or 'freedom', but this meaning is not applicable to raku as used in the West for it is used as a term to describe the process. In this method, biscuited ware is glazed and placed in a red hot kiln where it is rapidly fired until the glaze has melted, at which time it is removed from the kiln. The pot can then be reduced by burying it in a combustible material (sawdust, leaves, newspaper, etc.) and then quenched in water to arrest any tendency to reoxidize. The result is a fragile but decorative ware with rich mottled or crackled glazes on a black reduced body. This technique is in contrast to the traditional Japanese process in which the ware is low fired and glazed with a tin glaze, with no reduction process.

The important materials and equipment are a strong clay, suitable kiln and a good variety of glazes. Most rough open bodies will withstand raku firing, and additions of fireclay and grog to stoneware bodies will usually work well.

Suitable body recipes are:

Fireclay	50	Stoneware clay	80
Ball clay	25	Grog (coarse)	20
Grog	25		

The pots must be biscuit fired and, after glazing, be perfectly dry before being put into the hot kiln. The biscuit firing must not vitrify the pots or they may burst in the firing.

Kilns can be heated by any sort of fuel – wood, coke, coal, gas or electricity, the latter being quite safe provided the heating elements are protected by a layer of bricks and the current is switched off when the door is opened. A long pair of tongs to grip the pot and a pair of asbestos gloves are necessary to enable the kiln to be packed and unpacked.

The firing

Raku glazes are usually better applied thickly and the relationship of glazed and unglazed areas carefully considered as the blackened reduced body can be very attractive. The pots are put into the kiln when it is estimated to have reached a sufficiently high temperature which can either be judged by colour – a rich red orange – or measured with a pyrometer. During the firing, the glazes will begin to bubble as they melt and when they have settled evenly and have a shiny reflective surface, the glazes have matured. Depending on the efficiency of the kiln, this will take about 20–40 minutes. When the pots are taken from the kiln, they will oxidize as they are brought into the air, and, if reduction is required, it should now take place. Burying the pot inside a metal dustbin full of sawdust or other material and then covering the bin with a reasonably well fitting lid will ensure a well reduced glaze. Dark grey acrid smoke will be given off indicating a good reducing atmosphere. If copper is present in a glaze or in painted decoration, a rich lustrous surface will result from this heavy reduction. The body will be turned black by carbon.

After about 15 to 20 minutes, remove the pot, and to prevent reoxidation in the atmosphere, quench it immediately by placing it quickly in water. If the glaze is still molten when it is placed in the water, it will froth to give an unpleasant surface.

Most raku glazes are based on commercially available frits. Alkaline frits are completely safe when fired, and work well with small additions of copper. Lead frits are not likely to be completely non-soluble when fired and their use should be restricted to non-functional ware.

Alkali frit, lead frit and borate frit can be combined with about 10% whiting and 10% ball clay to give glazes which will work well. Additions of 5–10% tin oxide will give a rich white glaze which will usually crackle to give a large network of black lines. This contrasts well with the black matt body. Additions of colouring oxides will give the following results:

Copper	2–3%	turquoise
Cobalt	0.5%	blue
Manganese	1–2%	purple-brown
Iron	2–6%	creams-ambers.

After the pots have cooled, the glaze surface needs to be cleaned to remove soot and dirt with a stiff brush, wire wool, or an abrasive cleaning powder.

MEDIUM TEMPERATURE GLAZES

Glazes firing in the range 1180–1240°C (2156–2264°F) are still largely neglected by the studio potter who traditionally fires to either earthenware or high temperature stoneware temperatures. The advantages of the medium-range include lower firing costs, the benefits of well vitrified bodies and the use of fluxes from both higher and lower temperatures. The other main distinction of this temperature is the possibility of a greatly increased range of colours from such oxides as uranium and vanadium. Main fluxes are calcium borate frit or colemanite, lithium carbonate, cryolite, lead silicate and any alkaline frit. Nepheline syenite, because of its lower melting point, can be substituted for feldspar when experimenting with lowering the firing temperatures of stoneware glazes. The basic approach to glazes in this temperature range is exactly the same as that for other temperatures, and with suitable materials, the same textural effects as those obtainable at higher temperatures can be achieved.

A basic clear glaze with fairly wide firing range is:

Nepheline syenite	40
Calcium borate frit	40
Flint	10
China clay	10

Wood ash glazes can also be used at these lower temperatures:

Mixed wood ash	40
Nepheline syenite	30
Talc	15
Ball clay	15

Part Three
USING THE GLAZE

10
Applying and Firing the Glaze

A range of five or six glazes may prove to be more useful and versatile to the potter than 20 or 30 glazes, simply because the potential of the small group of glazes has been more fully explored. Thickness of application, oxide additions, effect over different clay slips and bodies, and firing conditions etc. offer many possibilities for a single glaze. It is difficult to explore all the possibilities of too large a range of glazes. In this chapter all the possibilities of using the glaze are explained.

A raw or slip glaze, to the studio potter, means one which is applied directly to the green (unfired) ware and then fired only once. This is in marked contrast to the pottery industry, where a raw glaze is defined by the raw state of the ingredients rather than the point at which it is applied to the pot. The pottery industry defines a raw glaze as one compounded from materials which have not been fritted and is applied to the biscuit ware followed by a second or glost firing. A glaze slop consists of powdered materials, suspended in water to form an homogeneous mixture into which the pot may be dipped, or from which glaze can be taken and poured, sprayed or painted onto the pot.

Certain conditions make this task much easier. First, consider the raw or slip glaze. Because this glaze is applied to unfired clay, account must be taken of the shrinkage that will occur during drying and firing, and care must be taken to ensure that the glaze will adhere to the raw clay before it is fired. Traditionally, slip glazes are made from at least 30—40% plastic clay (not china clay) which is often similar to that used in the body. This ensures a good bonding between body and glaze before firing, a similar rate of shrinkage during firing, and finally a match between glaze and body after firing. Naturally occurring clays such as Albany slip, London clay, or Fremington clay fluxed with either frit or an effective low-firing material such as nepheline syenite or cryolite can form the basis of such glazes. Only certain clay bodies and certain shapes will withstand raw glazing but the economic advantages for the production potter cannot be easily overlooked and make the consideration of this technique well worth while. A raw glaze often shrinks greatly during drying and when applied to biscuited ware will crack and fall off the pot during firing.

Glazes for use on biscuit ware need separate consideration. A glaze recipe usually includes both plastic and non-plastic material, such as ball clays which are plastic and minerals such as feldspar and china clay which are non-plastic. The physical difference between these two types of glaze material affects the binding strength of the dry glaze, and consequently its ability to resist powdering or flaking off the pot. For this reason a glaze can be made easier to apply and to handle by incorporating a certain proportion of plastic ingredients – up to 20–25% if possible. Too high a proportion of plastic material will cause the glaze to crack and crawl, as described earlier, and this can be partially remedied by substituting some of the raw clay for calcined clay. If a good proportion of plastic clay is not included in the glaze recipe, certain other materials can be added to act as binders. The most useful of these binders is bentonite which is a very fine wind-blown clay with a level of plasticity about 20 times as great as ordinary ball clay. Because of this extraordinary ability and the attendant swelling of the particles, not more than 2–5% is usually added to the glaze. Yet this makes a significant difference to the handling ability; adherence is improved and the tendency of the glaze to settle into a solid mass at the bottom of the glaze barrel is also reduced. Too large an addition of bentonite will make a glaze sticky and difficult to pass through a sieve. A typical bentonite analysis shows 64% silica, 21% alumina, 4% iron plus small quantities of other fluxes. Because of its high iron content bentonite cannot be added (except in very small amounts) to very white bodies and glaze without having an effect upon the colour of the body and glaze.

Other additions to the glaze batch which will help suspension, handling, and adherence, without affecting the firing properties of the glaze, are the natural gums, such as gum tragacanth or arabic, starches, glues, dextrine, and the recently developed thermoplastic resins. Natural gums and starches are useful in small quantities of glaze for immediate use, but their disadvantage is that after a short period they decay and sour in the glaze barrel. This will, of course, be affected by storage conditions. Dextrine (made by heating starch with acid) is a popular binder which works effectively in the glaze in additions of less than 5%. Synthetic cellulose binders such as CMC are also effective. These will burn out of the glaze without difficulty at fairly low temperatures. Methylcellulose, polyethylene emulsions and polyvinyl alcohol have all been successfully used to harden glazes.

A useful method for determining the length of time different materials will remain suspended in water before settling can easily be demonstrated by preparing a small batch of glaze from a single material. Nepheline syenite, for instance, will settle almost at once to form a solid layer at the bottom of the glaze bucket. This layer is extremely difficult to dislodge and it is therefore a good rule of thumb to incorporate a small percentage of bentonite whenever such a material is included in the recipe. Control of grain size and the grinding of glaze materials, not often within the scope of studio potters (few of whom have the necessary equipment) does affect the physical handling of the glazes. Some materials, for example, can be too finely ground, giving rise to the problems of crawling during the firing of the glaze, and in the case of lead compounds can increase their solubility. Most materials need only to be ground sufficiently to pass through a 120 mesh, though most commercially available materials will pass through a 300 mesh. Too coarse a material will result in a glaze mix which is not sufficiently intimate and will raise the effective melting point resulting in an unequal melt. Fine grinding of colouring oxides and pigments is essential if colour specking, especially when cobalt compounds are used, is to be avoided. This can be achieved by milling for two or three hours, though for small quantities a pestle and mortar may be used.

The control of glaze thickness and viscosity can be a problem for studio potters who may find themselves with either a glaze which seems thin, but gives a thick layer on the pot, or a glaze which seems thick, but gives a thin layer on the pot. Apart from experience in handling a particular glaze, there are several ways in which this situation can be understood:

1   The specific gravity (S.G.) of a glaze slip, which is a measure of the amount of solid present in the liquid, can be checked. An instrument called a hydrometer can be used to measure S.G. A simple hydrometer can be made by fixing a weight on to the end of a wooden stick which is then floated in the glaze slop. When a glaze is known to have the correct thickness the depth to which the 'hydrometer' sinks into the slip can be marked on the stick. If, on subsequent occasions, the mark is below the surface of the glaze then too much water is present and, either more dry glaze materials must be added, or, the glaze must be allowed to settle and the excess water syphoned off. If the mark is above the glaze surface, more water must be added.

2   The pint weight of the glaze can be measured. As the term implies this is the weight of exactly one pint of glaze slip. For an average glaze, for use on a porous biscuit, $31\frac{1}{2}$ oz. to a pint is considered correct. For a glaze which is to be applied on to a vitrified body 34 ozs to the pint is required.

3   Certain materials have a flocculating effect in the glaze mix, that is, they make the glaze less fluid without an increase in pint weight. They are normally acids or acid salts. Good examples are calcium chloride, sodium chloride (this must be remembered when this material is used as a glaze constituent), ordinary vinegar (acetic acid). These materials when added to a glaze batch have a flocculating effect, which for certain glazes, helps give a more even coating. For some glazes, particularly those in which tin oxide is present (these need an even covering for best effect) this remedy has been found to be successful. There are other materials which have a deflocculating effect, that is, they make the mixture more fluid. These materials are alkaline or alkaline salts. A good example of the use of deflocculation is the use of sodium silicate in casting slip to enable a slip of high solid content to be made and so speed up the casting rate and thus make possible production of thicker casts. Many materials, though usually thought of as being insoluble, are in fact slightly soluble in the glaze batch and the longer a batch is stored in the wet state, the greater the amount of

material dissolved. Whiting, for example, is slightly soluble. Some frits, though compounded to give an insoluble material, still have one small degree of solubility. Wood ash, though washed three or four times, will often retain some soluble salts. If a glaze batch containing wood ash is kept, a solid deposit will often form on the edge of the barrel due to the crystallizing out of these soluble salts.

MIXING THE GLAZE

Preparing and mixing the glaze are tasks which are made simpler and more efficient if one or two rules are observed. A carefully worked out recipe must be accurately weighed. If colouring oxides are added then these must be weighed with the greatest care. An error in weighing, resulting in a slight overdose of cobalt oxide, can for example turn an attractive pale blackbird egg blue into a livid midnight navy.

The following points are worth noting:

1   The pans of the weighing scales and balances should be sufficiently large to accommodate comfortably the amounts of material to be weighed. Metric weights – grammes and kilogrammes, make the job of increasing or decreasing amounts simple; ounces and pounds present complicated arithmetical problems.

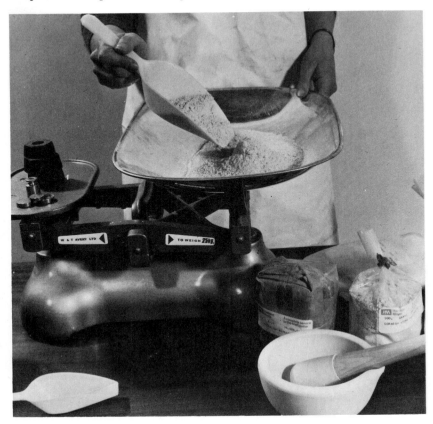

43 Weighing raw materials in a good sized scale pan. Note the handy scoops and pestle and mortar. Photograph – Harrison Mayer Ltd.

2   Use a large glaze barrel. The light and smooth surfaced plastic buckets and bins with well fitting lids are excellent. Zinc bins are often corroded by the glaze and are in addition heavy and difficult to clean. A barrel which will not contain the complete mixture within three quarters of its total capacity (i.e. leaving one quarter free space for mixing) is too small and will be more trouble than it is worth.

44 A small motorized porcelain ball mill. Photograph – Harrison Mayer Ltd.

3   Always add the glaze ingredients to the water. This prevents the formation of lumps and aids mixing. Sandwich plastic and non-plastic ingredients if possible. Use hot or warm water if it is available; this helps break down lumps more quickly. Mix the ingredients thoroughly in the water by hand or with an electric mixing machine.

45 Passing glaze through a sieve with a stiff glaze brush. Photograph – Harrison Mayer Ltd.

4   The slop mixture can now be mixed, either by sieving once or twice (60 or 80 mesh sieve is ideal) to form a completely homogeneous mix, or it can be ball milled. Sieving is a straightforward process in which the mixture is passed through the sieve with the aid of a stiff brush. The mixture is then checked for correct consistency. Glazes are easier to sieve if too much, rather than too little, water is present. The excess water can be removed after the glaze has settled. (With a well suspended glaze this can take 24 hours). It is a sensible precaution to keep two sets of glaze sieves and brushes, one set for white, oxide-free glazes, and the other set for stained or coloured glazes. This will keep contamination to a minimum since it is extremely difficult to clean all traces of coloured glaze from a sieve, particularly those which contain cobalt.

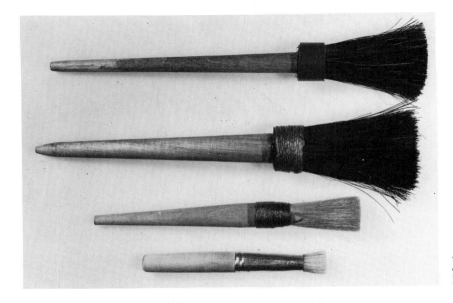

46 A variety of stiff glaze brushes. Photograph – Harrison Mayer Ltd.

Ball milling involves the use of a relatively complex piece of machinery which must be run at the correct speed. A small ball mill will consist of a jar loaded to half capacity with porcelain balls and the glaze slop. The loaded jar is rotated for a period of time the duration of which will be determined by the effect required. For example, one hour would be sufficient to bring about a good homogeneous glaze which need not be sieved. Continued milling would result in further grinding of the ingredients which could affect the behaviour of the glaze. In the ball mill the volume occupied by the balls should be approximately half the volume of the jar. Speed of rotation must be sufficient to allow the balls to fall and mix. Too slow a speed will result in poor mixing and too fast a rotation will, due to excessive centrifugal force, pin the balls to the sides of the mill. Ball milling has the advantage of requiring little physical effort and will also help to reduce or eliminate specking.

APPLYING THE GLAZE

47a & b Dipping the pot inside and outside. a) holding the pot so that no air is trapped inside b) draining the glaze.

Applying wet glaze to ware fired to 950–1000°C (1742–1832°F) can be done by dipping, pouring, spraying or painting. Stoneware and earthenware clays fired to a biscuit temperature of 1000°C (1832°F) are porous and strong. Porcelain fired to this temperature is porous but not strong. The high porosity can be reduced using a higher biscuit temperature, or, if this is not possible, partially nullified by wetting the ware before glazing. Raw glazing pots which have not been biscuit fired need suitable glazes and methods; usual practice is to glaze the insides by pouring and swilling, allowing the clay to dry to the leather hard state before the outsides are glazed by dipping the invested pot into the glaze. Spraying and painting glaze on raw pots requires little special treatment except that outlined below.

Some clay bodies can be dipped into glaze just as normal biscuit ware. Some can be dipped best when they are leather hard, others when they are bone dry. With these pots it is usual to leave a foot which can be firmly gripped during the glazing, as it is tricky to hold the rim without damaging it. For raw glazing the glaze needs to be thicker than that for biscuited work.

Painting on glaze has several advantages. It requires only a small amount of glaze which will be limited to the painted areas. The glaze needs to be prepared more thickly than usual and mixed with a suitable binder such as gum arabic or tragacanth, and applied with a full soft brush. More than one coat will be necessary to achieve an even covering and each layer must be allowed to dry before the next layer is painted on. Unless a binder is added to the glaze, subsequent layers will lift off the previous layers. Painting is a slow but useful method for applying glaze to unfired pieces of individual or special pots or those pots which have limited handling possibilities. Glazing unfired ware also has the advantage of enabling the process to be completed in a single procedure without the delay of the biscuit firing which often interrupts the original conception. Glaze thickened with gum can be effectively painted onto fired glaze and reglazing fired pieces can be done by this method.

Glazes containing a high proportion of clay can often be applied onto biscuit ware more successfully by painting than by dipping, a process which often wets the biscuit too much, causing the glaze to crack off during drying and to crawl during firing.

48a & b Dipping the outside of the pot. a) holding the pot upright. b) after the pot has been glazed.

49 Glaze mops for applying glaze and touching-up bare spots Photograph – Harrison Mayer Ltd.

Dipping as a method of glazing is the technique used by most studio potters engaged in making repetition wares; it requires no special equipment, is quick and efficient. All that is required is sufficient volume of glaze contained in a large enough barrel so that the object to be dipped can be completely immersed and agitated. Too small an amount of glaze, or too small a barrel makes the method very difficult to handle. Depending upon the shape and size of the object to be glazed, it is normal practice to grip an open pot by its rim and foot and immerse it completely ensuring that the inside is completely filled with glaze. Leave the pot immersed in the glaze for a few seconds, gently agitating it all the time; lift out, shake off the surplus liquid, and place the pot to dry. A glazed pot can be handled when the glaze has lost its shine, which usually occurs within a minute or two. Other shapes are handled according to their needs. Leaving the pot in the glaze for longer than a few seconds will not necessarily cause a thicker glaze layer to form on the pot, for once the walls of the pot become saturated the outer layer of glaze will not adhere and will be washed off. A thick glaze layer can be obtained by allowing the pot to dry until the glaze has lost its shine and then dipping it again. This may be repeated several times. During glazing, keep the glaze well stirred, to prevent the settling of the materials. It is not always possible to dip thin walled pots because of the speed at which the walls become saturated. In such instances the inside is glazed first and allowed to dry and then the outside is glazed separately.

Pouring is a useful method of glazing large pots, for certain shapes and for certain decorative and accidental effects. With large pots, the inside is first swilled with glaze and drained. The pot is then supported on struts across a bowl and glaze poured over the outside. If a sufficiently large volume of glaze is used, and the pot slowly revolved on a turntable, an even coating can be achieved. However some shapes need to be supported by hand whilst the glaze is poured and this makes an even coating more difficult to obtain. Many potters prefer poured glaze effects because the fired results are often more in character with the properties of liquid glaze. Overlapping, running and dribbling, which arise as part of the glazing process, are enjoyed, and their effects often deliberately incorporated. This is in marked contrast to the attitude of the purists who argue that glaze serves only a secondary function, and its ability to create dramatic effects should not be allowed to distract from the form of the pot. Pouring can be used as a more formal decorative technique. It can be poured onto the walls of a pot to form apron shaped areas of glaze depending upon the angle at which the pot is held. Overlapping 'aprons' will introduce further variations.

Spraying glaze is an ideal method to use for large or awkwardly shaped objects. It is a method which has the advantage of requiring only small quantities of glaze. It enables very thick or very thin layers of glaze to be built up and it is an ideal method for the glazing of vitrified pots. The fired appearance of sprayed glaze tends to have its own particular qualities: glazes containing colouring oxides tend to develop a more speckled appearance and if the glaze has been applied thinly, this specking effect is heightened.

The disadvantage of spraying is that sophisticated and expensive electrical equipment is required. This will include a compressor, a spray gun and a spray booth fitted with a powerful extractor fan. The extractor fan should be sufficiently powerful to remove the unwanted fine glaze mist which forms inside the booth. This glaze dust is dangerous and a wise precaution is the wearing of a face mask with replaceable gauze inserts. Certain shapes are difficult to spray successfully; on a cup for example, the glaze spray often misses the underside of the handle and the very bottom of the inside. Short bursts of glaze sprayed onto the slowly revolving pot enables an even glaze layer to be built up. Spraying too long on one area will saturate the surface and the glaze will run off.

50 Spraying a small pot in a spray booth.

Glaze to be used for spraying needs to be thoroughly sieved to remove lumps, which quickly clog the nozzle of the gun. A turntable inside the spray booth enables the pot to be rotated while being sprayed and the spray gun is best held 30–40 cm (12–16 in.) away. Pots with a non-porous surface, such as some industrial biscuit or fired glazed pots are more successfully sprayed if they are heated first either in an oven or special heating cabinet, otherwise the glaze takes too long to dry to the condition in which it can be handled.

A note here about glaze powders which, because they contain soluble salts must be applied in the dry state. These materials, (discussed on page 33) when present in a glaze, enable many special effects and colours to be achieved. Glazes which incorporate soda ash are an example of this sort of glaze. The presence of a small percentage of copper in these glazes produces rich and pleasant turquoise blues and greens. These glazes can be prepared by first normal weighing, then grinding in a pestle and mortar, and then mixing by dry sieving the materials twice through a coarse sieve. The powder is then sieved into position (only on flat surfaces) and fired in the usual way. For bright colours a light coloured background, such as a white glaze or white slip, will bring out the full richness of the colour. Such glazes are usually reserved for decorative pots as the surface is often heavily crazed.

PREPARING GLAZED WARES FOR THE KILN

Once glazed the pots can be fettled ready for placing in the kiln. Fettling will include gently rubbing down any large runs or dribbles of glaze, and touching up any bare or thin patches of glaze with a glaze mop (a large, rounded, full soft-haired brush). Goat's hair is often used for these mops. A small jar of glaze kept for touching-up removes the necessity of agitating a large barrel or bucket of glaze, merely to obtain a small quantity for touching up. These jars of glaze, suitably labelled, are handy when kept near to the kiln in case of accidental chipping of the glaze. The foot of the pot must be wiped clean of glaze with a small wet sponge, a job made easier if the foot has been painted or banded with either hot liquid paraffin wax or wax emulsion before being glazed. Waxing is almost essential when pots are fired with lids placed in position; both surfaces are waxed before, and cleaned after glazing. A thin layer of alumina and china clay may then be painted or dabbed on to prevent sticking. The covering over of finger marks by dabbing or painting on glaze must be carefully done to prevent a messy effect; glazes with a high clay content are best left to dry before retouching, while those with a low plastic content need to be touched up as soon as the glaze has lost its shine. All stoneware and porcelain pots are fired sitting directly on the kiln shelf without the use of stilts and spurs which are employed for low temperature earthenwares. The use of spurs enables the pot to be glazed all over, completely sealing the surface and eliminating the cleaning procedure. When spurs are used for supporting earthenware pots the glaze should not be applied thickly or the points of the spur will become deeply embedded in the glaze and will be difficult to remove.

Incidentally, the grinding off of the spur points, using a carborundum stone, should be done as soon as ware is unpacked from the kiln as these points and the thin slivers of glaze on the base of the pot are razor sharp and can cause deep cuts. In the pottery industry these points and slivers are referred to as glaze daggers.

DECORATIVE USE OF THE GLAZE

Double glazing is a decorative method which can give distinctive if slightly unrepeatable results because it depends for its repeated success on having the glazes and pots with walls at the same thickness each time. Briefly, the technique consists of applying one glaze over another in thicknesses which depend upon the glazes and effects required. A stiff white glaze and a runny dark glaze are often used together. Sometimes a white opaque glaze is applied over a dark slip glaze which is applied onto the green unfired pot before biscuit firing: this also eliminates the physical problems which can arise when double glazing biscuited ware. With double dipping the usual method is to immerse the pot in a slightly thinner mix of glaze, this layer is then allowed to lose its shine before the pot is dipped in the slightly thinner than usual mixture of the second glaze. If the first glaze is allowed to dry out before the second glaze is applied, then the first glaze will often bubble and blob up and an uneven coating will result. Occasionally the glaze will even fall off the surface as it dries. Spraying on succeeding layers of glaze will eliminate many of these problems. Glaze layers can easily be tested for thickness and spraying also eliminates the saturation of the first layer which occurs in dipping.

51 Emmanuel Cooper. Lidded jar, stoneware, double glazed. A stiff white glaze over a fluid iron glaze gave this bubbly volcanic effect. When reversed, with the iron glaze over the white glaze, gives a rich dry matt brown glaze breaking with orange and green flecks.

A useful, as opposed to decorative aspect of double glazing is the reglazing of fired pieces which have accidentally glazed too thinly. Applying glaze to fired surfaces is, as has been explained earlier, greatly helped by using a thicker glaze than usual to which a binder such as gum arabic has been added. Heating the pot beforehand also helps

The double glazing technique can be extended to include wax and paper resist as well as 'accidental' double glazing such as splashed, flicked, and dropped glaze. Whichever technique is used, the only precautions which need to be followed are those explained earlier in this chapter.

Trailing, which is the technique for piping on lines of glaze, is primarily associated with coloured clay slips but can be used equally well with glaze if the glaze has been thickened by the addition of a gum. Trailing glaze using a rubber bulb type of trailer is the most efficient method of application, but the glaze must be applied on top of the first glaze before it dries to prevent the applied lines from lifting off as they dry.

FIRING THE GLAZE

Temperature measurement

Accurate measurement of temperature and heat work is important if glaze effects are to be repeated. While it is not the purpose of this book to deal with the purchasing and operating of kilns, a note on temperature measurement in the kiln is necessary. Potters evolve their own particular methods of using the available guides, and what is always apparent is that all potters have their own system which is repeated for each firing. No two potters have exactly the same system, and, because of this, one potter's successful glaze is another potter's failure. Good advice is to work out your own method of measurement and stick to it for each kiln. Kiln packing must also be remembered, for if this varies greatly, the firing will be affected. A densely packed kiln will require more heat work than a kiln which is loosely packed.

Basically, there are two main methods of judging the temperature inside the kiln. One is with the use of instruments – the thermocouple and pyrometer – which indicate temperature; the other is by the use of pyrometric cones, which are formulated to melt and slump at predetermined temperatures.

Thermocouples and pyrometers are scientific instruments; the system consists of a thermocouple made up of two dissimilar metal wires welded together at one end, and encased in a porcelain sheath which is inserted into the kiln. The thermocouple is connected by a measured length of cable to a pyrometer which is calibrated to indicate temperature, usually in degrees centigrade. Heat in the kiln affects the metal wires and generates a small electric current which is measured and related to the temperature dial. Thermocouples can also be used to operate 'soak' or 'switch off' instruments set at predetermined temperatures.

Pyrometric cones are temperature and time indicators (pyroscopes) which have been used by the ceramic industry since they were invented by Seger in the nineteenth century. They are slender, trihedral pyramids made of ceramic materials, and are constituted so as to deform when the required temperature has been reached. In Britain, the Staffordshire cones are a British adaption of the German Seger cones. In the USA 'Orton' cones are similar, but have temperature-related numbers. For greater accuracy the cones should be heated at the rate recommended by the manufacturers. For example, a cone which is heated at 140°C (284°F) an hour will require 40°C (104°F) more heat, at stoneware temperature, to make it squat, than a cone heated at 60°C (140°F) an hour.

52a & b
a) *Pyrometric Staffordshire cones placed in stand ready for kiln.*
b) *Cones after being fired.* Photographs – Harrison Mayer Ltd.

Cones are a reliable and easily-seen guide for recording and helping to control the precise point at which firing reaches maturity. As cones measure temperature–time treatment, they are best used in conjunction with a temperature measuring device.

There are roughly eighty different cones, whose deformation temperatures differ in steps of from 10° to 50°C (50°–122°F) between adjacent numbers. They are numbered from 022–01 and 1–42 (excepting 21–25 inclusive) the respective ranges of temperature being from 600°C to 1080°C (1112°–1976°F) and from 1100°C to 1200°C (2012°–2192°F). To each number, a temperature has been designated based on a steady rise of 4°C (39.2°F) per minute, but, as the cones are measures of heat work, their performance depends on the rate of heating. If the rate is slower than 4°C (39.2°F) a minute, the effect would be to lower the temperature required to deform a particular cone. If heated more rapidly, the reverse would apply. For this reason, the firing schedule should be fairly constant to achieve similar glaze effects.

Cones are made in two sizes; standard size, about 5 cm ($2\frac{1}{2}$ in.) long, for normal use, and small size, about 2.5 cm (1 in.) long, usually used in confined areas or in small experimental kilns.

Before being placed in the kiln, the cones are prepared by either placing them in a special fireclay stand or by supporting them in refractory clay. It is usual to have three cones of consecutive number placed in a row, about 3 mm ($\frac{1}{8}$ in.) apart with the surfaces carrying the numbers in line and at an angle of 15°, which is provided in the shape of the cone when a stand is used. Plastic clay should be worked with a penknife around the base of each cone and allowed to dry before being placed in the kiln. If the setting material is left wet, the moisture given off in the kiln may affect the fusion of the cones. The cone below the required temperature will indicate when correct temperature is near. The cone above will check any overfiring.

Once prepared and dried, the cones are placed in the kiln so that they can be clearly seen through the spyhole. Correct placing will ensure that cones receive the full heat of the kiln without being flashed by direct flame contact or intense local heat, or cooled by currents of cold air. Cones placed out of sight in the corners of the kiln can be used to record, after the firing has finished, the heat work achieved.

At top temperature, the lowest cone number should have squatted, the critical centre cone bent so that its tip just touches the stand, and the highest one should remain almost upright. Cones that have not collapsed, whether because they were temperature check cones or because the firing was interrupted, cannot be used in subsequent firing. This is because they have already been subjected to heat work and would give an inaccurate result.

Cones must always be stored in a cool dry place because exposure to moisture or damp can affect their squatting temperature.

Buller's rings are similar to cones in that they measure heat work in this case measured, not by collapse, but by shrinkage. Buller's rings are particularly useful because they enable temperature/heat work achieved to be measured very accurately, and are a useful check if placed in different parts of the kiln. Each ring is effective for the range 960–1400°C (1760–2562°F). Rings can either be removed during the firing or used after the kiln has cooled. Shrinkage is measured by putting the rings onto a special gauge which measures shrinkage and relates this to temperature.

Holdcroft's bars are similar to cones, but are placed horizontally on a refractory stand. Instead of squatting they sag and are placed in the kiln so that their behaviour can be seen during the firing. Like cones, bars are produced with different compositions and are selected for the temperature required.

OXIDATION AND REDUCTION

The potter often talks about oxidation and reduction in the kiln. For some potters, this is yet another part of the mystery which involves all effects obtained in the kiln. For others, it is part of a well-understood scientific phenomenon. This section is an attempt to bridge the gap with an explanation of the factors involved and how to achieve reduction effects.

53a & b
a) *Holdcroft bars in stand before being fired.*
b) *After firing.*
Photographs – Harrison Mayer Ltd.

Most of the materials used by the potter contain oxygen in combination with the main ingredients in the form of oxides. In fact, the commonest method of classifying the major components of a glaze composition is by comparing the ratio between the element expressed as the oxide. The three groups – RO/R_2O, R_2O_3, and RO_2, have oxygen in different ratios. Oxygen is one of the commonest elements found in the earth, comprising some 60% of the total of all the known elements and, furthermore, it is highly reactive, always seeking to establish stable bonds with other elements. Whenever chemical changes take place, it is almost inevitable that oxygen will be involved and the extent to which the presence or lack of it can effect changes is of particular interest to the glaze chemist.

Most of us are familiar with the process known as oxidation by which different materials combine with oxygen. A common example is that of combustion in which carbon in such materials as wood, coal, or oil combines with oxygen from the air. Burning, a rapid combustion, is a chemical reaction which liberates heat and light. During burning carbon dioxide is given off as gas and the ashes which are left behind consist mainly of the oxides of inorganic materials present in the original material. For successful combustion to take place, a good supply of air is necessary. If for any reason this supply is limited by, for example, combustion taking place in confined space, only a partial combustion will occur; in the case of wood, charcoal would be formed. The rusting of iron is another familiar example of oxidation. In this reaction, iron (Fe) combines with oxygen from the atmosphere preferably in the presence of water to become rust (Fe_2O_3). An experiment to demonstrate this can be made by placing a piece of iron in a jar inverted in water. As the iron forms rust combining with oxygen in the air in the jar, the water level in the jar will rise to replace the space of the lost oxygen.

Potters often speak of an oxidizing firing for a kiln which admits a surfeit of oxygen – that is in fact, under normal atmospheric conditions which allow all reactions involving oxygen to be completed. This is a particularly important process during the first firing between 400°C (752°F) and 850°C (1568°F), which is sometimes known as the oxidation period. During this period any carbonaceous matter present in the clay must be free to burn out, by combining with oxygen from the atmosphere to form the gas carbon monoxide or carbon dioxide. If this reaction is prevented from occuring by either a lack of atmospheric oxygen or too rapid a temperature rise, which causes the body to vitrify and trap in the carbon, problems of bloating can arise later in the firing.

The opposite of oxidation is reduction and this is the chemical process which prevents oxidation taking place. This process is used by the potter to 'reduce' the atmosphere of the kiln by restricting the amount of oxygen available in the atmosphere. In such conditions, oxides behave differently and, more importantly, give different results. Such conditions affect, not only the body, but the glaze. Silica and alumina are hardly affected at all by the reducing atmosphere, but some oxides, particularly iron and copper, are affected. Most clay bodies contain some iron and, in a normal oxidizing atmosphere, this will colour a body red, brown, yellow, or buff.

The same body, fired in a reducing atmosphere will appear as dark purple or black, dark grey or light grey. This is mainly due to the iron, present originally as ferric oxide (Fe_2O_3) losing oxygen to become ferrous oxide (FeO), which has a different colour and also behaves differently in the glaze, where it acts as a vigorous flux, in contrast to the more inert Fe_2O_3 material. This is particularly important when considering whether a body will be suitable for an oxidized or reduced firing, since, when fired oxidized, bodies are capable of containing much higher quantities of iron. One of the most attractive effects of reduction is on clay bodies containing 1–2% iron which take on a pleasant toasted appearance where the surface colour has been darkened to give a rich effect.

Iron in the glaze behaves in ways similar to iron in the body, becoming a most active flux in a reduced glaze, and giving different colours, the details of which are on page 48.

Copper, too, is greatly affected by the atmosphere in the kiln though copper is usually added to glazes rather than to bodies. During an oxidized firing, copper remains as cupric oxide (CuO) which usually gives a green colour in glazes. In a reducing atmosphere, the cupric oxide loses oxygen to become cuprous oxide (Cu_2O) or colloidal copper (Cu). Cuprous oxide gives red colours in the glaze, and colloidal coppers appear as specks of iridescence.

Generally speaking, a reducing atmosphere tends to make a glaze more fluid and active, and glazes suitable for use in a reducing atmosphere are able to contain higher amounts of alumina and silica; often glazes used successfully in a reduction kiln will appear underfired in an oxidation kiln. Conversely, successful oxidation glazes will be too fluid in a reduction kiln.

Kiln practice
Reduction in a flame burning kiln can easily be achieved by depriving the fuel of sufficient oxygen so that the flame burns with a yellowish smokey flame. This flame, hungry for oxygen to complete its combustion process, seeks the oxygen necessary from the most readily available source. Copper and iron are the two metal oxides which are least stable and readily release their oxygen. Reduction in the kiln is achieved by partially closing secondary air inlets and the damper, or by increasing the fuel input. The amount of primary air may also be restricted. All kilns seem to differ in the balance required between one method and the other, and it is often a question of delicate adjustment to find the most effective method. Some kilns cannot be reduced and at the same time maintain temperature rise, and short alternating bursts of reduction and oxidation are required. For this purpose a thermocouple and pyrometer are essential to indicate changes in temperature. Most potters begin reduction at 1000°C (1832°F) (after the carbon burning period is over) and continue until top temperature is reached. A short, cleansing oxidation period ends the firing so that the body oxidizes to a brighter, lighter colour. Too long a period of oxidation at the end of the firing will affect the glaze.

Reduction effects for the potter working with an electric kiln are not so easily achieved and have to be especially created. This can be achieved either by reducing the atmosphere or by adding materials to the glaze which act as local reducing agents.

Exposed wire elements in electric kilns are vulnerable to corrosive attack during the reduction process which severely shortens their life. For this reason it is really only economical to reduce during alternate kiln firings so enabling the protective layer on the elements to be re-established. Even so, shorter element life will result. It is also only practical to reduce the kiln for short periods which will particularly affect the glazes rather than the body, and this is most effectively done towards the end of the firing. Electric kilns fired by silicon carbide rods or 'Globars' as they are sometimes called, are more or less immune to attack from reducing atmospheres in the kiln; for the potter who wishes to reduce the kiln, and fire regularly with electricity, these provide an excellent alternative to gas.

Because of the effect of the reducing atmosphere on the kiln furniture, ensure that this is the correct type recommended by the manufacturer. Coat the top of kiln shelves and the ends of props with high alumina batt wash to prevent surfaces sticking. Silicon carbide shelves are specially made to withstand the effects of a reducing atmosphere and, though expensive, will not bend or warp. When packing the kiln bear in mind the flame flow, that is the movement of the flame across the kiln, and pack the shelves accordingly. In large kilns a bag wall is built in front of the firebox to direct the flames round the kiln. Open shelves allow flames to pass through, while a block of shelves impede the flow. An ideal kiln pack is one in which the flame is evenly spread throughout with the temperature constant top to bottom and back to front. This may be achieved by leaving extra spaces between some shelves and closing up others; here experience of a particular kiln will enable successful results to be obtained. Beware of protecting the indicating cones from the flames or over exposing them – the reaction of the cones to the heat is a very important indicator especially in reduction kilns. Also ensure that the thermocouple inside the kiln is relatively exposed, a rod in the roof protected by, say, a bowl may not give an accurate indication of the kiln temperature generally.

The firing is started slowly, allowing time for steam to be released. At this stage the atmosphere should be strongly oxidizing with a gentle flow of air through the kiln. The chimney damper and the secondary air inlets should be open. A test with a lighted taper held in front of the front spy hole should show a slight pull of the flame into the kiln. (For the rate of temperature rise see chapter 1 page 4).

At 1000°C (1832°F) reduction can commence; the damper and the secondary air inlets are partially closed. This restriction of the amount of air available causes the flame to lengthen and burn inside the chamber of the kiln around the shelves and pots and a reducing atmosphere results. Too heavy a reduction will cause sooting and little or no temperature rise. A useful test for a successful reducing atmosphere is to hold a lighted taper by the open spy hole in front of the kiln. In a reducing kiln a slight flame should burn from the spy hole which pushes the flame of the taper away. In other words the flames inside the chamber are under pressure. At this stage a pyrometer is very useful. A careful watch should be kept on the dial to note that a steady temperature rise occurs. If the temperature falls, too little air is present and the inlets should be opened slightly; too rapid a temperature rise may indicate little or no reduction and inlets must be closed slightly.

By about 1200–1220°C (2192–2228°F) reduction is almost complete. Some potters like to reduce to about 1250°C (2282°F) but for most sorts of body and glaze the desired effects have now been achieved and sealed by the melted glaze. Some glazes (such as the Sang de boeuf) may need reduction to higher temperatures, and here experience of individual glazes is essential. But generally the final temperature rise to 1260–1280°C (2300–2336°F) is achieved by opening the chimney damper and secondary air inlets slightly to clear the kiln atmosphere and to give an oxidizing period. Known as the purge or cleansing time, it is a chance for the body to oxidize slightly and take on a light, brighter colour. Too long a period of oxidation may result in some loss of quality: potters generally reckon on the final purge lasting about 30–60 minutes, though again this depends on individual kilns and tastes.

When final temperature has been reached the burners are turned off, the chimney damper and all air inlets closed. Large kilns may need 'clamming', that is the process in which slight cracks round the door and brickway generally are filled with a wet mixture of equal parts clay and sand. This can be easily removed later and reused.

When the kiln has cooled to 400°C (752°F) the chimney damper can be opened slightly, and at 200°C (392°F) all inlets can be opened and the door or wicket as it is often called 'cracked' to peep inside.

For some effects, it is more convenient or necessary to reduce the kiln as it cools, for example, to produce a black body. This sort of reduction can be achieved by either having the burners on a low flame, with inlets and dampers closed, or by inserting a lighted gas poker as the cooling continues with the burners off.

Whenever flame burning kilns are used, whether gas or oil, care is needed to ensure a steady or even flow of fuel. Kilns can be fitted with an automatic cut-off device which comes into operation if the fuel supply is stopped, however briefly. This prevents any unlighted fuel from entering a red hot kiln so causing an explosion. The most effective insulation round the kiln is air. Kilns should not be built too near a wall, and exhaust chimneys, which get very hot during the firing, need plenty of space round them to eliminate fire risks.

In the electric kiln a reducing atmosphere is achieved by either introducing a direct gas flame, such as a lighted gas poker, or by introducing combustible materials containing carbon, which will burn giving off quantities of smoke. Moth balls, wood chips, oil rags and grease have all been tried with varying degrees of success. The rate at which such materials are pushed or dripped into the kiln, depends both on the size of the kiln and the degree of reduction required. In kilns not specially built for this purpose, the spy holes are obvious entry points. All doors and ventilation holes should be sealed – a plastic mixture of equal parts sand and fireclay serves as an effective seal; this can easily be brushed off once the kiln has been fired. Reduction can start at any point after 1000°C (1832°F), though continuous attention will be needed. A thin plume of smoke issuing from the kiln will denote a reducing atmosphere, but it should be remembered that this smoke is partly composed of carbon monoxide which is a poisonous gas. The kiln room should, therefore, be well ventilated to ensure that the exhaust gases from the kiln are not inhaled in anything but the weakest form.

As an alternative to reducing the whole atmosphere in the kiln, pots can be fired in sealed saggers which also contain slow burning carbonaceous materials. This method involves no complicated firing procedure, and the kiln is fired in the normal way. German studio potters have achieved remarkable reduction effects in this way. Charcoal, coal, graphite, wood or sawdust, or a mixture of these materials, will burn slowly to affect the atmosphere, and the pots inside the saggar. A fine clay with a low shrinkage will help to keep the saggar sealed; any leakage will minimize the effects of the burning fuel.

The effects of adding a reducing agent to the glaze materials so that its effect is directly on the surrounding glaze has been dealt with to some extent on page 112. Silicon carbide is the most popular of these and is an effective agent for reduction effects.

Most research has been directed at the production of copper reds with successful results. Silicon carbide has a refractory effect in the glaze, and, unless very finely ground (which the potter cannot usually do, as it is an extremely hard material) it will tend to give rough glaze surfaces. Additions to the glaze are between 3% and 5%. It can also be added to slips and used under a variety of glazes, often with amazing results.

There are other alternatives to silicon carbide, usually little explored because they do not come within the range of the potter's chemicals. Graphite or finely ground wood charcoal are easily and cheaply available sources of carbon, which can be used in the glaze as a reducing agent. About 10% of carbonaceous material is added to the glaze which is applied and fired in the usual way.

Other materials which will cause reduction effects in the glaze are very small quantities of aluminium powder or coal ash, which is refractory and contains approximately 42% silica and 24% alumina, as well as iron and other impurities, with carbon. Dicalcium silicate is a refractory material which will suspend itself in a glaze to give the optical opalescent effects of a reduced kiln.

11
Qualities Desirable in a Glaze

All potters have their own notion of what aesthetic and practical qualities a glaze should possess, and a list of the qualities that would constitute such a glaze will not suit many people – other than the person compiling the list. There are, however, some general guidelines and points which make glazing and glaze mixing an easier and less mysterious operation, and this chapter is a more personal look at aspects of this problem.

From a practical point of view, the more limited the potter's laboratory, the deeper the knowledge of materials will become as the experiments proceed. Some potters limit their glaze materials to what they see as seven major ingredients – feldspar, china clay, flint, whiting, dolomite, barium carbonate and colemanite. From these materials they claim that an almost endless range of different sorts of glazes can be constructed, though we would add nepheline syenite to this list. After your own series of tests with most of the ingredients in your laboratory you may want to make your own selection and this will probably involve imposing a limit on the number of materials with which to experiment to enable a deeper understanding of the obtainable possibilities.

Materials which can be ordered in reasonable quantities and re-ordered whenever necessary are essential if the glazes are to form the basis of a standard repeatable range. Of course there are many potters who are not particularly interested in repetition effects, but want only specific glazes for a limited time. Other potters want a reliable and repeatable range of glazes to use as and when necessary, and for them the correct choice of basic materials is vital. It is no good mixing up a batch of glaze which is admired and ordered in quantity if, because of the nature of the materials involved, the effect is unrepeatable. This restricts experiments with materials which are in limited supply, to more or less one off glaze batches. It is also worth bearing in mind the cost and ease of preparation. Materials with specified analysis bought ready prepared for use from the supplier are the most reliable and easiest to use. Opposed to this are materials listed in the second section on page 28 such as local clays and wood ash, which will vary in composition and, in addition, require considerable work to prepare them for use. The initial cost of obtaining such materials is negligible and many can even be collected free, but the cost, in time and preparation, may be considerable.

The firing and handling of the glaze also needs to be made as practical as possible. Glazes which settle out quickly into a hard solid mass need the addition of a suspender (see page 129) while other glazes, with little plastic content, will dry on the pot to form a powdery surface which makes the work of kiln packing even more complicated. A gum or some other suitable binder (page 129) will give the glaze better handling qualities.

Finding the critical firing point of a glaze is often a matter of luck. An iron-rich glaze which needs to move over the surface of the clay to bring out the full rich effects of a typical tenmoku glaze usually needs to soak at the end of the firing period and at a temperature nearer to 1280°C (2336°F) rather than 1260°C (2300°F). Yet at this sort of temperature, and especially if it is maintained, white magnesium glazes pick out the iron in the underlying clay and the result is a rich mottled grey brown glaze instead of the desired speckled opaque white, so these are not good companions in the kiln. However, with a working knowledge of your kiln and its hottest and coolest parts according to the shelf arrangements, you can safely incorporate the two glazes in a single firing. Generally speaking, open spaces heat up quickly, while areas in which shelves are packed close together tend to take longer to heat up and these arrangements can balance out the hot and cool spots in the kiln.

The economics of kiln packing are also a primary concern for the production potter who does not want to waste any kiln space. Kiln shelves are thick and solid and are extremely expensive to fire, therefore the whole area needs to be utilized. All these considerations need to be taken into account when production is planned; for example, small plates and saucers, which will stand in between and around large dinner plates, are necessary to fill up these shelves.

Related to this problem is the maturing temperature range of the glaze. The wider this range, the easier the firing becomes. Glazes high in clay tend to have a wide maturing range while those rich in iron or ash tend to have a critical firing temperature which, if not reached, yield dull effects, and if surpassed causes the glaze to run down the pot onto the kiln shelf.

AESTHETIC CONSIDERATIONS

Apart from the practical aspect of the qualities a good glaze should have, there are the aesthetic considerations. To many potters, it is the semi-matt Chinese glazes of the Sung and Ming Dynasties which possess the perfect classical effects. Often imitating the qualities of Jade, such glazes were thick and unctuous – mutton fat is how they are often described; others were thin and runny, often moving over the pot to reveal a delicate and finely engraved design underneath, carved into the surface of the pot. Such glazes have been compared to the sky after rain – brilliant, deep and fresh. Chinese potters never added metal oxides to their glaze mixtures, such pale colours that arose did so as a result of tiny quantities of colouring oxides present as impurities in the raw materials. They also came about as a result of the method of firing and the available materials which brought out these 'impurities' in the glaze and developed the deep opalescent qualities of the glaze as opposed to their surface colours. Such glazes also strengthened the high fired ware upon which they were used as well as providing smooth, practical surfaces. At their best, the glaze and shape were united to form a complete whole.

However, tastes, needs, and working methods are not always the same. The slipware potters of Britain knew nothing of the Chinese successes, yet, in terms of their own skills and knowledge of a few basic techniques, their achievements are equally great. Directly trailed designs employing coloured clay slips finished with a layer of transparent lead glaze which brought out the colours, provided a very functional ware. No difficult technical problems were met (lead solubility was not a major concern then) and the pots fulfilled a need in society. Slipware potters made ware which was practical to use and economical to produce: out of these basic requirements came something else – beauty.

As technical knowledge expanded in the eighteenth century and big industry loomed on the horizon, Josiah Wedgwood saw possibilities for the pottery industry. He revolutionized the preparation of materials, the methods of production, and the marketing of the wares. Different techniques were developed which produced different sorts of pots, and the pottery industry and the country potter took their first step in opposite directions. New aesthetic considerations were introduced and one which appealed to a very wide section of the community. Elegant and practical and cheap is no mean description of the popular Wedgwood wares. It was a description which suited these early industrial wares until about 1830 when industrialization seems to have lost sight of aesthetic considerations and the pots lost their pleasant shapes and simple decoration to become gaudy and unbalanced.

There were people who were aware of the lost qualities and sought to re-introduce them in the production of Art Pottery. These artists wanted to use the methods of the country potters and combine this with an industrial excellence to produce art pots on a par with the work of all fine artists. The results ranged over a wide area of success and failure, but the *fin de siècle* idea finally terminated at the end of the First World War. Many art potters found only the glazing of the pots interesting and some used dull, lifeless shapes on which to produce exquisite and technically accomplished effects – which still leave potters in awe in terms of their achievement. Other art potters wanted all the romance and mystery of the fire to result in freely applied and arbitrary effects which merged completely with the pot.

But what has this to do with our aesthetic awareness today? We work in very different conditions. As potters, we are not limited by the locality of materials – suppliers' catalogues list materials from all over the world and often do not even bother to give their country of origin. Written technical knowledge is greater and more readily available now than it has ever been.

Ignorance is no longer an excuse. As potters, we are freed from the shackles of fulfilling a functional need in society, and are at liberty to practise skills for our own and our customers' delight. Studio potters produce a luxury product which, while it may enhance the quality of daily life, is not essential; and everyone could find mass produced (and cheaper) substitutes if necessary. Studio potters have to largely create, rather than to fulfil a need.

With such an open framework in which to work, studio potters have little to direct their steps except their own sensitivity and what is practical for them. A small electric kiln will produce different effects from those of a large wood-fired kiln and the two production methods must not be confused. Taste, national or international, is never easy to estimate, but because potters work for other people in the sense that pots are to be used, rather than admired, the creative process has not been completed until the pots have been sold. A studio full of cups and saucers which no one wants, apart from the potter, will not be satisfactory either creatively or practically. To make what both the potter and the public like is a basic tenet of the studio potter, and this happy state usually grows out of a healthy working and selling situation, rather than from a drawing board. Giving the public what it wants can mean educating both the potter and the public in the widest possible sense. Glaze and shape are all part of the total effect and each must be related physically and aesthetically to the other.

Potters making tablewares have, paradoxically, the easiest and the most difficult task with regard to the glazes they choose. It is easiest in the sense that the glazes must fulfil their function; they must be strong, smooth to the touch, and resist staining. They must be non-poisonous, permanent, well-fitted to the body without either crazing or chipping off the edges and rims. A shiny glaze is practical, but the public do not care for shiny surfaces and seem to prefer instead matt or semi-matt glazes which appear to them more a part of the body of the pot. This is where the task gets more difficult; the glazes must be attractive, repeatable and stand the test of time. A customer setting out to buy a dinner set may want, or can only afford, to buy in small quantities – difficult matching problems are a potter's nightmare. Also, in this sense, being attractive must of necessity omit the spectacular and dramatic for the quieter more neutral qualities which lend themselves to food backgrounds without becoming mere wall paper. This elusive attractive glaze must also be pleasant to look at, and inviting to touch and use. Potters are lucky when they have discovered such a glaze and it is usually used for many years.

The ceramist whose concern is not with production tablewares but either with making individual pots, such as bowls, or with making objects which do not act as any sort of container, has almost the whole range of glaze technology to explore. Such a potter rarely uses a large kiln and the economics of production do not rely on filling up kiln space but on the success of the finished piece having the desired qualities. Temperature, body, and firing conditions can be altered according to needs and the 'effects' sought after and the potter can have an exciting time creating the enormously wide and rich variety of possible glazes, most of which are outlined in this book. It is still not sufficient, however, merely to get an effect. The marriage between object and glaze must be complete physically and aesthetically and there is no magic formula with which to do this.

Sculptors, working with clay, often want to use a glaze on their work. For them a true glaze would mask the subtlety and detail of their work under a layer which served no useful purpose. In this case pigments, which colour only the surface of the clay, offer a possible solution. No gloss is required and a dry but stable pigment can enrich the surface and enhance the form without distracting the eye from the whole object. Almost any of the metal oxides can be successfully used. They can be rubbed into the surface dry or mixed with water and painted or sprayed on. Further rubbing will heighten or reduce concentration of colour or tone. Clay slips, too, can be used in this way to give a thin, vitreous yet matt surface. White slips can form a useful light coloured background. All the oxides and many of the materials can be tested on their own to see their effect. Iron oxide and the ochres will give rich shades of brown and mahogany. Manganese oxide, on its own or mixed with clay, will give solid blacks and browns with subdued highlights. Zinc oxide gives a matt yellow surface. Oxides can also be tried mixed with clay or feldspar. The range is very wide and the recipes on page 163 give some useful starting points. Many potters, too, find the pigments useful in providing coloured clay areas which emphasize form and pleasantly contrast with areas of glaze.

The possibilities for different types of glaze are endless, yet the results still must be assessed by the two leading questions. One, does the glaze do its job – and only individual circumstances can define what that job is – and, two, does it do it well – in other words, do you and other people like it? Again, it must rely on the individual situation. What may be liked in one situation may be grotesque in another. Thinking and feeling, looking at the work of previous potters and contemporary potters will help but, finally, it is all up to the individual potter.

Part Four

HISTORY

12
The History of Glazes

How, where or when the discovery was made that certain substances, when heated, fuse to form a glass is not known. That such materials could be applied to the surface of clay, and, after heating, give a vitrified surface which we recognize as glaze, is another discovery lost in antiquity. On circumstantial evidence, the technique seems to have been used first in the Middle East, and is probably an Egyptian or African invention, made over 7000 years ago. How the invention or discovery was made cannot be attributed to any known fact, yet fables relate how, after a bonfire of seaweed on a sandy shore, lumps of glass were discovered in the ashes. Other fables speak of malachite grinding stones, which, when heated in the presence of an alkali, acquired a glazed surface.

The earliest known examples of vitrified glaze surfaces are on steatite heads from Badari in Upper Egypt and date back to about 5000 B.C. The origin of glazed objects is confused even further by the fact that the Egyptians glazed materials other than clay. Whether the Egyptian potters were not interested in glazing clay, or whether they tried and failed is a matter, so far, for speculation. Quartz and soapstone (steatite) objects such as amulets, scarabs and statuettes, were made and glazed until 2000 B.C. when this material was replaced by a synthetic mixture known as Egyptian faience. This mixture consisted of fine white sand mixed with natron – a naturally occurring form of sodium carbonate which acts as a powerful flux at low temperatures. The mixture, which could not have been very plastic, was shaped largely in moulds; it was heated until the entire mass fused together. Faience vases and statuettes were made for over 2000 years.

Glazed objects made from this sort of material embellished palaces and temples of the Assyrians and Babylonians, and the rich turquoise colours must have looked particularly attractive. At the Palace of Sargon near Mosul, Iraq (722–705 B.C.) lions, bulls, ravens, and other forms of animal life were depicted.

Around 2000–1500 B.C. the techniques of making glass was discovered and this knowledge spread far and wide – even as far as China. With the making of glass came an awareness that grinding cold glass (frit) formed the basis for a glaze. In the library of Ashur-barri-pal, Assyria, dating to the seventh century B.C., clay tablets have been found on which is written in cuneiform characters the composition of a procedure for glazing.

The difficulties of applying a glaze to a pot were numerous. Alkaline glazes are highly fluid and inevitably craze or drop off the pot surface. In any case, the use of glaze requires a knowledge of quite complex technology. Firstly, the glazed objects must be carefully placed and supported in the kiln, secondly such objects must be protected from ash and grit and the direct flame, and thirdly, a crucial temperature must be reached. Such requirements imply the use of a sophisticated kiln in which the placing chamber is well protected from the flames. Such kilns have been excavated in the Middle East though our knowledge of them is still limited. The Greeks were able to operate particularly sophisticated firing techniques which enabled them to control and alter the atmosphere in the kiln to produce their famous red and black wares.

Large deposits of alkaline materials occur naturally in the Near East and potters in the Middle and Near East continued to use and develop alkaline glazes. These glazes needed a highly siliceous body containing 85% or more quartz to adhere successfully. Such a glaze was almost impossible to use on a clay base without the application of a thick layer of siliceous slip to the body of the vessel. The use of alkaline glaze over white slip or over a highly siliceous body became widespread and painted and incised decoration was a characteristic feature of Islamic wares. Around the eighth or ninth century A.D., tin oxide was added to the glaze to render it white and opaque, and, in many cases, to imitate more closely the much-admired Chinese porcelains imported via the silk route.

In Mesopotamia, around 1000 B.C., successful experiments were being made with the glazing of brick surfaces; the glazes were coloured with additions of various colouring oxides and were opacified by the addition of a sort of antimony (roméite) and tin oxide. The bricks, built into decorative walls and palaces, can still be seen today. However, the widespread glazing of pottery vessels had to await the discovery that lead, which was also used in glass manufacture, could be used in glazes to give a much more workable material. Lead glazes tend to be more thickly applied and more glossy in appearance than alkaline glazes and their use was preferred for vessels and large objects. The first known lead glaze recipe has been deciphered from writing on a cuneiform tablet found near Tall 'Umar (Selucia) on the Tigris in Mesopotamia. In modern notation, the recipe can be read as glass 243.0, lead 40.1, copper 58.1, saltpetre 3.1, lime 5.0. The tablet also describes the preparation of clay bodies and from the information, experimental glazed pottery objects have been made. Examples of lead glazed ware have been found which date to this period, at Atchara in Turkey, and suggest that the use of lead glaze was well established by that time. The glaze used still tended to be too thick and was inclined to flake off. It was not until the late Hellenistic period that a thinner and more adhesive glaze was developed and used throughout the Middle East.

In contrast to the Middle East, China developed a very different sort of glaze that involved skills which were not understood in Europe until the eighteenth century.

Chinese potters fired their pots to a temperature greatly in excess of temperatures achieved elsewhere. This high firing technique seems to have been used first in the Shang dynasty (1550–1025 B.C.) and is closely allied to the technique of preparing bronze. High temperature firing needs special kilns to produce the heat, a body which is sufficiently refractory to withstand the heat, and, to produce the glaze, rocks which melt around 1200°C (2192°F). Shang potters also used pure kaolin (china clay) of which there are large deposits in China. The kilns they used were divided clearly into stoking chamber, and firing chamber with a flue connecting the two. The discovery that ground feldspar, applied evenly over the surface of the pot, gave a hard, vitrified glaze was made at this time. Glazes were coloured white, olive green, or dark brown.

During the Han dynasty, 206 B.C.–A.D. 220, there were other notable developments. The high fired feldspathic glaze wares continued to be used, but a low temperature glaze was also introduced. This employed the use of lead, as a flux, and this was probably imported from Western Asia. Green or brown lead glazes were used in Honan, Skensi and Shantung. Little is known about the history of the lead glaze after its brief appearance in the Han period until it reappeared around A.D. 550, when it was of greatly improved quality and richness.

The development of Chinese stonewares continued towards greater refinement, with glazes which were applied more thinly, becoming clearer and brighter, and the clay bodies becoming whiter and denser. Some of the pots have patches of different colours showing that serious attempts were made to control the atmosphere of the kiln and so ensure the rich oxidized browns as well the pale blues and greens from a reduced kiln atmosphere.

The silk route, extending across Central Asia from the Mediterranean Coast via Baghdad, Samarkand, Kashgar, Tunhuang to Central China was responsible for the trading of goods and ideas. Chinese pots were taken to the Middle East where whiteness and strength of these high-fired wares stimulated the Arab potters; from Arabia came lead frit and cobalt ore which the Chinese potters used to produce earthenware of great richness and colour.

During the Chinese Tang dynasty, the white porcelain wares reached a new level of sophistication and elegance. A fine thinly potted white body with a thin layer of transparent glaze accurately foretold the brilliant porcelains of the later Sung period. It was during the Sung dynasty that work of classical simplicity was made which cannot be equalled. High fired stoneware vessels, well potted and with thick unctuous glazes coloured either white or pale green adorned the palaces and temples. Delicately made porcelains, with matt white glazes, or shiny pale blue transparent glazes, were a triumph of technical skill and aesthetic expression. Such pots, the predecessors of the blue and white wares and the delicately decorated enamel wares of Ming China, were used as the measure against which the work of other potters was compared. Chinese glazes were imitated throughout Europe and the Middle East and technologists sought to discover the secrets of their manufacture.

In contrast to this highly refined and elegant Chinese ware, the stonewares of Japan, first developed around A.D. 1200 show a liveliness and vigour which came from a more intimate use of their method of firing. The Japanese learned the art of high temperature firing from the Koreans, but discovered and liked the fact that wood ash from the firing chamber settled on the exposed parts of their pots, to give a rich, mottled glaze and this became a characteristic feature of their work. The high temperature firing vitrified the body and made the addition of a shiny glaze unnecessary. Some potters relied only upon the rich colourings and flashings of ash on their pots, while others mixed ash with feldspar and applied these mixtures to the pots to give runny richly coloured glazes, which are still admired and copied today.

The discovery that lead compounds could be used in glazes to extend the possible colour range and render the glazes usable on most types of clay, to give a tougher surface, was the most important development in Europe, and laid the basis for the main types of glazes to be used for 1500 years. The use of lead compounds in glazes had been widespread in the Near East during the first century B.C. Yellow and green glazes were used on a luxury type of ware, made in moulds, largely in imitation of contemporary silver work. Roman potters made lead glazed ware, usually coloured green, yellow or brown, at various centres throughout the Empire. In Europe, St Remy-en-Rollat, Lezoux, and later Cologne and Bonn, were all popular centres of production.

Technology in the Roman Empire continued to develop other sorts of glaze. The method of producing frit ware, from a mixture of quartz sand and natron, and further grinding up such a mixture and applying it to the surface to give a glaze, reached its peak in Egypt at this time. The practical working difficulties of handling such a non-plastic body resulted in only small pieces being made, but as skills improved, pots and vessels of larger size were produced, all with brilliant colours. Turquoise was the most common, but this was extended to include black, red, apple-green, purple, yellow and white.

The development of a practical alkaline glaze which could be applied to a normal clay body probably took place in Parthica during the early days of the Roman Empire. The glaze, which involved the use of alkaline salts as its base, was stained in various tones of green and blue by the use of copper and iron oxides. Small amounts of lead were added, as was tin, and the glaze was used in the Near East for many hundreds of years.

Both lead and alkaline glazes were opacified by the addition of tin oxide around the sixth or seventh century. Such glazes were popular because they imitated the whiteness of the Chinese porcelain wares and provided an attractive surface for painted decoration. The Islamic potters used the tin glaze and some decorated it with rich lustre colours produced in a highly reduced kiln atmosphere. The Moors took the technique of tin glazing and the secrets of the manufacture of lustre decoration to Spain where wares of great decorative beauty were developed. From Spain, the use of tin glaze was taken to Italy and provided Italian Renaissance potters with 'canvases' on which to work. Gradually tin glazing extended throughout Europe and centres were established. Delft, in Holland is one of the most famous; here the Dutch blue and white Delftware was produced.

One other major method of glazing was to be discovered. This was vapour glazing and this occurred in Germany towards the end of the fourteenth century. Earlier, in the twelfth century, the presence of suitable refractory clays had resulted in the production of unglazed proto-stoneware in the Rhineland. Two hundred years later it was discovered that ordinary household salt, when thrown into the kiln at top temperature, volatilized into soda which combined with the silica and alumina of the body to form a strong, thin, colourless, glassy film on the surface of the pot. Part of this reaction liberated chlorine gas into the atmosphere. Colour in the glaze was introduced by washes on the pot of iron slips, and later, cobalt and manganese. Fine white wares, as well as the brown coloured wares, were produced.

In Europe generally, the use of lead glazes was the major form of glazing. Potters in Byzantium had retained the technique of lead glazing which during the Middle Ages made its way across Europe and eventually into Britain. Salt glazing continued to be the main glazing method in Germany though it was a technique which was also used with great success in Britain in the seventeenth and eighteenth centuries. Salt glazing was introduced into America by immigrant potters where it formed the basis of an indigenous style of lively and imaginative pots.

During the eighteenth century, the basis of modern glazes was developed. In Germany, Böttger's discovery of how to make porcelain made the work of the European potter acceptable to the upper classes. In Britain, the work of Josiah Wedgwood and other potters, with the use of refined bodies and carefully calculated glazes, laid the foundation for the modern ceramic industry. All the basic techniques were known and waiting to be refined and developed. The nineteenth century saw the importation into Europe of the Chinese and Japanese stonewares and these stimulated efforts to produce stoneware glazes in Europe and America for the first time.

Today, the industry has refined its glazes to ensure almost perfect quality control. Some industrial producers are beginning to react against this and are introducing casual 'accidental' effects such as specking, running, bleeding and so on, which very much imitate the work of the studio potter. Potters generally have a wealth of information at their disposal; experiments to discover new and rich effects often take them along paths very similar to those of their ancestors of long ago.

APPENDICES

1 Health Hazards

Common sense is usually the best and most reliable guide to any sort of safety measures, and, if it is used in good measure, then most of the health hazards will be avoided. But in ceramics there are some hazards which must either be avoided completely or calculated with careful precision. Here particular reference is made to the use of raw lead and lead compounds. It is very tempting to look at our potter predecessors who used raw lead as a 'natural' material and assume that it is a perfectly safe material. We now know that this is not so, and there has been a swing of the pendulum by some potters against the use of any lead in glazes. This, however, is to deny the earthenware potter the use of one of the most effective fluxes. With a good knowledge of the hazards which the material involves, all materials available to the potter can be used safely.

There is one other general point which is worth making. A studio potter, working alone, is not subject to any factory regulations or official inspection. This situation changes as soon as someone is employed, when all the regulations which apply to the factory come into force. There is not the space here to detail all of the Factory Act, but the relevant parts will be summarized. Most regulations, however, are applicable in kind, if not in law, to all studio potters. Basically all potters use the same sorts of materials and run the same risks, and need, therefore, to take as much care in ensuring our own safety as well as that of any employees.

The main areas in which hazards occur are from inhaling dust, handling toxic materials, inhaling exhaust gases from kilns, fire risks, and finally, solubility from metals in glazes.

Dust is the potter's worst enemy. Government standards lay down maximum permitted levels of airborne dust, and factory regulations detail methods by which dust must be avoided. Most of the raw materials supplied by the manufacturers are extremely finely ground, and when disturbed float around invisible to the naked eye. Flint and quartz are the biggest danger, and normally each batch is supplied with 5–10% additions of moisture to prevent fly-up when used. Silicosis – the lung condition arising from the inhalation of silica dust – is an incurable disease and must therefore be avoided. Flint and quartz are the most concentrated danger and both these materials can be present in clay and in fritted glaze material. Other glaze materials, such as the heavy metals which included zinc, barium, lead, antimony, chromium, cobalt, copper, nickel and vanadium are poisonous if taken internally as well as being dust risks. Depleted uranium oxide is poisonous as well as being slightly radioactive. This material is safest when stowed in a metal box – preferably lined with lead – but the quantities usually stored and used by the studio potter offer little danger of contamination from radioactivity.

All materials are safest stored in containers with lids which are reasonably well fitting and which can be wet wiped. Plastic buckets or bins are ideal, though rows of used coffee or sweet jars are handy substitutes. Sacks, either of hessian or plastic, and packets are to be avoided. They cannot be cleaned and, when disturbed, scatter dust liberally. Good workshop practice involves transferring materials from their delivery containers into storage containers, no matter how small the quantity. Clear labels with the name of the supplier and reference number placed both inside and outside the container, will enable repeat orders to be placed easily. Empty packages should be disposed of carefully to eliminate any danger from contamination. Spilt glaze or dry materials should be mopped up immediately and not paddled around the workshop – something we often tend to forget in the excitement of glazing. Raw materials should also be added to water and dropped in as near the surface as possible.

Avoiding dust completely is almost impossible – minimizing it requires careful thought and regular workshop hygiene. Basically, this must involve no dry sweeping or dusting and no sprinkling of raw materials or dry mixing. Wipe surfaces and lids with wet sponge, and sweet floors with a proprietary brand of oiled sawdust (various sorts of mixtures are available). Sawdust damped with water only lays the dust until the water dries, and then leaves it ready to be disurbed. Incidentally, the oiled sawdusts leave most sorts of floors looking rather handsome. In factories no bins can be kept on the floor which must be hosed down with water every day after work has ceased. All shelves etc. must be washed clean.

Industrial vacuum cleaners are efficient at sucking up dust from corners etc. and are useful, but they are not a real alternative to thorough sweeping or hosing. Ventilation, too, is important. Small cubby-holes for glaze mixing tend to concentrate the dust and should be avoided. Needless to say, glaze spraying should only be done in a special booth fitted with an extractor fan sufficiently strong to remove all the unwanted fine glaze mist which, because of its fineness, is a particularly dangerous hazard. Resist the temptation to spray larger pots outside the booth – think of other ways of applying the glaze. Also ensure that the exhaust from the extractor fan is directed so as to avoid any pollution of other working areas. Ideally, spray booths should be fitted with a water curtain, which catches the unwanted glaze and prevents it from entering the atmosphere.

Ingesting glaze materials is an unlikely event, but it is amazing how potters tend to assume that without any clear warning to the contrary, most glaze materials are non-toxic! The fact that most materials are supplied in bulk seems to inspire confidence in their safety. This is not the case. All the heavy metals mentioned earlier, plus selenium and cadmium, are poisonous if eaten. Do not eat or drink anything in the workshop, and wash hands with soap and running water after handling any glaze material.

Mention of the poisonous exhaust fumes from the kiln has already been made. A pale blue smoke hanging in the atmosphere emitted from the kiln at around 700–900°C (1292–1652°F) will include a good quantity of carbon monoxide, and will 'taste' at the back of the throat. This is a gas which must be avoided. Improve the ventilation with either a through current of air or a powerful extractor fan. Experiments with materials inserted into the kiln to cause a reducing atmosphere will also need to be carried out in a room with efficient ventilation. This is especially applicable when either 'Calor' or natural gas is burnt in the kiln. These exhaust fumes are particularly dangerous. When firing kilns with oil or gas, room ventilation is even more important to prevent the build-up of dangerous levels of carbon monoxide gas and ensure the supply of oxygen in the atmosphere is not seriously depleted.

Raw and fritted glaze materials present no fire hazard. They are not liable to burn, nor do they have a flash point. However, mediums used for applying and cleaning screen printing pigments do have low flash points. Such materials must *not* be stored near the kiln, nor used in the presence of exposed flames. Most of these materials also give off strong fumes which are harmful to health, and so should be used only in a well ventilated room.

Finally, there is the problem of the solubility of metals, and metal release from fired work. This is a problem where common sense is of little use. The metals involved are lead, cadmium, and selenium, and the dangers occur with earthenware glazes and low temperature enamels (on-glaze colours) where the low melting glass may have a substantial acid solubility. The problem concerning lead has been dealt with at some length in chapter 2, and ways of avoiding the solubility problem have been suggested. Governments of all countries have laid down strict safety limits of low metal release tolerance, and these apply equally to imported ware. If the ware does not fall within the safety limits, it will not be allowed in; in the case of home produced ware it cannot be marketed.

With a well balanced glaze, applied and fired as instructed, there is no danger at all. Only when carefully balanced glazes are altered, either by the addition of raw materials or colouring oxides, or put over coloured slips is there a danger that such glazes may be rendered soluble in acid solutions. Therefore, any material which may induce metal release when added to a glaze should not be used in manufactured glazes, without subsequent testing. (When in doubt consult the manufacturer.)

In the case of coloured enamels, it is safest to avoid their use on surfaces which will come into contact with food and drink. Usually they are restricted to small areas of decoration which can be arranged either on the outside of containers or on the rims of plates.

To sum up, it is consoling to note that most ceramic materials are quite safe in use. Where hazards do exist, correct handling will eliminate the risk.

Precautions to follow, in summary, are:

1   Avoid getting any ceramic materials into the mouth, and do not consume food or drink while in the workshop.
2   Wear protective clothing which can be removed after work. Keep the clothing clean by regular washing.
3   Use soap and running water to wash the hands and arms after work.
4   Keep your workshop clean by wet washing and sweeping with suitable materials.
5   Avoid draughty, dusty conditions, and ensure adequate and proper ventilation.
6   Keep materials in lidded containers and close the lids after use.
7   Do not smoke in the workshop area.

2 Glaze and Slip Recipes

I STONEWARE GLAZES

CLEAR/SEMI-CLEAR

Standard clear/milky
1290°C (2354°F)

Whiting	15
Feldspar	35
China Clay	15
Flint	35

Clear/semi matt
1260°C (2300°F)

Whiting	20
Feldspar	40
China Clay	20
Flint	20

WHITE AND MATT GLAZES

Dolomite-white smooth matt
1260°C (2300°F)

Whiting	5
China Clay	35
Feldspar	45
Dolomite	15

Dry yellow/white matt glaze
1260°C (2300°F)

Whiting	35
China Clay	45
Feldspar	20
Dolomite	5

Dry yellow white matt
1250°C (2282°F)

Whiting	40
Feldspar	10
China Clay	50

Dolomite-white speckle
1260°C (2300°F)

Feldspar	33
China Clay	15
Ball Clay	15
Whiting	15
Talc	17

Calcium white matt glaze
1260°C (2300°F)

Whiting	20
China Clay	20
Feldspar	60

Good for added iron oxides, 2% gives yellow/cream, 8% gives broken red.

Opaque white – crawling tendency
1260°C (2300°F)

Whiting	10
Feldspar	25
China Clay	20
Flint	45

Smooth speckled matt
1250°C (2282°F)

Whiting	45
Feldspar	30
China Clay	20
Flint	5

Dry clay matt
1250°C (2282°F)

Whiting	45
China Clay	45
Feldspar	5
Flint	5

Good for added colouring oxides.

Clay matt
1250–1280°C (2282–2336°F)

Whiting	45
China Clay	45
Ball Clay	10

A useful clay matt in oxidation and reduction. Especially useful as a base for added oxides.

CRYSTALLINE GLAZES 1260°C (2300°F)

Frit High Alkali (P. 2250)	70
Flint	10
Whiting	5
China Clay	5
Feldspar	10
+Rutile	3
Zinc Oxide	50
Nickel Oxide	1

Soak at 1100°C for 1–2 hours when cooling. Dark yellow brown crystals. Additions of colouring oxides will give coloured crystals.

Attractive shiny glazes, with crystal growths 1250–1260°C (2282–2300°F)

Feldspar	36		Feldspar	46		Borax Frit	45
Whiting	13		Whiting	9		Whiting	10
Zinc Oxide	24		Zinc Oxide	28		Zinc Oxide	27
(light)			Flint	28		Flint	30
China Clay	5		Rutile	4		+Rutile	4
Flint	22						
Rutile	4						

All work well with small additions of colouring oxides.

TENMOKU

Shiny black breaking red on edges
1265°C (2309°F) oxidation

Feldspar	34
Flint	34
Whiting	16
Ball Clay	10
China Clay	6
+ Iron Oxide	8

Matt tenmoku – good satin surface
1260°C (2300°F) reduction

Feldspar	40
Flint	20
Whiting	10
China Clay	10
Ball Clay	5
+ Iron Oxide	12%

Shiny rich blue/black
1260°C (2300°F) reduction

China Stone	56
Whiting	14
China Clay	10
Flint	20
+ Iron Oxide	9%

Good Black Tenmoku
1260°C (2300°F) oxidation, excellent in reduction.

Feldspar	33
Flint	40
Whiting	17
China Clay	10
+ Iron Oxide	11%

BLUE, GREEN, PURPLE

Bright blue/green
1260°C (2300°F) oxidation or reduction

Nepheline Syenite	50
Barium Carbonate	50
Copper Carbonate	1.5%
+Bentonite	3

Dark purple
1260°C (2300°F)

Nepheline Syenite	50
Barium Carbonate	50
Nickel Oxide	0.5%
+Bentonite	3

Green/blue matt
1260°C (2300°F)

Barium Carbonate	25
Nepheline Syenite	55
China Clay	8
Flint	8
Lithium Carbonate	4
Copper Carbonate	2%

Matt dark blue green
1260°C (2300°F)

Barium Carbonate	45
Feldspar	45
China Clay	10
Copper Carbonate	2

Blue/navy, matt
1260°C (2300°F)

Barium Carbonate	26
Flint	10
China Clay	10
Feldspar	46
Dolomite	8
+ Cobalt Carbonate	1.5
Rutile	3

OIL SPOT GLAZES AND IRON RED 1260°C (2300°F)

Spotted red/brown

Fremington clay	21
Feldspar	33
Nepheline Syenite	46
+ Iron Oxide	2%

Dark Brown
1260°C (2300°F)

Fremington Clay	80
Nepheline Syenite	20
+ Iron Oxide	3%

ARTIFICIAL REDUCTION EFFECTS

Pale blue turquoise
1260°C (2300°F)

Feldspar	30
Zinc Oxide	3
Whiting	10
China Clay	5
P. 2250 Frit	15
Flint	30
Cryolite	5
Tin Oxide	2
Silicon Carbide	0.5
Copper Carbonate	0.5

Cloudy pink/blue
1260°C (2300°F)

Calcium borate frit (or colemanite)	3
China Clay	2
Whiting	20
Flint	30
Feldspar	40
Talc	5
Tin Oxide	1
Silicon Carbide	0.5
Copper Carbonate	1

Blue/red semi matt
1260°C (2300°F)

Frit 2250 (Podmore)	30
Feldspar	20
Calcium Borate Frit (or Colemanite)	10
Flint	35
China Clay	5
Silicon Carbide	0.5
Copper Carbonate	0.3
Tin Oxide	1

ASH GLAZES

White/yellow, matt speckled
1260°C (2300°F)

Mixed Ash	40
Feldspar	40
China Clay	20

Orange/yellow/white, matt
1260°C (2300°F)

Feldspar	18
Mixed Ash	37
Whiting	18
China Clay	22
Ball Clay	5

Good with banded or painted iron decoration.

OTHER STONEWARE GLAZES

Yellow with green speckled areas
1260°C (2300°F)

Soda Feldspar	42
Barium Carbonate	22
China Clay	12
Whiting	12
	12
	2

Copper red in reduction
1260°C (2300°F)

Barium Carbonate	20
Feldspar	55
Dolomite	5
China Clay	5
Flint	10
+ Copper Carbonate	1.5%
Tin Oxide	2.5%

Red, matt, oxidation
1255–1260°C (2291–2300°F)

Soda Feldspar	25
Dolomite	15
China Clay	25
Bone Ash	10
Flint	25
+ Iron Oxide	10%
Zinc Oxide	
Uranium Oxide	

II   EARTHENWARE GLAZES

Low solubility lead glaze
1100°C (2012°F)

Lead Bisilicate	73
Whiting	7
Feldspar	20

N.B. Do not add any colouring oxides or use over coloured slip for pots to be used for food or drink.

Bright lead glaze
1150°C (2102°F)

Lead Bisilicate	50
China Clay	15
Cornish Stone	30
Whiting	5

Lead glaze 1080°C (1976°F)

Lead Bisilicate	73
China Clay	12
Cornish Stone	13
Flint	2

Lead 1060–1120°C (1940–2048°F)

China Clay	15
Whiting	5
Feldspar	10
Lead Bisilicate	70

Alkaline glaze matt
1080–1100°C (1976–2012°F)

Soda Feldspar	35
Whiting	7
China Clay	4
Flint	7
Borax Frit	47

Alkaline glaze clea⌐
1080–1100°C (197⌐–2012°F)

Soda Feldspar	3⌐
Whiting	⌐
China Clay	⌐
Flint	⌐
Borax Frit	5⌐

Turquoise 1080°C (⌐976°F)

Alkaline Frit	⌐2
China Clay	⌐8
Flint	⌐0
+ Copper Oxide	1.5%

III   SLIP RECIPES

Red

Red Clay	100
Iron Oxide	5

White

Ball Clay	50
China Clay	20
Feldspar	20
Flint	10

for green add 5% copper carbonate.
for blue add 3% cobalt carbonate.

Black No. 1

Red Clay	100
Iron Oxide	4
Manganese Oxide	3

Black No. 2

Stoneware Body	100
Iron Oxide	10
Manganese Oxide	10

Red Slip

Yellow Ochre	50
Ball Clay	40
Iron Oxide	10

Silicone carbide slip

China Clay	3⌐
Ball Clay	3⌐
Feldspar	3⌐
Flint	1⌐
Silicon carbide	⌐

3 The Use of the Slide Rule

Most slide rules consist of four or more lettered scales which slide against each other, and calculations are made by reading across one to the other. Scale C and D are usually used for multiplication or division, and a movable hairline, or cursor, is provided to make reference from one to the other. The position of decimal points is ignored throughout the calculating process and are inserted in the answer by inspection or judgment.

Division

To divide 4 by 2:

1   Set cursor over number (4) on scale D.
2   Slide scale (C) until the second number (2) is under cursor and over first number (4).
3   Answer is found on scale D opposite 1 or 10 on Scale C.
    = 2.

Further examples:

a)   1.24 divided by 68. Set as above but ignore decimal point, i.e. 124 divided by 68.
     Answer on Scale C (under 10) = 183.

     but, 1.24 divided by 68 = 0.0183, i.e. $68 \overline{\smash{\big)}\ 1.2400}^{\ 0.0183}$

b) $1.342 \div 2.684 \quad = 5 \quad = 0.5000$
c) $0.4362 \div 4362 \quad = 1 \quad = 0.1$
d) $0.04362 \div 0.4362 = 1 \quad = 0.01$

Multiplication

Example:
4×2

1   Find 4 on Scale D and set 1 on Scale C over it.
2   Set cursor on 2 on Scale C.
3   Answer is shown on Scale D under the cursor = 8.
N.B. for certain calculations, number 1 on Scale 1 will be taken as 1 or 10 (1).

e.g. $5 \times 3 = 15$

Further examples:

a) $0.13 \times 0.13 = 169 \quad = 0.0169$
b) $0.13 \times 1.3 \ = 169 \quad = 0.169$
c) $1.3 \times 1.3 \ = 169 \quad = 1.69$
d) $13 \times 13 \ \ \ = 169$

Fixing the decimal point for multiplication can be done by (a) considering the problem by substituting 'of' instead of '×' or (b) counting up the decimal points in the problems and positioning the point in the answer, counting from right to left.

To Calculate Percentage Composition:

1 Total ingredients.
2 Divide each individual ingredient by total and multiply by 100.
3 Check result – sum total = 100.

e.g. Feldspar   120
      Dolomite   55
      Whiting   20
      Clay   32
      Flint   118
                  ———
                  345

Feldspar: $\dfrac{120}{345} \times 100 = 35$ (calculated to nearest whole number)

etc.

Expressed as percentage:

Feldspar   35
Dolomite   16
Whiting   6
Clay   9
Flint   34
            ———
            100

4 Table of Elements

Elements of particular interest to potters arranged in alphabetical order of their chemical symbol

Symbol	Name	Atomic Number	Atomic Weight
Al	Aluminium	13	26.98
B	Boron	5	10.82
Ba	Barium	56	137.36
C	Carbon	6	12.011
Ca	Calcium	20	40.08
Cd	Cadmium	48	112.41
Co	Cobalt	27	58.94
Cr	Chromium	24	52.01
Cu	Copper	29	63.54
F	Fluorine	9	19.00
Fe	Iron	26	55.85
H	Hydrogen	1	1.0080
K	Potassium	19	39.100
Li	Lithium	3	6.940
Mg	Magnesium	12	24.32
Mn	Manganese	25	54.94
Na	Sodium	11	22.991
Ni	Nickel	28	58.71
O	Oxygen	8	16
P	Phosphorus	15	30.975
Pb	Lead	82	207.21
Sb	Antimony	51	121.76
Se	Selenium	34	78.96
Si	Silicon	14	28.09
Sn	Tin	50	118.70
Sr	Strontium	38	87.63
Ti	Titanium	22	47.90
U	Uranium	92	238.07
V	Vanadium	23	50.95
Zn	Zinc	30	65.38
Zr	Zirconium	40	91.22

5 Substances of Ceramic Interest

Albite	Soda felspar, $Na_2O.Al_2O_3.6SiO_2$; mol. wt 524
Amphiboles	Group of ferro-magnesian minerals.
Anatase	Titanium dioxide.
Andesine	Soda-lime felspar.
Angelesite	Naturally occurring lead sulphate.
Anorthite	Lime felspar, $CaO.Al_2O_3.2SiO_2$; mol. wt. 278.
Azurite	Naturally occurring basic carbonate of copper $2CuCO_3.Cu(OH)_2$.
Barytes	Barium sulphate ($BaSO_4$).
Basic slag	By-product of 'basic' process of steel production containing calcium phosphate amongst other constituents.
Bauxite	Natural hydrated alumina.
Biotite	One of the mica group. A complex silicate of very variable composition containing Mg, K, Fe and Al.
Bole	Ferruginous clay.
Braunite	Mainly manganese oxide with some iron oxide.
Brown ironstone	Natural hydrated oxide of iron.
Brookite	Titanium dioxide (TiO_2).
Burnt sienna	Orange-red pigment made from terra sienna.
Calcite	Calcium carbonate ($CaCO_3$).
Carborundum	Silicon carbide.
Caulk or Cawk stone	Old name for barytes.
China Pitchers	Approx. $\left. \begin{array}{l} 0.90\ CaO \\ 0.10\ K_2O \end{array} \right\} 0.35\ Al_2O_3 \left\{ \begin{array}{l} 1.36\ SiO_2 \\ 0.24\ P_2O_5 \end{array} \right.$: Mol. Wt. 212
Cullett or Cullit	Broken glass
Derbyshire spar	Fluorspar (CaF_2).
French chalk	see Steatite.
Fuller's earth	Impure hydrated silicate of alumina.
Galena	Lead sulphide (PbS).
Haematite	Ferric Oxide (Fe_2O_3).
Halloysite	A form of clay approximately $Al_2O_3.2SO_2.2H_2O$; mol. wt. 295.
Limonite	Hydrated iron oxide.
Litharge	Lead oxide (PbO).
Meerschaum	$2MgO.3SiO_22H_2O$.
Ochre, brown	Limonite.
Ochre, red	Haematite, red.
Ochre, yellow	Limonite.
Pegmatite	Granitic rock, composed chiefly of quartz and feldspar, e.g., meldonite.
Plaster of Paris	Calcium sulphate ($2CaSO_4.H_2O$).
Sillimanite	$Al_2O_3.SiO_2$.
Soda	Sodium oxide.
Soda ash	Sodium carbonate (Na_2CO_3).
Steatite	Talc ($3MgO.4SiO_2.H_2O$).
Terra sienna	Ferruginous earth with manganese.
Thivier's earth	A ferruginous earth.

Tincal	A form of borax.
Umber	Earthy mixture of iron and manganese oxides.
Yellow ochre	Ferruginous calcareous clay.
Zircon	Zirconium silicate ($ZrSiO_4$).
Zirconite	General term for materials composed of zirconium oxide.

6 Common Ceramic Materials

	Chemical Symbol	Mol. wt.	Melting Point °C	°F
Albite	$Na_2O.Al_2O_3.6SiO_2$	524.3	1170	2138
Alumina	Al_2O_3	102	2050	3722
Alumina Hydrate	$Al(OH)_3$	Eq. wt. 78	—	—
Alumina Hydroxide	$Al_2(OH)_6$	156	—	—
Antimony Trioxide	Sb_2O_3	291.6	—	—
Barium Carbonate (Witherite)	$BaCO_3$	197.4	1360	2480
Bone Ash (Calcium phosphate)	$3CaO.P_2O_5$ or $Ca_3(PO_4)_2$	310.2 Eq. wt. 103	1670	3038
Borax	$Na_2O.2B_2O_3.10H_2O$	381.5	200	392
Boric Acid	$B_2O_3.3H_2O$	123.7	—	—
Boric Oxide	B_2O_3	70	577	1070
Boro-calcite	$CaO.2B_2O_3.6H_2O$	304	—	—
Calcium Carbonate (Whiting)	$CaCO_3$	100.1	—	—
China Clay	$Al_2O_3 2SiO_2 2H_2O$	258.1	1770	3218
Colemanite	$2CaO.3B_2O_3.5H_2O$	412 Eq. wt. 206	—	—
Cornish Stone (China Stone)	$K_2O.Al_2O_3.8SiO_2$	678	1230	2246
Chromic Oxide	Cr_2O_3	152	2435	4415
Cobalt Oxide	CoO	74.9	1935	3515
Copper Carbonate	$CuCO_3$	221.2	—	—
Copper Oxide	CuO	79.6	1326	2418
Cryolite	$Na_3.AlF_6$ or $3NaF.AlF_3$	210 Eq. wt. 420	1020	1868
Dolomite	$CaCO_3.MgCO_3(CaO.MgO.2CO_2)$	184	—	—
Feldspar (Orthoclase Potash)	$K_2O.Al_2O_3.6SiO_2$	556.5	1250	2282
Feldspar (Albite Soda)	$Na_2O.Al_2O_3.6SiO_2$	524.3	1200	2192
Feldspar (Anorthite Lime)	$CaO.Al_2O_3 2SiO_2$	278	1551	2284
Ferric (iron) Oxide	Fe_2O_3	159.7	—	—
Fireclay	$Al_2O_3.6SiO_2$	463.8	—	—
Flint (Quartz)	SiO_2	60.1	1600	2912
Fluorspar	CaF_2	78.1	1330	2425
Galena (lead sulphide)	PbS	239	—	—

Appendices

	Chemical Symbol	Mol. wt.	Melting Point °C	°F
Ilmenite	$FeO.TiO_2$	152	—	—
Lead Bisilicate	$PbO.2SiO_2$	343.3	815	1499
Lead Monosilicate	$PbO.SiO_2$	283.3	766	1410
LeadOxide (Litharge)	PbO	223.2	888	1630
Lead Sesquisilicate	$2PbO.3SiO_2$	646.9 Eq. wt. 323.4	—	—
Lepidolite	$(LiK)_2.(FOH)_2.Al_2O_3.3SiO_2$ or $LiFKF.Al_2O_3.SiO_2$	446	—	—
Lithium Oxide	Li_2O	29.9	—	—
Magnesia (Magnesium Oxide)	MgO	40.3	2800	5072
Manganese Carbonate	$MnCO_3$	115	—	—
Manganese Dioxide	MnO_2	87	1650	3002
Meerschaum (Sepiolite)	$2MgO.3SiO_22H_2O$	297.5 Eq. wt. 148.7	—	—
Nepheline Syenite	$K_2O.3Na_2O.4Al_2O_3.8SiO_2$	1168 Eq. wt. 389	1250	2282
Nickel Oxide	NiO	75	1990	3614
Petalite	$Li_2O.Al_2O_3.8SiO_2$	612	1250	2282
Potassium Carbonate (Pearl ash)	K_2CO_3	138.2	896	1645
Silicon Carbide (Carborundum)	SiC	40.3	—	—
Silica Oxide	SiO_2	60.3	1713	3116
Silver Sand	SiO_2	60.3	—	—
Sodium Oxide (Soda)	Na_2O	62	—	—
Sodium Carbonate (Soda Ash)	Na_2CO_3	106	852	1565
Spodumene	$Li_2O.Al_2O_3.4SiO_2$	373	—	—
Strontium Oxide (Strontia)	SrO	104	2430	4406
Talc (Steatite, french chalk)	$3MgO.4SiO_2.H_2O$	380 Eq. wt. 127	—	—
Tin Oxide (Stannic Oxide)	SnO_2	151	1127	2061
Titanium Oxide (Anatase)	TiO_2	80	1560	2844
Vanadium Pentoxide	V_2O_5	182	—	—
Wollastonite	$CaSiO_3$	116	—	—
Zinc Oxide	ZnO	81	1975	3587
Zirconium Oxide	ZrO_2	123	2550	4622

Equivalent weights

The *Atomic weight* is the total number of protons and electrons present in a single atom. The *Molecular weight* is formed by the total of all the atomic weights present in the molecule.

Some materials have 'equivalent weights'. This defines the molecular weight of the material which must be taken to yield one complete unit of the oxide desired in the glaze. Most materials have the same molecular and equivalent weights. The exceptions are:

	Mol. wt.	Eq. wt.			
Bone Ash	310	103	Alumina Hydrate	78	156
Colemanite	412	206	Nepheline Syenite	1168	389
Cryolite	210	420	Talc	380.1	126.7

7 Some Frits Available

These tables are reproduced in the form supplied by the manufacturers.

PERCENTAGE COMPOSITION OF SOME FRITS AVAILABLE UK

Harrison Mayer Ltd

	PbO	CaO	Na_2O	K_2O	MgO	ZnO	Li_2O	Al_2O_3	SiO_2	TiO_2	B_2O	ZrO_2
Lead Bisilicate 36.2.191	65.0	—	—	—			—	2.8	32.2	—	—	—
Standard Borax 36.2.192	—	15.0	9.0	1.2			—	7.5	49.0	—	18.3	—
Alkaline Leadless 36.2.193	—	6.4	12.3	2.0		10.9	—	4.0	56.1	—	8.0	—
Zircon Opaque Leadless 36.2.194	—	—	7.2	0.2		5.2	—	5.7	54.4	—	10.6	10.4
Lead Borosilicate 36.2.195	18.0	7.2	5.2	1.3		—	0.3	6.7	51.0	—	10.2	—

Podmore & Sons Ltd

	PbO	CaO	Na_2O	K_2O	MgO	ZnO	Li_2O	Al_2O_3	SiO_2	TiO_2	B_2O	ZrO_2
Lead Bisilicate P2241	64.9	—	—	—	—	—	—	2.6	32.5	—	—	—
Lead Sesquisilicate P2242	68.7	—	—	—	—	—	—	—	28.5	2.9	—	—
Calcium Borate frit P2244	—	27.10	—	—	—	—	—	4.78	17.74	—	50.60	—
Borax Frit P2245	—	8.86	11.15	8.66	0.03	—	—	9.00	48.70	—	13.60	—
Borax Frit P2246	—	15.02	8.66	1.29	0.05	—	—	7.47	48.90	—	18.66	—
Borax Frit P2247	—	7.31	3.60	2.73	0.15	—	—	9.37	62.00	—	14.84	—
Zircon Frit P2252	—	7.4	6.0	—	—	2.3	—	4.5	55.0	—	14.7	9.7
Borax Frit	—	3.68	5.44	—	2.20	0.90	—	6.70	65.80	—	15.35	—

MOLECULAR FORMULAE OF SOME FRITS AVAILABLE UK

Podmore & Sons Ltd

	Na_2O	K_2O	CaO	MgO	ZnO	Al_2O_3	SiO_2	B_2O_3	ZrO_2
P2250 High Alkali	0.5	0.3	0.2	—	—	0.1	1.5	0.1	—
P2251 Borax Frit	0.485	0.057	0.458	—	—	0.425	4.35	1.16	—

Fulham Pottery

3002 Standard Borax	0.336	0.32	0.632	—	—	0.146	2.6·	0.6⸱4	—
3003 Transparent Alkaline	0.5	—	0.5	—	—	—	2.6	0.6	—
3005 Zircon	0.414	—	0.413	0.112	0.061	0.351	4.08	0.827	0.426

PERCENTAGE COMPOSITION OF GLAZE FRITS AVAILABLE USA

Ferro Corporation

Lead Frits	F	Na_2O	K_2O	CaO	MgO	BaO	PbO	Al_2O_3	B_2O_3	SiO_2
3304		1.1	—	—	—	—	54.4	4.0	—	40.5
3403		0.3	1.4	0.1	—	—	67.8	2.3	—	28.1
3419		6.4	—	—	—	—	59.2	—	14.5	19.9
3467		2.4	1.7	8.0	0.6	—	17.2	9.1	4.5	56.5
34493		1.5	1.9	4.6	—	—	31.3	3.1	12.9	44.7
3496		2.4	1.4	4.2	—	—	33.1	4.9	4.3	49.7

Leadless Frits	F	Na_2O	K_2O	CaO	MgO	BaO	PbO	Al_2O_3	B_2O_3	SiO_2
3110		15.3	2.3	6.3	—	—	—	3.7	2.6	69.8
3134		10.3	—	20.1	—	—	—	—	23.1	46.5
3289		5.5	—	—	—	27.4	—	5.4	12.4	49.3
5301	9.0	14.0	5.5	2.4	—	—	—	12.1	12.5	44.5
3831		4.6	12.0	12.2	—	17.9	—	10.6	—	42.7

PERCENTAGE WEIGHT FORMULAE OF FRITS AVAILABLE USA

Pemco Products Group

	Na_2O	K_2O	CaO	BaO	PbO	ZnO	Al_2O_3	B_2O_3	SiO_2	ZrO_2
Pb–41	—	—	—	—	72.2	5.4	—	9.0	13.4	—
Pb–316	—	—	—	—	61.3	—	7.0	—	31.7	—
Pb–349	1.8	2.7	10.4	—	17.1	—	6.2	8.0	53.3	—
Pb–740	1.2	—	—	—	56.8	20.0	2.0	—	20.0	—
Pb–742	3.6	—	4.5	—	31.0	—	3.4	13.0	43.5	1.0
Pb–1038	2.7	0.3	—	—	43.5	7.6	5.0	5.0	35.9	—
Pb–1114	1.9	1.4	9.8	—	31.6	—	3.5	11.1	40.7	—
P–25	14.7	5.4	0.5	—	—	0.7	12.1	16.9	49.7	—
P–311	6.5	0.7	14.1	—	—	—	10.0	14.4	54.3	—
P–626	5.6	—	—	27.4	—	—	5.4	12.4	49.2	—

8 Typical Percentage Compositions of American Materials

	BUCKINGHAM POTASH FELDSPAR	NEPHELINE SYENITE	KONA F-4 SODA FELDSPAR	KONA A-3 POTASH FELDSPAR	G-200 POTASH FELDSPAR	K-200 POTASH FELDSPAR	EUREKA POTASH FELDSPAR	OXFORD POTASH FELDSPAR	CORNWALL STONE	KINGMAN POTASH FELDSPAR	CUSTER POTASH FELDSPAR	CLINCHFIELD POTASH #202 FELDSPAR
SiO_2	66.3	60.2	66.8	71.6	65.76	66.00	69.8	69.4	71.1	66.5	68.5	68.1
Al_2O_3	18.4	23.3	19.7	16.3	19.28	18.30	17.11	17.04	16.8	18.4	17.5	17.5
TiO_2									0.50			
Fe_2O_3	0.07	0.077	0.04	0.07	0.06	0.07	0.01	0.09	0.16	0.08	0.08	0.09
CaO	0.40	0.3	1.8	0.4	0.98	0.20	Tr.	0.38	1.6	0.10	0.30	0.20
MgO	Tr.	Tr.	Tr.	Tr.	Tr.	Tr.	Tr.		0.05	Tr.	Tr.	Tr.
Na_2O	2.7	10.6	7.0	3.7	3.20	1.50	3.5	3.22	2.29	2.7	3.0	2.6
K_2O	11.8	5.1	4.5	7.8	10.36	13.00	9.40	7.92	6.57	12.0	10.4	10.9
L.O.I.	0.3	0.4	0.2	0.1	0.31	0.26	0.2	0.3	1.25	0.2	0.3	0.3

	KEYSTONE POTASH FELDSPAR	CEDAR HEIGHTS A.F. GOLDHART CLAY – 200 MESH	CEDAR HEIGHTS BONDING CLAY 50 MESH	CEDAR HEIGHTS REDART CLAY	KENTUCKS #4 BALL CLAY	TENNESSEE #5 BALL CLAY	TENNESSEE #10 BALL CLAY	BARNARD SLIP CLAY	ALBANY SLIP CLAY	CALCINED CHINA CLAY	E.P.K. CHINA CLAY (FLORIDA)	GEORGIA CHINA CLAY	A.P. GREEN MISSOURI FIRE CLAY
SiO_2	64.76	57.32	57.32	64.27	52.1	53.3	50.4	52.38	59.48	53.08	45.91	45.20	52.00
Al_2O_3	19.94	28.50	28.50	16.41	31.2	31.1	33.2	10.60	11.54	44.40	38.71	38.02	30.00
TiO_2		1.98	1.98	1.06	1.6	1.4	1.6	0.85	0.90	0.95	0.34	1.95	1.50
Fe_2O_3	0.04	1.23	1.23	7.04	0.8	1.0	0.9	20.27	4.13	0.40	0.42	0.49	1.00
MnO	0.17							3.23	0.08				
CaO		0.08	0.08	0.23	0.4	0.3	0.3	Tr.	6.28		0.09	0.26	0.05
MgO	2.48	0.22	0.22	1.55	0.3	0.2	0.3	Tr.	3.35		0.12	0.30	0.03
Na_2O	12.24	0.30	0.30	0.40	0.3	0.8	0.5		0.40	0.31	0.04	0.02	0.05
K_2O	0.35	0.88	0.88	4.07	1.0	1.5	0.7	3.77	2.75	0.39	0.22	0.04	0.20
L.O.I.		9.39	9.39	4.78	12.4	11.4	12.1	8.27	10.40		14.16	13.51	10.00
		Sulphur 0.24	Sulphur 0.24										

9 Analysis of Materials Supplied by Harrison Mayer Ltd

(Reference number in brackets)

Alumina Hydrate   (36.0.001)

Al_2O_3	65.0
SiO_2	0.25
Fe_2O_3	0.01
Na_2O	0.35
H_2O	34.40

Alumina Calcined   (36.0.002)

Al_2O_3	99.10
SiO_2	0.03
Fe_2O_3	0.03
CaO	0.05
Na_2O	0.57

Ball Clay, Black   (36.0.003)

SiO_2	46.0
TiO_2	0.8
Al_2O_3	32.2
Fe_2O_3	1.0
MgO	0.3
CaO	0.3
K_2O	2.1
Na_2O	0.3
Loss on ignition	17.0

China Clay, No. 1   (36.0.012)

SiO_2	47.06
Al_2O_3	36.94
Fe_2O_3	1.09
TiO_2	0.23
$(K.Na)_2O$	1.81
Loss on ignition	12.10

China Clay, No. 2   (36.0.013)

SiO_2	48.30
Al_2O_3	36.90
Fe_2O_3	0.68
TiO_2	0.04
$(K.Na)_2O$	2.18
Loss on ignition	11.64

Cornish Stone, Hard Purple   (36.0.014)

SiO_2	72.60
Al_2O_3	15.40
Fe_2O_3	0.19
TiO_2	0.04
CaO	2.10
K_2O	4.32
Na_2O	3.62
Loss on ignition	1.62

Ball Clay, Blue   (36.0.004)

SiO_2	55.0
Al_2O_3	30.0
Fe_2O_3	1.3
TiO_2	1.2
CaO	0.22
MgO	0.66
K_2O $\}$ Na_2O	3.44
Loss on ignition	8.60

Bentonite   (36.0.006)

SiO_2	55.44
Al_2O_3	20.14
Fe_2O_3	3.67
CaO	0.49
MgO	2.49
K_2O	0.60
Na_2O	2.76
Loss on ignition	13.50

Bone Ash   (36.0.007)

SiO_2	0.51
Al_2O_3	0.27
Fe_2O_3	0.06
CaO	53.30
MgO	1.10
$(K.Na)_2O$	0.55
P_2O_5	42.50

Borax Crystals   (36.0.008)

Na_2O	16.25
B_2O_3	36.52
H_2O	47.23

Borax Anhydrous   (36.0.009)

Na_2O	30.8
B_2O_3	69.2

Borocalcite   (36.0.011)

SiO_2	4.50
Al_2O_3	0.18
Fe_2O_3	0.12
CaO	26.30
MgO	0.50
$(K.Na)_2O$	0.50
B_2O_3	44.50
Loss on ignition	22.3

Boric Acid   (36.0.010)

B_2O_3	56.30
H_2O	43.70

Cornish Stone,
Mild Purple   (36.0.015)

SiO_2	72.8
Al_2O_3	15.7
Fe_2O_3	0.19
TiO_2	0.03
CaO	1.37
MgO	0.12
K_2O	4.56
Na_2O	3.71
Loss on ignition	1.37

Dolomite   (36.0.019)

SiO_2	1.05
Al_2O_3	0.56
Fe_2O_3	0.40
CaO	31.41
MgO	20.77
$(K.Na)_2O$	0.15
Loss on ignition	45.53

Felspar, Potash   (36.0.020)

SiO_2	65.2
Al_2O_3	19.0
Fe_2O_3	0.10
CaO	0.38
K_2O	12.00
Na_2O	2.89
Loss on ignition	0.39

Feldspar Soda   (36.0.021)

SiO_2	67.90
Al_2O_3	19.00
Fe_2O_3	0.11
CaO	1.88
K_2O	2.78
Na_2O	7.48
Loss on ignition	0.29

Quartz   (36.0.040)

SiO_2	99.50
Al_2O_3	0.13
Fe_2O_3	0.06
Loss on ignition	0.17

Talc   (36.0.046)

SiO_2	58.30
Al_2O_3	0.15
Fe_2O_3	0.22
CaO	0.42
MgO	33.40
Loss on ignition	7.33

Wollastonite   (36.0.048)

SiO_2	51.40
Al_2O_3	0.50
Fe_2O_3	0.76
TiO_2	0.03
CaO	46.20
MgO	0.25
Loss on ignition	0.70

Molochite

SiO_2	54.50
Al_2O_3	42.50
Fe_2O_3	0.75
TiO_2	0.08
CaO	0.10
MgO	0.10
K_2O	1.75
Na_2O	0.10

Mineral Flux, No. 4

SiO_2	80.18
Al_2O_3	11.12
Fe_2O_3	0.14
CaO	1.64
K_2O	2.20
Na_2O	4.16
Loss on ignition	0.23

Feldspar, Mixed   (36.0.022)

SiO_2	65.80
Al_2O_3	19.00
Fe_2O_3	0.10
CaO	0.68
K_2O	10.20
Na_2O	3.72
Loss on ignition	0.33

Flint

SiO_2	98.6
Al_2O_3	0.26
Fe_2O_3	0.02
CaO	0.47
K_2O	0.11
Na_2O	0.01
Loss on ignition	0.33

Nepheline Syenite   (36.0.36)

SiO_2	57.62
Al_2O_3	23.84
Fe_2O_3	0.11
CaO	1.51
K_2O	8.30
Na_2O	7.60
Loss on ignition	0.99

Petalite   (36.0.037)

SiO_2	76.70
Al_2O_3	16.50
Fe_2O_3	0.07
CaO	0.89
MgO	0.16
K_2O	0.50
Na_2O	0.60
Li_2O	3.55
Loss on ignition	0.83

10 Conversion Tables and Glaze Calculations

CENTIGRADE AND FAHRENHEIT

°Centigrade	°Fahrenheit	°Centigrade	°Fahrenheit	°Centigrade	°Fahrenheit
1	33.8	30	86.0	500	932.0
2	35.6	40	104.0	600	1112.0
3	37.4	50	122.0	700	1292
4	39.2	60	140.0	800	1472
5	41.0	70	158.0	900	1652
6	42.8	80	176.0	1000	1832
7	44.6	90	194.0	1100	2012
8	46.4	100	212.0	1200	2192
9	48.2	200	392.0	1300	2372
10	50.0	300	572.0	1400	2552
20	68.0	400	752.0	1500	2732

To convert °C into °F multiply by 1.8 and add 32.
To convert °F into °C multiply by 0.55 and subtract 32.

CONVERSION TABLE FOR PYROMETRIC CONES, BARS AND RINGS

°C	°F	British Cones	Seger Cones	Orton Cones	Hold-croft's Bars	Buller's Rings	°C	°F	British Cones	Seger Cones	Orton Cones	Hold-croft's Bars	Buller's Rings
600	1112	022	022	—	1	—	795	1463	—	—	016	—	—
605	1121	—	—	022	—	—	805	1481	—	—	015	—	—
615	1139	—	—	021	—	—	810	1490	—	—	—	7½	—
650	1202	021	021	020	2	—	815	1499	014	014a	—	—	—
660	1220	—	—	019	—	—	830	1526	—	—	014	—	—
670	1238	020	020	—	3	—	835	1535	013	013a	—	—	—
690	1274	019	019	—	—	—	840	1544	—	—	—	8	—
700	1292	—	—	—	4	—	855	1571	012	012a	—	—	—
710	1310	018	018	—	—	—	860	1580	—	—	013	9	—
720	1328	—	—	018	—	—	875	1607	—	—	012	10	—
730	1346	017	017	—	5	—	880	1616	011	011a	—	—	—
750	1382	016	016	—	—	—	890	1634	—	—	—	11	—
760	1400	—	—	—	6	—	895	1643	—	—	010	—	—
770	1418	—	—	017	—	—	900	1652	010	010a	—	—	—
790	1454	015	015a	—	7	—	905	1661	—	—	011	12	—

°C	°F	British Cones	Seger Cones	Orton Cones	Holdcroft's Bars	Buller's Rings
920	1688	09	09a	—	13	—
930	1706	—	—	09	—	—
935	1715	—	—	—	14	—
940	1724	08	08a	—	—	—
950	1742	—	—	08	15	—
960	1760	07	07a	—	16	1
970	1778	—	—	17	—	—
980	1796	06	06a	—	—	—
985	1805	—	—	—	18	—
990	1814	—	—	07	—	—
1000	1832	05	05a	—	19	5
1015	1859	—	—	06	—	—
1020	1868	04	04a	—	—	—
1030	1886	—	—	—	—	10
1040	1904	03	03a	05	20	—
1060	1940	02	02a	04	21	—
1065	1949	—	—	—	—	15
1080	1976	01	01a	—	22	—
1100	2012	1	1a	—	23	20
1115	2039	—	—	03	—	—
1120	2048	2	2a	—	24	—
1125	2057	—	—	02	—	—
1135	2075	—	—	—	—	25
1140	2084	3	3a	—	25	—
1145	2093	—	—	01	—	—
1200	2192	6	6a	—	26	35
1205	2201	—	—	5	—	—
1230	2246	7	7	6	26a	—
1240	2264	—	—	—	—	40
1250	2282	8	8	7	27	—
1260	2300	—	—	8	—	—
1270	2318	—	—	—	27a	—
1275	2327	—	—	—	—	45
1280	2336	9	9	—	28	—
1285	2345	—	—	9	—	—
1300	2372	10	10	—	29	—
1305	2381	—	—	10	—	—
1320	2408	11	11	—	—	—
1325	2417	—	—	11	30	—
1335	2435	—	—	12	—	—

°C	°F	British Cones	Seger Cones	Orton Cones	Holdcroft's Bars	Buller's Rings
1350	2462	12	12	13	31	—
1380	2516	13	13	—	32	—
1400	2552	—	—	14	—	—
1410	2570	14	14	—	—	—
1430	2606	—	—	—	33	—
1435	2615	15	15	15	—	—
1460	2660	16	16	—	—	—
1465	2669	—	—	16	34	—
1475	2687	—	—	17	35	—
1480	2696	17	17	—	—	—
1490	2714	—	—	18	36	—
1500	2732	18	18	—	—	—
1505	2741	—	—	—	37	—
1520	2768	19	19	19	38	—
1530	2786	20	20	20	—	—
1535	2795	—	—	—	39	—
1550	2822	—	—	—	40	—
1580	2876	26	26	23	—	—
1595	2903	—	—	26	—	—
1605	2921	—	—	27	—	—
1610	2930	27	27	—	—	—
1615	2939	—	—	28	—	—
1630	2966	28	28	—	—	—
1640	2984	—	—	29	—	—
1650	3002	29	29	30	—	—
1670	3038	30	30	—	—	—
1680	3056	—	—	31	—	—
1690	3074	31	31	—	—	—
1700	3092	—	—	32	—	—
1710	3110	32	32	—	—	—
1722	3131	—	—	$32\frac{1}{2}$	—	—
1730	3146	33	33	—	—	—
1745	3173	—	—	33	—	—
1750	3182	34	34	—	—	—
1760	3200	—	—	34	—	—
1770	3218	35	35	—	—	—
1785	3245	—	—	35	—	—
1790	3254	36	36	—	—	—
1810	3290	—	—	36	—	—
1820	3308	—	—	37	—	—

11 Suppliers and Bibliography

UK

Raw materials, frits, kilns, etc

Harrison Mayer Ltd
Meir
Stoke-on-Trent ST3 7PX

Wengers Ltd
Eturia
Stoke-on-Trent

Podmore and Sons Ltd
Caledonian Mills
Stoke-on-Trent

Thomas E. Gray Ltd
17 The Headland
Kettering, Northants

Clay

Fremington Red Earthenware Clay
C. H. Brannam, Litchdon Potteries,
Barnstaple, Devon

Chemical Suppliers

BDH Chemicals Ltd
Poole, Dorset BH12 4NN

Hopkin and Williams
Freshwater Road, Chadwell Heath Essex
PO Box 1, Romford RM1 1HA

Depleted Uranium U_3O_8

British Nuclear Fuels
Risley, Warrington, Lancs

Laboratories that will test for metal release

Ceramic Department
North Staffs Polytechnic
College Road, Stoke-on-Trent

Harrison Mayer Ltd
Meir
Stoke-on-Trent ST3 7PX

British Ceramic Research Association
Queens Road
Penkhull, Stoke-on-Trent

Ellis Testing and Research Laboratory
Aldbury
Nr Guildford, Surrey

USA

American Art Clay Co (Amaco)
477 West 16th Street
Indianapolis Ind 46222

Westwood Ceramic Supply
Company
14400 Lomitas Avenue
City of Industry
Calif 91744

B. F. Drakenfeld and Co Inc
Washington PA 15301

Hammill and Gillespie, Inc
225 Broadway
New York NY 10007

Pemco Products Group
5601 Eastern Avenue
Baltimore
Maryland 21224

Leslie Ceramics Supply, Co.
1212 San Pablo Avenue
Berkeley, CA 94706

Standard Ceramic Supply Company
Box 4435
Pittsburgh, PA 15205

Rovin Ceramics
6912 Schaefer Road
Dearborn, MI 48126

Cedar Heights Clay Company
50 Portsmouth Road
Oak Hill, OH 45656

Ferro Corporation
4150 East 56th Street
Cleveland, Ohio 44101

Harrison Bell (associate
company of Harrison
Mayer Ltd)
3605A Kennedy Road
South Plainfield
New Jersey

Laboratories which will test for lead and cadmium release

Pittsburgh Testing Laboratory
850 Poplar Street
Pittsburgh, PA 15220

Bio-Technics Laboratories, Inc.
1133 Crenshaw Blvd.
Los Angeles, CA 90019

The Twining Laboratories, Inc.
Box 1472
Fresno, CA 93716

Coors Spectro-Chemical Laboratory
Box 500
Golden, CO 80401

MAGAZINES

Ceramic Review (UK)
17a Newburgh Street
London W1V 1LE

Pottery Quarterly (UK)
Northfield Studio
Tring. Herts

Ceramics Monthly (USA)
Box 4548, Columbus
Ohio 43212 USA

Studio Potter (USA)
Box 172, Warner
N. H. 03278 USA

The New Zealand Potter
15 Wadestown Road
Wellington 1
New Zealand

Pottery in Australia
48 Burton Street
Darlinghurst
NSW 2010
Australia

SPECIALIST BIBLIOGRAPHY

Minerals and Rocks, Brian Simpson, Octopus Books, 1974. A beautifully illustrated and readable account.
Clay and Glazes for the Potter, Daniel Rhodes, Pitman Publishing. A well-established favourite amongst potters for its complete look at all the materials and processes of the potter.
Ceramic Glazes, Felix Singer and W. L. German, Borax Consolidated Ltd., London, 1960. A scientific explanation of the technology of glazes as well as much practical information.
Ceramic Glazes, C. W. Parmelee, Chaners Books. A detailed and scientific explanation of how to make commercial glazes.
Pioneer Pottery, Michael Cardew, Longman, London, 1972. Contains an excellent account of stoneware glazes for the reduction potter as well as much other valuable information.
The Chemistry and Physics of Clays, Rex W. Grimshaw, Ernest Benn Ltd, 1971. The classic reference book.
A Handbook of Ceramic Calculations, A. Heath, Webberley Ltd, Stoke-on-Trent, 1937. The traditional procedures for all ceramic calculations in industry.
The Podmore Ceramists' Handbook, Podmore and Sons, Stoke-on-Trent. An invaluable reference book for scientific and technical information.
Glazes for Special Effects, Herbert H. Sanders, Watson-Guptill, New York. Working notes and recipes for making richly coloured and textured glazes using American materials.
Chinese Stoneware Glazes, Joseph Grebarnier, Watson-Guptill/Pitman. Traditional Chinese glazes are explained and practical advice describes how they can be made.

Oriental Glazes, Nigel Wood, Pitman/Watson-Guptill. A detailed look at how the classic Chinese and Japanese glazes can be understood and made.
Ceramic Review Book of Glaze Recipes, E. Lewenstein and E. Cooper, Ceramic Review, 1978. Over 200 recipes from professional potters.
Glaze Projects, Richard Behrens, Professional Publications Inc, Ohio. A formulary of leadless glazes.
Ceramic Glazemaking, Richard Behrens, Professional Publications Inc, Ohio. Experimental formulation and glaze recipes.
Calculations in Ceramics, Redford and Griffiths, MacLaren, 1963.
Literature Abstracts of Ceramic Glazes, Koenig and Earhart, College Offset Press, Philadelphia, 1951.
Recipe Book for Glazes and Colours, Fritz Viehneger, Verlag de Sprechsaal, Coburg, 1959.
The Glazer's Book, A. B. Searle, Technical Press Ltd, 1948.
The Chemistry of Pottery, Karl Lagenbeck.
A Potter's Book, Bernard Leach, Faber, Transatlantic Arts Inc.
Ceramic Formulas: The Complete Compendium, John W. Conrad, Macmillan Publishing Co Inc, 1973.
Ceramic Science for the Potter, W. G. Lawrence, Chilton Book Company, 1972.
Pottery Decoration, Thomas Shafer, Watson-Guptill Publications, 1976.
Kilns: Design, Construction and Operation, Daniel Rhodes, Chilton Book Company, 1968.
Stoneware and Porcelain, Daniel Rhodes, Chilton Book Company, 1956.

12 Charts for Calculating Glaze Formulae and Recipes

Ⓓ RECIPE TO FORMULA

NAME:

1. RECIPE TO FORMULA (QUICK METHOD)

Oxides Present in Minerals:

Mineral & Formula	Quantity in recipe	Molecular wt.	= Molecular Proportion

TOTALS:

Reduce formula to unity by dividing all totals by total of bases.

3. Formula with one decimal point.

Ⓓ Formula to Recipe

Glaze Formula

Firing temperature

Name / Ref:

Oxides required										Ratio	x	Mol.		%	
Amount needed												Wt.			
Source															

Index

(Main references are in **bold** type)